Exhibition Experiments

Edited by

Sharon Macdonald and Paul Basu

Blackwell
Publishing

BLACKWELL PUBLISHING
350 Main Street, Malden, MA 02148-5020, USA
9600 Garsington Road, Oxford OX4 2DQ, UK
550 Swanston Street, Carlton, Victoria 3053, Australia

First published 2007 by Blackwell Publishing Ltd

1   2007

Library of Congress Cataloging-in-Publication Data

Exhibition experiments / edited by Sharon Macdonald and Paul Basu.
    p. cm. – (New interventions in art history)
Includes bibliographical references and index.
ISBN-13: 978-1-4051-3076-9 (hbk.)
ISBN-13: 978-1-4051-3077-6 (pbk.)
1. Museum exhibits. 2. Museums—Management. 3. Art museums—Management. I. Macdonald,
Sharon. II. Basu, Paul.

AM151.E965 2007
069′.5–dc22

                                    2006026269

A catalogue record for this title is available from the British Library.

Set in 10.5/13pt Minion
by SPi Publisher Services, Pondicherry, India
Printed and bound in Singapore
by Markono Print Media Pte Ltd

For further information on
Blackwell Publishing, visit our website:
www.blackwellpublishing.com

Contents

Illustrations

Notes on Contributors

Mieke Bal, cultural critic and theorist, holds the position of Royal Dutch Academy of Sciences Professor (KNAW). She is also Professor of Theory of Literature and a founding director of the Amsterdam School for Cultural Analysis, Theory and Interpretation (ASCA) at the University of Amsterdam. Her areas of interest include literary theory, semiotics, visual art, cultural studies, postcolonial theory, feminist theory, French, the Hebrew Bible, the seventeenth century and contemporary culture. She is also a video-artist. Her many books include *Travelling Concepts in the Humanities: A Rough Guide* (2002); *Louise Bourgeois' Spider: The Architecture of Art-writing* (2001); *Quoting Caravaggio: Contemporary Art, Preposterous History* (1999); *Reading "Rembrandt": Beyond the Word-Image Opposition* (1991). *A Mieke Bal Reader* has recently been published. Her video installation *Nothing is Missing* is currently touring internationally.

Paul Basu is Lecturer in Anthropology at the University of Sussex. His research interests center around the relationships between cultural memory, senses of place, and the performance of identities. His recent monograph, *Highland Homecomings* (2007), explores such issues in the context of genealogy and heritage-tourism in the Scottish diaspora. He has participated in numerous exhibition experiments, including designing a community museum/landscape interpretation centre in Scotland.

Laura Bear is Lecturer in Anthropology at the London School of Economics. She has written a novel, *The Jadu House* (2000) and an academic book, *Lines of the Nation: Indian Railway Workers, Bureaucracy and the Intimate Historical Self* (2007). Currently she is working on practices of the future in the remaking of the city of Kolkata. This work focuses equally on city planners and the lived experiences of families moving into new housing complexes linked to the software industry in Kolkata.

Clare Carolin is Senior Curator at the Hayward Gallery. She has curated and organized numerous exhibitions including retrospectives of work by Panamarenko, Malcolm Morley, and Sam Taylor-Wood and thematic exhibitions including *Eyes, Lies and Illusions* and *Fantasy Architecture: 1500-2036*. In 2002 she was responsible for the UK premier of Ann-Sofi Sidén's *Warte Mal!: Prostitution after the Velvet Revolution* at the Hayward Gallery. She has contributed articles and interviews to *Kalias: Revista de Arte, La Vanguardia de Barcelona, Lapiz, Contemporary Magazine*, and *The Art Newspaper*. She is currently developing a Hayward Touring exhibition on the subject of hidden practice, secrets, and code in modern and contemporary art and a major survey exhibition of art from the 1980s.

Neil Cummings and **Marysia Lewandowska** have collaborated since 1995. Their art projects include *Screen Test* (2005–6) commissioned for the British Art Show 6, *Enthusiasm* (2005–6) for the Whitechapel Gallery London, Kunst Werke Berlin and the Tapies Foundation in Barcelona, which evolved from *Enthusiasts* (2004), first exhibited the Center for Contemporary Art in Warsaw. They have produced various books including *Lost Property* (1996) and *The Value of Things* (2000). Cummings is Professor of Theory and Practice at Chelsea College of Art and Design, and Lewandowska is Professor in Fine Art at Konstfack, Stockholm. For more information on their projects visit www.chanceprojects.com.

Alexa Färber is Research Fellow in the Department of European Ethnology, Humboldt-University Berlin. Her publications include *Die Weltausstellung als Wissensmodus. Ethnographie einer Repräsentationsarbeit* (2006) and, as editor, *Hotel Berlin: Formen urbaner Mobilität und Verortung* (2005). She is currently working on a project entitled *Urban Culture and Ethnic Representation: Berlin and Moscow as Emerging "World Cities"?*

Cathy Haynes is currently Head of Interaction for arts producer Artangel where she is responsible for the Nights of London series of artist-led projects exploring the nocturnal city (www.artangel.org.uk/nightsflondon). She is co-editor of the occasional mini-publication Implicasphere (www.implicasphere.org.uk). She is also a doctoral candidate at Goldsmiths, University of London, researching the limits of the animal and the human in texts by Franz Kafka, Max Ernst and Georges Bataille. While working for Hayward Public Programmes, she devised and organized the talks program for Ann-Sofi Sidén's exhibition *Warte Mal!: Prostitution after the Velvet Revolution* at the Hayward Gallery, London.

Michelle Henning is Senior Lecturer in Media and Cultural Studies at the University of the West of England. She is the author of *Museums, Media and Cultural Theory* (2006), as well as a number of essays on cultural theory, digital photography, new media, and museums. She also works as a visual artist, and won the J. A. Clark Bursary for Creative Work in New Media in 1997. Her recent research was funded by the Arts and Humanities Research Council. She is currently researching how Romantic notions of natural symbolism and animist beliefs left their traces in early Modernism.

Bruno Latour is a philosopher and anthropologist working in Paris. He has written many books on the linkages between science and culture, including *Aramis or the Love of Technology* (1996) and *Pandora's Hope* (1999). Together with Peter Weibel, he curated *Iconoclash* and *Making Things Public* at the ZKM (Center for Art and Media). In 2005 he published *Reassembling the Social*.

Ann Lorimer is Visiting Assistant Professor of Anthropology at Reed College in Oregon. Her dissertation *"Reality World": Constructing Reality Through Chicago's Museum of Science and Industry* (2003) draws on fieldwork among museum visitors, staff, and exhibit creators, as well as archival research on earlier Chicago spectacles of capitalism. Her research interests include aesthetics, linguistic practice, material technologies, and political economy. She and her students at Reed are currently exploring the potentials and limits of commodity forms, such as fair-trade or sweat-free goods, that seek to facilitate collective agency.

Sharon Macdonald is Professor of Social Anthropology at the University of Manchester. Her books include *Theorizing Museums* (Blackwell, 1996, co-editor), *Reimagining Culture* (1997), *The Politics of Display* (1998), *Shifting Grounds: Experiments in Doing Ethnography* (special issue of *Anthropological Journal of European Cultures*, 2002, co-editor), *Behind the Scenes at the Science Museum* (2002), and *A Companion to Museum Studies* (Blackwell, 2006, editor). She is currently completing a project on post-war cultural policy and Nazi architectural heritage in Nuremberg, funded by the Humboldt Foundation and the Arts and Humanities Research Council.

Griselda Pollock is Professor of the Social and Critical Histories of Art, Director of the AHRC Centre for Cultural Analysis, Theory and History, and Co-Director of the Centre for Cultural Studies at the University of Leeds. Her many books include *Vision and Difference: Femininity, Feminism and Histories of Art* (1988), *Differencing the Canon: Feminism and the Histories of Art* (1999), and most recently *Encounters in a Virtual Feminist Museum* (2006), *Museums after Modernism: Strategies of Engagement* (Blackwell, 2006, co-editor), and *The Theatre of Memory: Trauma, Representation and Life Histories in* Leben oder Theater, *1940–42* (2007).

Nuno Porto is Assistant Professor of Social and Cultural Anthropology in the Department of Anthropology and Coordinator of the Museum of Anthropology at Coimbra University. He has conducted research on colonial museology in Angola. As an anthropologist he has been curator of several exhibitions and has published on photography, museums and art. His publications include *Science, Magic and Religion: Ritual Processes of Museum Magic* (2005, co-editor).

Ann-Sofi Sidén is an artist who trained in Germany, Sweden, and the US and whose work deals with themes of social event, vulnerability, control, violence, and surveillance. Her works have been shown at many galleries around the world, most recently in *Speed* at the Galerie Barbara Thuman in Berlin.

Peter Weibel is Chairman and Chief Executive Officer of ZKM, the Center for Art and Media, Karlsruhe, Germany. Between 1993 and 1999 he was Curator at the Neue Galerie Graz and commissioned the Austrian pavilions at the Venice Biennale. In addition to his activities as an artist and curator, Peter Weibel has published widely on art and media theory.

XPERIMENT! (Bernd Kraeftner, Judith Kroell, Isabel Warner) is a transdisciplinary research group based in Vienna. The members of the working party contribute (in)competencies and skills in fine arts (painting, installations), filmmaking, sociology, medicine, science and technology studies, etc. The members share an interest in experimenting with scientific ideas at the messy intersection of the sciences, health care, politics, publics, and the arts. The group participated with its recent work "What is a Body / a Person? – A Topography of the Possible" at the exhibition *Making Things*

Public curated by Bruno Latour and Peter Weibel at the Centre for Art and Media (ZKM) in Karlsruhe, Germany, at the 46. Oktobarski Salon in Belgrade, Serbia (November 2005) and at the exhibition *die wahr/falsch inc.* in Vienna, Austria (June–July 2006). E-mail collective@xperiment.at.

Introduction: Experiments in Exhibition, Ethnography, Art, and Science

Paul Basu and Sharon Macdonald

"*Nullius in verba*," "On the word of no man." In the 1660s, with these words taken from Horace, the scientific age was inaugurated. Adopted by the newly established Royal Society, this motto declared a break from Aristotelian epistemologies based on doctrine, rhetoric, and the authority of accepted truths which had dominated the scholastic world of the Middle Ages and Renaissance. What the new academicians proposed was a commitment to empirical evidence as the basis for knowledge, a commitment to establishing truths about the world through the staging of experiments. The experiment, meaning "from trying," thus became synonymous with the scientific method. Indeed, the popular image of the scientist remains that of a white-coated figure, surrounded by laboratory apparatus, peering into a test tube.

Historians of science have discussed the concept of the experiment at length. Like other disciplines, the natural sciences have had their reflexive turn and authors including Hacking (1983), Latour (1999), and Shapin and Schaffer (1985) have turned their critical attention to the experimental processes through which scientific knowledge is produced. While they have pointed out the heterogeneity of types of experimentation historically (especially Hacking 1975; see Schaffer 2005), central to many characterizations is that experiment is regarded as a knowledge-generating procedure – "experiment is the *creation* of phenomena" as Ian Hacking puts it (1983, p. 229, emphasis added). Via the assembly of particular apparatus and methods performed in a context that was at least theoretically open to the public, experimentalism was, according to Thomas Hobbes's critical account of 1660, an empirical intervention that aimed to "procure new phenomena" (see Shapin and Schaffer 1985, p. 115). Experiment thus entails the "systematic production of novelty" (Pickstone 2000, p. 13). Or, as Bruno Latour (1999) has explored, experiment can be seen as a transformative process – for the people as well as the materials involved. (For example, the experimenter is transformed by the experiment into an expert.) As we hope to demonstrate, such conceptualizations resonate in the chapters of this book, which are concerned not with scientific experiments so much as with experiments in exhibitionary practices.

Indeed, the realms of experiments and exhibitions are perhaps not so distinct. Shapin and Schaffer argue that the purpose of scientific apparatus is "to make visible the invisible" – in other words, to exhibit, to "hold out," to display. In the seventeenth century Robert Hooke, we might note, was the Royal Society's first *curator* of experiments. (The word "curator" was first used to refer to an officer in charge of a museum collection around the same time as the founding of the Royal Society.) Furthermore, the world's first university museum – the Ashmolean, which opened its doors in 1683 – was also a venue for the public demonstration of scientific experiments. The exhibitionary quality of public experiments – their drama, spectacle, and shock value – has been revived more recently in the gory showmanship of Gunther von Hagens, his hugely successful *Body Worlds* exhibition and televised autopsies.

If the contributors to this volume are agreed on one thing, however, it is that contemporary exhibitionary practices cannot be conceived merely as means for the display and dissemination of already existing, preformulated knowledges (the Aristotelian model rejected by the scientific experimentalists). Arguing that contemporary exhibitionary practice is – or should be – also an experimental practice, the contributors to this volume insist that exhibition, too, is a site for the generation rather than reproduction of knowledge and experience. In the following chapters, exhibition is thus conceived as a kind of laboratory, in which, to use the language of actor network theory (Law and Hassard 1999), various "actants" (visitors, curators, objects, technologies, institutional and architectural spaces, and so forth) are brought into relation with each other with no sure sense of what the result will be. The exhibitions discussed are, it might be said, experiments in meaning-making.

Initiating our Experiment

As editors, our experiment has been to bring together a diverse group of contributors – curators, artists, anthropologists, and other academics – to reflect on their own or others' exhibitionary experimentalism. Our experiment began with an open call for papers for a panel entitled "Exhibition Experiments: Technologies and Cultures of Display" at the *Anthropology and Science* decennial conference of the Association of Social Anthropologists held in Manchester in 2003.[1] The abstract for the panel invited contributions on experimentation with exhibitionary form, media, and technologies of display and suggested that presentations might reflect upon the motivations, effects, potential, and limitations of exhibitionary experimentation and also possible parallels with, or differences from, ethnographic experimentalism (discussed below). Papers were selected which best met with this remit and that collectively offered a broad range of examples, so that ideas could be investigated across diverse contexts. The panel drew a large audience and produced lively discussion. This discussion then fed into the second phase of our project in which we reviewed the knowledge generated so far, further refined our remit to focus more specifically on cases which involved a substantial element of experimenting with the idea and practice of exhibition itself, and then – following leads from the conference debate, from our panellists and others with whom we discussed the ideas – invited further contributions, from a wider array of disciplines, in order to open up the experiment for a second time.

As with the exhibitions discussed in this book, our experiment involved gathering contributions without sure knowledge of what the outcome would be. Certainly, we were aware that there seemed to be a good deal of exhibition experimentation going on and had noted some apparently shared themes, but the extent to which such diverse experiments would be motivated by like concerns, would share similar ideas, or would be subject to related reflections by those involved was open to question. What we were interested to find was that, despite the diversity of the contributors' professional backgrounds and the contexts of the exhibitions they write about, there was a remarkable consistency in many aspects of their arguments and observations. Below, we pick out some of the areas that the chapters in *Exhibition Experiments* collectively bring to the fore.

Exhibiting Exhibition

The shift from Aristotelian to experiment-based empirical science entailed, as noted above, a making visible of the processes by which scientific knowledge was established. Mechanism was, at least ostensibly, laid bare, and theoretically was made open to "any man" or "the public." Whatever the opacities involved in practice – such as continuing flows of patronage, barriers to public inspection, mystifications of expertise, and so forth – the notion of transparency of method was central to the burgeoning idea of experiment.

The idea of exhibition experiment as involving a making visible of processes of exhibition itself is present in many of the chapters that follow, and several contributors note the increasing prevalence of "reflexive" or "meta-exhibitions." In Nuno Porto's discussion of ethnographic museums, for example, he notes cases such as the one at Neuchâtel, Switzerland, which produced reflexive exhibitions that paid attention to questions of collecting and colonial power regimes, such as *Collectors/Passions* (1982), from the early 1980s. Other accounts of the trend toward "institutional critique" (e.g. Putnam 2001; Foster, Krauss, Bois, and Buchloh 2004; Marstine 2005; Schneider and Wright 2006) generally emphasize the work of artists such as Christian Boltanski, Neil Cummings, Hans Haacke, Joseph Kosuth, and Fred Wilson. While much reflexive art work has been contained within artworks themselves – for example, Boltanski's "Inventory of Objects belonging to an inhabitant of Oxford" (1973; discussed by Schneider 2006) – an increasing trend has been toward installation (see Porto, chapter 8) in which art escapes its frame and infiltrates other parts of the museum, or even moves beyond it. *Browse* (1997) by Neil Cummings and Marysia Lewandowska, for example, consisted of a leaflet showing objects from both the British Museum and Selfridges department store – so highlighting the similarities between the two and raising questions about the nature of collecting. The leaflet was made available in both the museum and the store (see Putnam 2001, p. 112; Cummings and Lewandowska 2001). Chapter 6 provides further examples of their challenging work.

The range of aspects of exhibiting that have been subject to reflexive strategies is extensive. For those concerned that exhibiting exhibition risks becoming a repetitive and overly familiar move, the range of examples contained in this book suggests that the scope for experimenting with exhibition is as broad as the range of topics that exhibitions cover. The cases that Porto describes from the Museum of Anthropology of the University of Coimbra (MAUC), Portugal, for example, include an exhibition of materials from the Dundo Museum, Angola, considering photography in relation to colonial regimes of surveillance; and *Nomads,* an exhibition of, and about, objects that had traveled and been exhibited elsewhere.

These examples are very different from the reflexivity involved in the storyboard produced by Xperiment! – a group involved in the public communication of science – in which they seek to lay bare the ongoing processes by which they attempted to learn about the science and interests involved in genetic modification (chapter 5). Or take the example of *Capital,* an artistic intervention by Cummings and Lewandowska at the opening of Tate Modern in London in 2001. This involved exploring analogies between Tate Modern and the Bank of England, and the role that both play in assurances in circuits of capital. Drawing on ideas about gift exchange, *Capital* also sought to draw attention to questions of the visibility of some kinds of art patronage versus the invisibility of the financial contribution of ordinary taxpayers.

In a chapter that is centrally concerned with exhibiting exhibition, Mieke Bal provides a further example of an exhibition that seeks to expose what she here calls "the work of exhibition" – the narrative strategies and frames through which exhibitions position viewers and offer up particular, positioned, readings. It is worth noting that in a considerable corpus of previous writing and, more recently, her own curatorial work, Bal has herself made a major contribution to analyzing the "work of exhibition" (e.g. 1996, 2006). Her praise here, then, for an exhibition that she describes as "the most effective, gripping and powerful" that she has ever seen – and that derives this power from the way in which it illuminates its subject while simultaneously being a "meta-exhibition" or "exhibition exploring the nature of exhibiting" – deserves particular note. The exhibition, called *Partners* and curated by Ydessa Hendeles, is concerned with the uneasy relationship between German and Jewish populations. It deploys mixed media – photography and sculpture – in juxtapositions that prompt the visitor to be attentive to the politics of particular kinds of optics and commemorative practices; and in her analysis Bal seeks to understand its mechanisms via a set of illuminating analytical concepts inspired by the exhibition's own use of filmic and cinematic aesthetics.

What these chapters also show is that the work of experimentally exposing exhibitionary mechanisms can be undertaken through the full range of exhibitionary media – including both "conventional" media, such as art works and objects, and "new media" such as video or digital technologies (see especially chapter 1 by Henning and chapter 7 by Carolin and Haynes). Moreover, as Paul Basu shows in his chapter, even museum architecture can be used reflexively by architects such as Daniel Libeskind to disrupt conventional museological architectural tropes and thus to "critique the concept of the museum through the medium of the museum itself." He borrows from literary theory to refer to the strategy of "reflexive structuration, by means of which a text shows what it is telling" (Ulmer 1992, p. 140; see chapter 2), as "the *mise en abyme*." This terminology, which indicates the dangerous nature of the process involved, is revealing. Exposing your own practices is not necessarily easy. It can indeed feel like, if not quite a falling into the abyss, at least a kind of crisis.

Crises of Representation and Ethnography

Exposing practice has been a key feature not only of the first age of experimentalism – that associated with the project of the Enlightenment, in which the scientific method provided a reliable means of knowing the "Truth" – but also with what might be called a second age of experimentalism, associated with that post-Enlightenment "crisis of representation" in which notions of "objectivity," "certainty," and "Truth," as well as earlier claims of transparency, have themselves come to be questioned. While the crisis of representation has been reported across a wide range of disciplines, it has been particularly keenly felt within anthropology (Marcus and Fischer 1986). In response, anthropology has struggled with its methodological and textual practices to, among other things, respond to the conundrum of how to represent "otherness" when the very concept of otherness is perceived as a construction of the discipline's own practices. Ethnography and ethnographic experimentalism have, in turn, inspired or provided a critical prompt to other disciplines, and especially to artists, in dealing with questions of engagement and representation. This is evident in many of the chapters that follow.

Several of the contributors here, for example, use ethnographic methods. This includes anthropologists Alexa Färber and Anne Lorimer who carry out participant-observation fieldwork on the making of exhibitions. By doing so, they not only practice the "repatriation of anthropology" (Marcus and Fischer 1986) – that is, anthropology of their own societies – advocated as one means of contending with anthropology's perceived focus on otherness, but they also turn a method that was developed in a context of capturing the exotic back onto a practice (exhibiting) that was itself implicated in that process. Other contributors, who do not identify themselves as anthropologists, also employ ethnographic approaches. Members of Xperiment!, for example, effectively use the experimental ethnographic methods of "following the object" or "following the story" (advocated by George Marcus 1998; see also Latour 1987) in their attempt to grasp the complexity of the scientific and political processes that they seek to describe. Moreover, their unusual "text" – a large storyboard that can be walked upon – also exemplifies tenets of "second age" experimental ethnographic writing in its presentation of multiple voices and positions, and as unfinished and contingent. The work of Cummings and Lewandowska with Polish film enthusiasts also entails a kind of collaborative ethnography; and in its search for new forms for exhibiting and archiving develops the kinds of concerns that have been voiced by anthropologists. Ann-Sofi Sidén's work on prostitution likewise relies on ethnographic engagement, in this case with the sex workers who become the subject of her exhibition – *Warte Mal!* ("Hey, wait!" – a phrase with which they attempt to attract their clients). While this work can undoubtedly be seen as an example of what Hal Foster has called "the ethnographic turn in contemporary art and criticism" (1996, p. 181), it goes beyond many such works both in avoiding assuming ethnographic authority (a problem that Foster has identified in some "artist as ethnographer" pieces) and in the way in which her work artistically generates complex questions of voyeurism, alterity, realism, and genre, as discussed by a range of commentators in chapter 8.

Works such as these not only draw on ethnographic practices, they also offer experimental models that may in turn inspire transformation in practices in anthropology and other disciplines. As Schneider and Wright (2006a) observe in their discussion of the relationship between art and anthropology, there is considerable unplumbed potential in artistic practice that might be experimentally developed in anthropology. In particular, art offers techniques for moving beyond the overwhelming textual focus of anthropology's 1980s representational concerns, as exemplified in *Writing Culture: The Poetics and Politics of Ethnography* (Clifford and Marcus 1986). To escape logocentrism is not, however, necessarily to escape the criticisms to which it has been subject. Non-textual media – such as video, photography, painting, or interactive computer screens – can equally, though in interestingly different ways, raise problems of the kind put forward by the *Writing Culture* critiques (e.g. of authority and authorship, realism and transparency) – as we see in many of the chapters that follow.

Nevertheless, what exhibitions offer is the opportunity to mix media and to draw from different disciplinary traditions, and in the process to explore their differential potentials. Exhibitions also typically reach a wider public than do academic texts and offer different possibilities for engaging them – including physically and within the exhibition space itself (see below). It is notable that in recent years a number of the academics who have written most extensively on questions of representation have themselves turned to exhibition-making. George Marcus, for example, has been involved in exhibiting the work of Cuban artists, including Fernando Calzadilla and Abdel Hernández. Their artistic practices – partly influenced by *Writing Culture* debates – offer, he suggests, inspiring collaborative possibilities for ethnographic practice (Calzadilla and Marcus 2006). Mieke Bal, who writes here and who is one of the most well-known and original cultural theorists writing on art, has herself taken up the challenge to create an exhibition (Bal 2006). In doing so, she drew upon her understandings of the "affective syntax" and "work of exhibition" discussed here to create an experimental work that also aimed to avoid the dilemmas of the auteurist exhibitionary strategy that has become one of the most common responses to critiques of the absence of authorship in exhibitions. As she explains, openly acknowledging the authorial role of the curator does not necessarily challenge the curator's authority. More challenging strategies – involving exposing the work of exhibition through exhibition itself – are required. Likewise, Bruno Latour, whose writings have inspired experiments in ethnography, text, and exhibition (for example, the ideas of multiple "actants" and of "following" noted above; and see chapter 5), has worked with Peter Weibel at the ZKM to produce the exhibitions *Iconoclash* and *Making Things Public* discussed here; both exhibitions include exploration of themes of representation that he has previously tackled in his writing.

Exhibition experiments, then, expand the scope for engaging inventively and provocatively in questions raised by the so-called "crisis of representation" in anthropology and elsewhere. They do so on account of some characteristic qualities – to which we now turn.

Assemblages

All exhibitions entail the bringing together of unlikely assemblages of people, things, ideas, texts, spaces, and different media. Curators, designers, artists, anthropologists, sponsors, visitors, artworks, artifacts, antiquities, machines, installations, display cases, spotlights, photographs, moving images, catalogues, promotional materials, object labels, audio tours, gallery guides – we might say that these constitute the apparatus of the exhibition experiment. As Weibel and Latour note, they are highly artificial assemblages, brought together for no other reason than the experiment itself, and yet their purpose remains to make visible that which is otherwise invisible, to make tangible something intangible (Shapin and Schaffer 1985). The alchemy through which this transformation is brought about is another of the themes that run through many of the chapters of the book.

Reflecting on the social, creative, and bureaucratic negotiations involved in staging a major exhibition at Chicago's Museum of Science and Industry, Lorimer suggests that there is indeed "magic" involved in the design process. Charged with the task of translating concepts into material forms (giving "body" to the concept of "mind," for example), Lorimer argues that for exhibition developers the process of assembling the components of a display may be better understood as a process of discovery, in which the exhibition takes on a "ghostly" life of its own, disrupting its creators' intentions and leading to serendipitous encounters. As the apparatus of the exhibition is assembled, in the museum workshop as much as on the gallery floor, so the different components interact with each other, generating new and unanticipated outcomes.

It was this idea of putting together different elements and observing the outcome of their interaction that was central to the early appropriation of the concept of the experiment within literature and the arts. Whereas the label "experimental" is today perhaps too loosely employed to refer to art practice which is regarded as innovative or avant-garde, in the late eighteenth and early nineteenth centuries artistic experimentation was considered more closely analogous to scientific experimentation. The German poet and philosopher Novalis (1772–1801), for example, was particularly interested in chemistry and how chemists experiment with different substances, combining them and observing how they react together under different conditions. For Novalis, experimenting with words, the text, too, was like a chemistry laboratory in which compositions in different areas of knowledge and experience could be examined by observing how they react to one another (Fabian 2002).

Working at ZKM, the Center for Art and Media, in Karlsruhe, Germany – an institution which is itself dedicated to bringing together different areas of knowledge and experience across the sciences, the arts, and politics – Weibel and Latour describe *Iconoclash* and *Making Things Public* as assemblies of assemblies. In the context of *Iconoclash*, for example, these assemblages include not only the "totally improbable elements" that would go on display, including documents, scientific objects, religious icons, and artworks (both genuine articles and facsimiles), but also the input of no fewer than seven curators assembled for the project. Challenging the "sacrosanct autonomy" of a singular curatorial vision, which typifies the hierarchical structure of much exhibitionary practice, Weibel and Latour's exhibitions are thus also experiments in heteronomy. Rather than seeking agreement and a neat convergence of purpose, Weibel and Latour describe the desired outcome of these assemblages as the production of "interference patterns," which, as physicists experimenting with wave forms will explain, can be both constructive and destructive.

New media "remediate" old media, old media remediate new media (see Henning, chapter 1). Of all media, that most closely associated with the process of assemblage is film. In cinema it is classically the relationship *between* the assembled shots that constructs their meaning: "The essence of cinema", writes Eisenstein, "does not lie in the images, but in the relation between images!" (Aumont 1987, p. 146). It is interesting, therefore, that Mieke Bal uses cinema as her master trope in her analysis of *Partners*. By exploring the medium of the exhibition through the medium of cinema, one might say she remediates both. Bal is concerned with understanding the affective relationships both between the exhibition visitor and the artworks exhibited, and among the assembled artworks themselves. The emotional punch of *Partners*, Bal argues, results from the way in which the visitor encounters the discrete elements of the exhibition as she moves through it. In particular Bal is interested in exploring the "affective syntax" that results from the sequencing of and transitions between these elements as they are framed and animated by the dynamics of the visit. This may be understood as an essentially cinematic experience, consequent upon more than the mere juxtaposition of images or installations, and dependent upon more complex techniques such as dissolves, superimposition, zoom-ins, flashbacks, long shots, close-ups, and so forth.

Crucially, it is the visitor that provides the kinetic impetus to make the images of *Partners* "move," and the affective discourse of the exhibition thus remains "virtual, not actual, so long as visitors do not 'perform' the film" (Bal, chapter 3). It is to this issue of performance, another dominant theme in the world of exhibition experimentalism, that we now proceed.

From Mediation to Enactment

The "crisis of representation" discussed above and alluded to in many of the chapters forms the critical context for much contemporary experimentation in exhibitionary form. It is no longer tenable to claim that one can represent neutrally, objectively, or impartially – whether in an exhibition or in an ethnographic monograph. All representations are socially, politically, ideologically, institutionally, and technologically mediated. Exhibitions, as various authors here argue, must be understood as sites of cultural mediation; and mediation, furthermore, must be understood as a process that partly constructs that which it mediates. In exhibition experimentation, this shift from representation to mediation has provoked two responses. On the one hand there is what Henning (below) describes as "hypermediacy," in which the processes of mediation are accentuated and where media are used to reference other media. On the other hand there is what Henning describes as "immediacy," in which processes of mediation are suppressed or concealed; this is evident, for instance, in the so-called "return of the object," where contextualizing information or narrative interpretation is, to a greater or lesser extent, suspended (Bann 2003). In many of the exhibitions discussed by our contributors, hypermediacy and immediacy co-exist, drawing attention to both the politics and poetics of display.

An exhibition is, above all, a multimedia environment in which different media come to remediate each other. As Henning reminds us, as new media technologies are introduced into exhibitionary practice, so the space of exhibition and the way it is used by both exhibitors and visitors are transformed. The gallery or museum is thus constantly reimagined as it embraces new technologies and reanimates old ones. In this way, the museum becomes a fascinating context for pursuing a kind of archaeological excavation of media technologies, in which the impact of new information and communication technologies, for example, can be shown to be prefigured in earlier, long-taken-for-granted technologies such as the card index system and interactive mechanical devices adapted from fairground attractions. Through such technologies we are witnessing a convergence of the institutions of the museum, the library, and the archive. But is this an experimental moment of reimagination or actually a return to an earlier concept of the museum? With the renaissance of the museum as archive, the concept of the "open storage display" has become increasingly popular. As the store effectively becomes the exhibit, Henning poses an important question: what becomes of the medium of the exhibition itself?

With Henning's caveat in mind, that very little innovation is without precedent in contemporary exhibitionary practice, a significant shift in the function of the exhibition space is nevertheless apparent in many of the experiments discussed in this volume. This might be most succinctly described in Weibel and Latour's words as a "performative turn" in exhibition practice. The exhibition is thus no longer conceived as a medium for representation, but becomes, instead, a medium for "enactment." Cummings and Lewandowska thus write of breaking from that long tradition which separates the site of the production of an artwork (the artist's studio) from the sites in which an artwork is all too often passively consumed (the gallery or exhibition). They argue, rather, for the "exhibitionary context" in which the *work* of the work of art is activated. Hence, as we have already noted, it is in the act of visiting *Partners* that its cinematic syntax is animated.

An interactive relationship between installation and visitor is central to the *Knowledge Themenpark* at Expo 2000, discussed by Färber. The main attraction of *Knowledge* was a "swarm" of 72 slowly moving robots, among which visitors could roam in a dimly lit exhibition hall. The designers employed the poorly understood swarming behavior of certain animals as a metaphor for the "complexity and interconnection of knowledge," but it is evident from Färber's ethnographic account that it was the visitors' own "knowledge-seeking strategies" that were most forcefully articulated by the exhibition. As the visitors interacted with the slowly swarming robots and discovered that the movements of the robots could be influenced by their own behavior, they sought to comprehend what was happening and in so doing became part of the performance of the installation. *Knowledge* became an arena for the visitors' own experimentation, and in a manner that made it necessary for them to gather evidence through "acting" – what happens if I do this? Whereas the artists' group involved in developing the swarm wanted the exhibit to be experienced without further interpretation, the Expo organizers were more concerned to explain what the installation was meant to represent and what visitors were supposed to learn from it. Here there were clearly two different conceptualizations of exhibition converging on the same site: the one concerned with knowledge transmission and understanding, the other with enactment and experience.

Weibel and Latour's exhibition *Making Things Public* is concerned with democracy and that elusive concept, "the public" (see also chapters 5 and 9). "Democracy", Weibel and Latour argue, "cannot be represented, it can only be 'enacted'," and thus *Making Things Public* was, above all, conceived as a "field of enactment" – an "interactive artwork" in which the visitor becomes another among the many assembled "actants" which comprise the exhibition. This is perhaps most clearly evident in an installation within the exhibition, designed by digital artists Michel Jaffrennou and Thierry Coduys, entitled *The Phantom*, after Walter Lippmann's 1925 book *The Phantom Public*. *The Phantom* is described as a "quasi-invisible" work of art, which comprised a series of audio-visual effects distributed throughout the entire *Making Things Public* exhibition. The "behavior" of this installation is shaped by numerous factors, including local climatic changes, the time of day, push-buttons that visitors are invited to press at various points in the exhibition, as well as the visitors' own movements through the exhibition, which are tracked through unique radio frequency identifiers in their tickets. The idea, explain the curators, "was to give visitors a vague and uneasy feeling that 'something happens' for which they are at least sometimes responsible – sometimes in a direct way, but mostly in ways not directly traceable" – "just as politics", they go on, "passes through people as a rather mysterious flow" (Weibel and Latour, chapter 4). *The Phantom* – and, indeed, *Making Things Public* as a whole – does not represent political process in a series of discursive displays, it enacts it. As Weibel and Latour conclude, "it is an exhibition experiment that *is* what it shows" (emphasis added).

But the performative turn in exhibition experimentation is not reliant on such "hi-tech" computer-mediated technologies. In contrast to *Knowledge Themenpark* or *The Phantom*, note, for example, Cummings and Lewandowska's *Capital*. Every day for the duration of the exhibition, at unspecified times, this experiment involved the enactment of a gift exchange, whereby a visitor would be approached by a gallery or museum official and, with the words "This is for you," would be presented with a finely wrapped, limited-edition photographic print of a silver spoon bearing the Bank of England's crest. This simple, though astonishing, gesture would disrupt the normal behavior of the gallery (provoking intrigue among bystanders as well as affecting those directly involved) and would typically result in an animated conversation between gift-giver and receiver. Discussions would follow as to the nature of the exchange enacted and thereby exhibited: were debts being repaid through the gift (for instance, the public institution's debt to the taxpayer, whose invisible gift sustains the institution), or were new debts being incurred? It is the enactment of such disruptions in the placid order of things that constitutes the *work* of the exhibition experiment.

Spaces of Encounter

Through such experiments, the exhibition becomes transformed from a space of representation into a space of encounter. This causes us to consider experimentation in the architecture of exhibitionary spaces and how it shapes the possibilities of the encounters such spaces generate (cf. Giebelhausen 2003, 2006; MacLeod 2005; Lampugnani 2006). It is interesting to note the spatial metaphors that our contributors draw upon: within you will find reference to maps that are territories to be walked upon and narrated, labyrinths that simultaneously frustrate and enthrall, halls of mirrors that reflect back visitors' own implication in that which is exhibited. Such spatial forms urge us to engage with the concept of exhibition, not as a two-dimensional "text" to be "read," as Cummings and Lewandowska remark, in a "slow pan along gallery walls" (chapter 6), but as an immersive, three-dimensional environment, which calls visitors to explore actively with all their senses, and with their "muscular consciousnesses" as well as their intellects (Ingold 2000: 203).

Speaking from their respective professional and disciplinary backgrounds, the discussants of Sidén's *Warte Mal!* exhibition, staged at the Hayward Gallery in 2002, all remark on the architectural space of the installation. Concerned with prostitution in the Czech border town of Dubi, the exhibit takes the form of a central corridor off which lead numerous cubicles, each equipped with benches and with television screens and loudspeakers which play loops of seemingly unedited video interviews with Dubi's sex workers. Elsewhere, onto screens and walls, are projected other video clips, still photographs and excerpts from Sidén's diaries recording her experiences as an artist-ethnographer living among her informants. Unlike the peep-show arcades that the installation's layout evokes, or the Dubi hotel rooms rented by the hour by the prostitutes, the walls of the exhibition are transparent. Thus, as visitors enter this maze-like exhibition, moving from viewing booth to viewing booth, they watch with the unsettling knowledge that they are also watched: as they gaze, they cannot hide from the gaze of others. As Laura Bear notes, this causes visitors to reflect on their own role as "consumers of images of others' lives," and to question their position in relation to the images and lives they look at, listen to, and read about: are they witnesses, observers, voyeurs? Griselda Pollock suggests that the architectural organization of *Warte Mal!* has the effect of weaving a web around its audience, capturing them in threads of discourse and image and space. Unlike in many exhibitions that one can pass through with ease, the visitor to *Warte Mal!* becomes entangled in these texts, photographs and videos. As one metaphor suggests another, so curator Clare Carolin considers the exhibition as a "hall of mirrors" in which visitors find themselves "reflected and implicated in the issue of prostitution" – there is no escaping here, no recourse to the reassuring and passive consumption of an aesthetic display. The exhibition has agency, it entraps its audience (cf. Gell 1998).

The spatial dynamics of exhibition are foregrounded by Basu in his discussion of the labyrinthine aesthetic in the deconstructivist museum architecture of Daniel Libeskind. Basu approaches the labyrinth not only as an architectural device, but also as a narratological one. He is interested, for example, in extending Ricoeurian ideas of the temporal configuration of emplotment into the space of the museum, considering how visitors tread sense-making paths through an exhibitionary environment, and questioning what happens if such paths are disrupted by what amounts to a labyrinthine design. Whereas many museums are unintentionally (and, many argue, negatively) labyrinthine in their layout (cf. Duncan and Wallach 2004), Basu argues that Libeskind intentionally employs a labyrinthine aesthetic in his museum designs to complicate and critique what he characterizes as "the persuasive 'straightforwardness'" of the institution's grand narratives and taxonomies. Through the use of inter-secting, corridor-like galleries, complicating trajectories, dead-ends and inaccessible voids, this design principle is enacted in the very structure of the museum, making of its galleries an "active path," which insists on its visitors' cognitive and physical labors. Applying de Certeau's (1984) cri-tique of the fictive "totalizing view" of the city to the space of the museum, Basu contends that, rather than fulfilling the promise, implicit in all museums, of rendering their obscure texts readable, the labyrinthine museum purposely frustrates its visitors' expectations, thrusting visitors back into the troubling – but less illusory – realms of partial truths and uncertainties.

Navigations

It will be clear that the exhibition experiments described in this volume are not experiments in didacticism. The purpose of their experimentation is not to innovate ever more effective ways of disseminating knowledge that has been preformulated and authenticated by experts to those who are inexpert and presumably in need of it. No, the tenor of these experiments has been to reconfigure the way in which exhibitions work. Rather than making complex realities more vividly simple, patronizing audiences and perpetuating illusory securities, the issue has more often been how to engage with complexity, how to create a context that will open up a space for conversation and debate, above all how to enlist audiences as co-experimenters, willing to *try* for themselves. The exhibitions discussed in this book are, it might be said, as much about "not knowing" as they are about knowing. They are about navigations in realms of proliferating knowledges and surfeits of information, about the negotiation of competing truths. Visitors in such environments must play an active role as navigators, way-finders and meaning-makers; drawing their own observations and conclusions without the reassuring presence of an "authority" to defer to.

Thus Xperiment! conceive their exhibitions as laboratories or research centers of "shared incompetence," the purpose of which is not to decrease the "knowledge differential" between experts and non-experts, but to bring together different people with different knowledges in an arena that is foreign to all (the arena of shared incompetence). Concerned with communicating scientific knowledge in the public realm, Xperiment! are keen to position themselves as non-scientists and non-experts (despite their audiences' preference to construct them as such). Rather, as exhibitors, they argue that they are engaged *with* their audiences in "fuzzy," unclear, and confused navigations of their topic and of each other's knowledges. In these navigations, no mutual understanding is necessarily achieved, and, indeed, understandings are dynamic, shifting with every changing context. In the project they describe, in which their "fuzzy knowledge navigations" are directed toward exploring a genetically modified rice strain, the group find themselves acting in turn as ethnographers, cartographers, and storytellers. The project culminates with Xperiment! playing shifting roles (are they actors, artists, activists, a PR organization?) as they guide museum visitors around a 250-meter-square "map" of the ethico-scientific processes involved in the production of the rice technology. Exchanging stories with their audiences, they discovered that "a museum can be much more than a territory that represents facts." It can also be a territory of "interaction and experience, an environment that generates various kinds of communications that consistently produce in the participants 'a difference which makes a difference.'" Such is the potential of the exhibition experiment.

The Trouble with Experiment[2]

Exhibition experiments, as we have defined them here, then, are intended to be troubling. Experimentalism is not just a matter of style or novel forms of presentation. Rather, it is a risky process of assembling people and things with the intention of producing differences that make a difference. In their production of something new, experiments seek to unsettle accepted knowledge or the status quo.

But experiments can go wrong. They may turn out to be not troubling in the ways that were intended, or, indeed, not troubling at all. They may make little difference. Equally, trying to create experimental exhibitions may itself generate troubles – practically, institutionally, and politically. Moreover, experimentalism should not be exempt from critique but – if it is to continue to trouble in meaningful ways – needs to be contextualized, analyzed, and troubled itself. Thus, while the chapters here seek to highlight and explore different kinds of exhibition experiments, they also remain alert to some of their limitations and dilemmas.

As many of the chapters below remind us, exhibitions inevitably take place in particular institutional contexts which pose their own constraints of space, funding, personnel, and managerial demands. Exhibitions are generally expensive and this may make some museum directors, managers, and trustees reluctant to allow experimental exhibitions – which are by definition relatively unknown quantities – to go ahead. Furthermore, exhibition experiments may be politically sensitive or challenging – and it is to the credit of all of the institutions that hosted the exhibitions described in this book that they were willing to take the risk to do so. It is not always thus as, for example, with the banning of the work of Hans Haacke from the Guggenheim (Foster, Krauss, Bois, and Buchloh 2004, pp. 545–8) or the decision to withdraw John Latham's *God is Great* – an artwork consisting of the Bible, the Talmud and the Qur'an embedded together in glass – from a retrospective of his work at Tate Britain in the aftermath of the July 7th London bombings in 2005. (For further examples see Dubin 2006 and Conn 2006.) Moreover, as Anthony Shelton has pointed out in a review of developments in ethnographic exhibition, in many museums there has been a shift of control away from curatorial staff and toward managerialism such that "[m]useums … are no longer motivated primarily by either established or experimental academic programming, but by the delivery of external institutional objectives broadly related to social engineering policies and subordinated to supposed market forces" (2006, p. 76). "Blockbusteritis," as Steven Conn (2006) has called the increasing tendency of many major museums to mount large-scale shows of well-known artists, is but one symptom of an institutional preference for tried-and-tested formulae.

While the experiments described in this volume have managed to find suitable niches in the contemporary museum world, they have not necessarily avoided financial and other constraints. An institution such as the ZKM, which has extensive financial and technological resources and also offers exhibition-makers considerable freedom to experiment, is the exception rather than the rule. But, as is shown by the fact that it has produced so many intriguing experimental exhibitions that have become wider talking points, it is an exception that generates significant interventions. Yet, even at the opposite end of the spectrum in terms of available finance, imaginative curators and artists may succeed in producing innovative experimental exhibitions. We have noted Cummings and Lewandowska's simple but effective experiment at Tate Modern above. Or take the example of the MAUC, where, as Porto describes, budgets were often severely limited and personnel few, and there were additional constraints and demands, such as that a particular exhibition would attract school groups. Nevertheless, by engaging fully with ideas about ethnographic experimentalism, curators were able to create exhibitions that were challenging even while working within the constraints. Sometimes, indeed, constraints may play into effects judged experimental – as Lorimer describes in relation to some of the factors involved in the Brain exhibition in Chicago's Museum of Science and Industry coming to look so ghostly.

One niche constraint that may pose particular problems for experimentalism is that of genre. Experiments frequently seek to challenge conventional boundaries, but this very challenge may make them hard to place. *Warte Mal!* is an interesting case here because its use of anthropological techniques and video documentary made some visitors and reviewers question its status as art. This was compounded by its subject matter – prostitution – which, as Pollock comments, "is thought somehow to be beyond the realm of what one should see in an art gallery" (chapter 7). Moreover, as the curator of the show comments, multiply troubling exhibitions such as this are more likely to be shown at "international biennials or in more modest – often artist-run – spaces" than in larger galleries (see also Rectanus 2006). On the other hand, once a form of experiment – in this case the politically engaged use of documentary – has been tested in a relatively established institution (in this case the Hayward), it may be taken up by others. However, as Carolin further suggests, as an experimental form becomes appropriated into the mainstream, it may also shed some of its complexity and political edge.

The movement of experiments into the mainstream raises the question of whether an experiment remains experimental in all contexts, or when it is repeated. In the natural sciences one feature of experiments is that they should be replicable. Nevertheless, it is the first use of a particular experiment that establishes new knowledge – the replications are intended to confirm it. The repetition of an experiment, therefore, is less "experimental" in the sense that we have defined it above, than is the first, more risky and indeterminate, attempt. This is not to say that repeating exhibition experiments in different contexts is not worthwhile. Doing so may bring them to new audiences; and altered contexts may, perhaps as part of the indeterminacy of process that Lorimer in particular highlights, turn out to have results that are more novel than expected. (The opposite can also be the case as shown in Macdonald's ethnographic study of exhibition-making in the Science Museum, London (2002).) Equally, we are aware of the characteristic Euro-American obsession with novelty (Hirsch and Macdonald 2005); and would not wish to maintain that only the new should be valued. Claims to novelty are, indeed, part of the standard discourse of exhibition-production (Macdonald 2002, p. 115). But this is not to say that such exhibitions are necessarily experimental – that is, that they trouble existing knowledge and practice.

Many aspects of exhibitions that we now accept as standard were, of course, experimental innovations once. Henning points out that when the

Museum of Society and Economy in Vienna introduced spotlighting in the 1920s this was considered a noteworthy innovation. So too, some time later, was the use of film within exhibitions. And as Lorimer notes, an exhibition opening in a science museum in the early 1990s that contained few "authentic" objects and many interactive exhibits was then considered novel.

Even aspects of experimental exhibitions inspired by "second age" experimentalism have, however, entered mainstream practice. Reflexivity, for example, has become widespread – it is a common motif in exhibitions at world's fairs, as Färber describes (see also Harvey 1996); and including sections on collectors and collecting has become an almost ubiquitous addition to ethnographic displays. Reflexivity might, indeed, appear to have become a new orthodoxy. Yet crucial here is the purpose to which it is deployed and how unsettling it is allowed to be. A criticism that has been made of some reflexive ethnographic strategies is that apparently self-exposing moves may be token gestures, serving more to legitimate what is displayed than to unsettle it. Or, as Färber suggests in her analysis of exhibition-makers' creation of a text about an experimental exhibition that was part of an event widely judged a failure, reflexivity may be deployed by the authors in order to try to distance themselves from the event and gain subcultural capital through ironic self-positioning. Turning what might otherwise be seen as failure into a productive lesson is not only fully in line with notions of experiment but also a valuable ability of the entrepreneurial person favoured in late capitalism, argues Färber. The rise of a discourse of experimentalism might thus be seen not so much as a rise in willingness to challenge existing knowledge and generate new, but as "deeply inscribed into the cultural logic of late capitalism" (Färber, chapter 10), legitimizing a particular kind of cultural entrepreneurship. As Cummings and Lewandowska write, "[i]n these "new" economies the artist or enthusiast is an ideal employee; astonishingly self-motivated, endlessly creative, flexible, enthusiastic, resourceful and, financially, poorly rewarded" (chapter 6).

The point being made here is not, however, that experimentalism, and reflexivity, are necessarily only or even primarily part of such a logic. Rather, the call is for remaining alert to such possibilities – and to addressing such questions through experimental work. As Nicholas Mirzoeff, discussing the idea of "the experimental university," points out, there is always a "risk that knowledge production simply becomes knowledge commodification" (Mirzoeff 2004, p. 146); and, equally, there is always a risk that the experimental is co-opted to support that to which it might direct its challenge. Writing of the early modern period, when scientific experimentalism began to gain ground, Barbara Maria Stafford has shown how the lines between experimental science and trickery were sometimes elusive: "for the early moderns an analogy existed between the legerdemain of experimentalists in all fields and the maneuvers of the con man ... The potential for fraud lurked in any demonstration in which the performer created the illusion of eyewitnessing without informing the beholder how the action was done" (1994, p. 79). Likewise, in relation to contemporary exhibition experiments, there may be illusions of laying bare mechanism or producing new knowledge without actually doing so.

This raises crucial questions about reception. For, as Thomas Hobbes pointed out in his objections to Robert Boyle's claims about the superiority of experimental knowledge in the late 1660s, "there [are] immense problems for the very notion of witnessing" (Shapin and Schaffer 1985: 114). Part of Hobbes's objections concerned the point that even if people are all brought together to witness a particular event, this does not necessarily mean that they "see" the same thing or make the same inferences. In relation to exhibitions, we typically know rather little about how they are received (cf. McClellan 2003; though see also Hooper-Greenhill 2006); and too much research remains rather crude (ibid.). There is undoubtedly a need for more subtle approaches that observe the kinds of language and metaphors that visitors use in their own comments, as do both Xperiment! and Lorimer in chapters 6 and 10 respectively. While such studies show that there is surely always scope for readings beyond those anticipated, it is also clear that visitor readings are produced in relation to the complexities of the exhibition's affective syntax, assemblages, and spaces. This includes, importantly, the extent to which visitors are sufficiently provoked to experiment with forming and voicing their own views.

Experimental Intervention

As we have noted above, this book too has been an experiment. By bringing together the chapters which follow, we hope not only to generate new knowledge about experimental exhibitions but – like the exhibitions described here – to provoke readers to consider the potential of exhibition experiments not only to meddle in the world of museums but also to intervene and make trouble beyond.

Notes

1   We thank all of those who participated in the panel and its discussion, and the conference organizers for their support.
2   This is borrowed from the title of chapter IV of Shapin and Schaffer 1985.

References

Aumont, J. (1987) *Montage Eisenstein.* Bloomington: Indiana University Press, and London: BFI Publishing.

Bal, M. (1996) *Double Exposures: The Subject of Cultural Analysis.* London: Routledge.

Bal, M. (2006) Exposing the public. In S. Macdonald (ed.), *A Companion to Museum Studies.* Oxford: Blackwell, pp. 525–42.

Bann, S. (2003) The return to curiosity: shifting paradigms in contemporary museum display. In A. McClellan (ed.), *Art and its Publics.* Oxford: Blackwell, pp. 117–30.

Calzadilla, F. and Marcus, G. E. (2006) Artists in the field: between art and anthropology. In A. Schneider and C. Wright (eds.), *Contemporary Art and Anthropology.* Oxford: Berg, pp. 95–115.

Clifford, J. and Marcus, G. E. (eds.) (1986) *Writing Culture: The Poetics and Politics of Ethnography.* Berkeley: University of California Press.

Conn, S. (2006) Science museums and the culture wars. In S. Macdonald (ed.), *A Companion to Museum Studies.* Oxford: Blackwell, pp. 494–508.

Cummings, N. and Lewandowska, M. (2001) *The Value of Things.* London: August.

de Certeau, M. (1984 [1980]). *The Practice of Everyday Life.* Trans. S. Rendall. Berkeley: California University Press.

Dubin, S. C. (2006) In-civilities in civil(ized) places: "culture wars" in comparative perspective. In S. Macdonald (ed.), *A Companion to Museum Studies.* Oxford: Blackwell, pp. 477–93.

Duncan, C. and A.Wallach (2004 [1978]) The museum of modern art as a late capitalist ritual: an iconographic analysis. In D. Preziosi and C. Farago (eds.), *Grasping the World: The Idea of the Museum.* Aldershot: Ashgate, pp. 483–500.

Fabian, L. (2002) Novalis' Combinatorial Poetics. *Nordlit* 11: 59–79.

Foster, H. (1996) *The Return of the Real.* Cambridge, Mass.: MIT Press.

Foster, H., Krauss, R., Bois, Y.-A., and Buchloh, B. H. D. (2004) *Art Since 1900: Modernism, Antimodernism, Postmodernism.* London: Thames & Hudson.

Gell, A. (1998) *Art and Agency: An Anthropological Theory.* Oxford: Oxford University Press.

Giebelhausen, M. (ed.) (2003) *The Architecture of the Museum: Symbolic Structures, Urban Contexts.* Manchester: Manchester University Press.

Giebelhausen, M. (2006) Museum architecture: a brief history. In S. Macdonald (ed.), *A Companion to Museum Studies.* Oxford: Blackwell, pp. 223–44.

Hacking, I. (1975) *The Emergence of Probability.* Cambridge: Cambridge University Press.

Hacking, I. (1983) *Representing and Intervening: Introductory Topics in the Philosophy of Natural Science.* Cambridge: Cambridge University Press.

Harvey, P. (1996) *Hybrids of Modernity: Anthropology, the Nation State and the Universal Exhibition.* London: Routledge.

Hirsch, E. and Macdonald, S. (2005) Introduction: creativity or temporality? *Cambridge Anthropology* (special issue on *Creativity or Temporality*) 25 (2): 1–4.

Hooper-Greenhill, E. (2006) Studying visitors. In S. Macdonald (ed.), *A Companion to Museum Studies.* Oxford: Blackwell, pp. 362–76.

Ingold, T. (2000) *The Perception of the Environment: Essays in Livelihood, Dwelling and Skill.* London: Routledge.

Lampugnani, V. Magnago (2006) Insight versus entertainment: untimely meditations on the architecture of twentieth-century art museums. In S. Macdonald (ed.), *A Companion to Museum Studies.* Oxford: Blackwell, pp. 245–62.

Latour, B. (1987) *Science in Action.* Cambridge, Mass.: Harvard University Press.

Latour, B. (1999) *Pandora's Hope: Essays on the Reality of Science Studies.* Cambridge, Mass.: Harvard University Press.

Law, J. and Hassard, J. (eds.) (1999) *Actor Network Theory and After.* Oxford: Blackwell.

Macdonald, S. (2002) *Behind the Scenes at the Science Museum.* Oxford: Berg.

MacLeod, S. (ed.) (2005) *Reshaping Museum Space: Architecture, Design, Exhibitions.* London: Routledge.

Marcus, G. E. (1998) *Ethnography through Thick and Thin.* Princeton: Princeton University Press.

Marcus, G. E. and Fischer, M. M. J. (1986) *Anthropology as Cultural Critique: An Experimental Moment in the Human Sciences.* Chicago: Chicago University Press.

Marstine, J. (ed.) (2005) *New Museum Theory and Practice.* Oxford: Blackwell.

McClellan, A. (ed.) (2003) *Art and its Publics: Museum Studies at the Millennium.* Oxford: Blackwell.

Mirzoeff, N. (2004) Anarchy in the ruins: dreaming the experimental university. In N. Thompson and G. Sholette (eds.), *The Interventionists: Users' Manual for the Creative Disruption of Everyday Life.* Cambridge, Mass.: MIT Press, pp. 143–6.

Pickstone, J. (2000) *Ways of Knowing: A New History of Science, Technology and Medicine.* Manchester: Manchester University Press.

Putnam, J. (2001) *Art and Artifact: The Museum as Medium.* London: Thames & Hudson.

Rectanus, M. W. (2006) Globalization: incorporating the museum. In S. Macdonald (ed.), *A Companion to Museum Studies.* Oxford: Blackwell, pp. 381–97.

Schaffer, S. (2005) Public experiments. In B. Latour and P. Weibel (eds.), *Making Things Public: Atmospheres of Democracy.* Karlsruhe: Zentrum für Kunst und Medientechnologie, and Cambridge, Mass.: MIT Press, pp. 298–307.

Schneider, A. (2006) Appropriations. In A. Schneider and C. Wright (eds.), *Contemporary Art and Anthropology.* Oxford: Berg, pp. 29–51.

Schneider, A. and Wright, C. (eds.) (2006) *Contemporary Art and Anthropology.* Oxford: Berg.

Schneider, A. and Wright, C. (2006a) The challenge of practice. In A. Schneider and C. Wright (eds.), *Contemporary Art and Anthropology.* Oxford: Berg, pp. 1–27.

Shapin, S. and Schaffer, S. (1985) *Leviathan and the Air-Pump: Hobbes, Boyle, and the Experimental Life.* Princeton: Princeton University Press.

Shelton, A. A. (2006) Museums and anthropologies: practices and narratives. In S. Macdonald (ed.), *A Companion to Museum Studies.* Oxford: Blackwell, pp. 64–80.

Stafford, B. M. (1994) *Artful Science: Enlightenment Entertainment and the Eclipse of Visual Education.* Cambridge, Mass.: MIT Press.

Ulmer, G. L. (1992) Grammatology (in the stacks) of hypermedia. In M. C. Tuman (ed.), *Literacy Online.* Pittsburgh, Pa.: University of Pittsburgh Press, pp. 139–64.

1

Legibility and Affect: Museums as New Media

Michelle Henning

Remediation

When museums started collecting and displaying artists' films, they "brought the night into the museum" (Dercon 2000). The white-cube art space inverts into the dark-cube. The possibility of projecting film in the gallery space was already written into the modern art museum, with its neutral-coloured walls, windowless galleries and dependence on controlled artificial lighting. Even so, film changes the way people use the museum: if the film is long, they may need to sit down, and the gallery becomes a cinema or auditorium; if it has a linear narrative structure, their entry into and exit from the space may be regulated. The introduction of different media into museums has an impact which is simultaneously banal and far-reaching.

The art museum adapts its display practices to the requirements of different media. At some point, simple adaptions become major, and the museum becomes a noticeably different institution. This is true of the adaptions made as the museum embraces new (computer-based) media art. The difficulties of how to exhibit this are to do with the audience's relationship with computers and the impact of fitting a gallery with them (see Graham and Cook 2002). New media art can often not be mutually experienced: watching someone else using an interactive projection is not the same as doing it yourself, but two people may stand in front of an object, a painting, a film projection, and experience it simultaneously. In a gallery or museum, to use a computer is to perform for others, or to withdraw from the public space of the gallery into a private pursuit. New media art may also require skills or experience that the audience does not have. Another problem is that it can (like performance art) be constantly changing and unrepeatable (Paul 2005).

One response to these difficulties has been to turn the gallery into a quasi-domestic space, the digital media "lounge." Some artists have expressed disappointment with these dedicated spaces, which reduce the control the artist has over the installation and viewing context. Museums have also begun to make more use of the internet. Since the late 1990s, many have been extending their web provision, sometimes showing specially commissioned projects only on the web, and treating their websites as an additional gallery. The Walker Art Center in Minneapolis has eight actual galleries, and opened a ninth on the internet in 1997. Under the direction of Steve Dietz, Gallery 9 became one of the best-known online exhibitions of internet art. In 2001, some institutions even planned to extend into broadcast and cable: Sandy Nairne, Head of National Programmes at the Tate, envisaged "a Tate digital channel" (Morris 2001, pp. 27–8). Glenn Lowry at MoMA described that museum's website as a "parallel museum" which could attract an audience who may never visit the actual museum (Morris 2001, p. 33). A number of artists and museums or galleries have also used the internet to link the physical space of the gallery to other spaces, or to govern events and performances within and outside the gallery space.

In this essay I want to explore some of the ways in which current developments resemble the exhibition experiments of the late 1920s. In that brief period, the exhibition and the museum were reinvented and reimagined through new technologies and media, and the virtual museum was anticipated. By considering this moment of possibility before the actualization of new media, via some of the categories associated with new media, I hope to offer some new ways of thinking about the meeting of museums and new media. I am interested here, not only in the art museum but also in other artistic experiments with new media and technologies in exhibition design.

New media and old are sometimes distinguished too sharply, on the presumption of abrupt and absolute distinctions between the "virtual" and the "real," and the "digital" and the "analogue." In new media theory, a more interdependent relationship between old and new media is suggested by the concept of "remediation." New media theorists Jay David Bolter and Richard Grusin use this term to describe how media borrow from one another, and incorporate one another. They argue that new media do not function independently of other media, and see remediation as "a defining characteristic of the new digital media" (Bolter & Grusin 2000, pp. 45, 55). They outline various ways in which new media remediate other media, from being a supposedly transparent means of accessing other older media forms, through to absorbing older media so that they appear as their technically updated descendents. But old media can remediate new media too, as they reinvent the latest techniques and media for their own purposes (Bolter & Grusin 2000, p. 48).

One way in which the museum would be remediated by new media is via the virtual museum. By this I mean not only the websites produced as "parallel museums" by existing institutions, but all websites which are produced and understood as museums. Secondly, the museum is remediated through the introduction of new media and computer technologies into its exhibitionary and archival practices, in the form of new media art, information kiosks and touchscreens, and databases. A third kind of remediation might be found in exhibition design, as it mimics and appropriates new media conventions and styles. For instance, I have noted elsewhere how natural history exhibits relating to biodiversity seem to resemble networks, and "branching tree" structures. In their use of diverse exhibitionary techniques, many contemporary displays take on a multimedia character similar to new media (Henning 2006).

Bolter and Grusin understand remediation as a mimetic process, by which new media approximate the "real." It is tightly connected with notions of "immediacy" and "hypermediacy." The first term refers to the ways media are self-effacing, concealing the act of mediation; the second refers to the multiplication of media and the ways in which media texts emphasize their mediated character through referencing and quoting other media (Bolter & Grusin, 2000, pp. 5–9). These two things are co-dependent. In dioramas, for instance, realism and authenticity are under-written by the use of the conventions of Romantic painting combined with representational conventions drawn from photography and film. In other types of display, the authenticity of artifacts is enhanced by supplementing them with video footage or sound recordings. According to Bolter and Grusin, all media, but especially new media, acquire their realism either by denying their own mediation or "by multiplying mediation so as to create a feeling of fullness, a satiety of experience, which can be taken as reality" (Bolter & Grusin 2000, p. 53).

Bolter and Grusin's theory of remediation is a theory of representation, based in a particular version of post-structuralist theory. When they argue that "there is nothing prior to or outside the act of mediation," they are close to the claims of cultural theory that there is nothing outside discourse (Bolter & Grusin 2000, p. 58). Though this has become almost a mantra for some writers, there are other schools of thought, which challenge this through an attention to aesthetics, affect, sensation, and mimesis (Massumi 2002; Sedgwick 2003). They allow us to see how what passes for cultural theory is sometimes little more than a series of statements that everything which might be thought to be outside discourse or representation (such as inarticulable but felt sensations) is in fact a "discursive construction" (Sedgwick 2003, p. 109). Bolter and Grusin note the barrage of sensations provided by hypermedia, but understand this as simply as underwriting the text's claim to the real. Insofar as cultural theory sees everything as mediated or discursively constructed, it is unable to register movement, matter, sensation. Media studies frequently leaves out one of the most interesting things about media: their affective pull, their production of feelings which do not invariably support the ideational content of a given text.

Affect

When I think about the introduction of media into the museum, I think about that impact that film has on the gallery, making it into a dark space, bringing in the night. This is something not reducible to the operations of discourse or ideology, though darkness does have social consequences. In theater, for instance, stage lighting required the darkening of the auditorium, reducing social activity amongst the audience and changing the communicative relationship between audience and actors. Nevertheless, there were different ways and degrees of darkening the auditorium, depending on the value attached to the social space of the theater (Schivelbusch 1995, pp. 206–10). Generally though, in theater, and later in cinema, darkness magnified the intensity of the experience and allowed the viewer to isolate themselves and concentrate their attention (Schivelbusch 1995, p. 221). This happened regardless of content, and on the level of affect. The remediation of the museum might also be thought in terms of an affective impact.

Perhaps the art museum is not the best example, since its organizational and technical changes are often driven by the acquisitions policy.

The "hybrid and participatory" character of new media art necessitates changes in the roles of the curator, the artist and the audience, and requires art museums to adapt (Paul 2005). Art museums are in this sense reactive. The appropriation of various media and technologies within exhibition design more generally is reactive in a different way: responding to the pressures of the market and wider demands for hi-tech and interactive experiences. However, the early remediation of the museum had a very different social context and significance. It was begun in the 1920s by European avant-garde exhibition designers, artists, and museum directors who purposively introduced technologies and media to the museum. Their experimental museums and exhibitions are usually associated with an avant-garde and socialist enthusiasm for technical rationalization, standardization and industrialization. I will argue that their exhibition experiments worked to increase the legibility, accessibility, and affective intensity of exhibits, and pointed towards the potential of exhibitions as democratic, participatory media.

In the late 1920s the *Gesellschafts- und Wirtschaftsmuseum* (Museum of Society and Economy, henceforth GWM) in Vienna introduced spotlighting to its displays. A decade later, Otto Neurath, the director of the museum at that time, stated: "Being conscious of the fact that the working man has time to see a museum only at night, the Gesellschafts- und Wirtschaftsmuseum was open at night. The lights were placed so that the brightest rays came onto the pictures" (Neurath 1936, p. 46; see figure 1.1). It is interesting that this use of artificial lighting was considered innovative and worthy of comment. Before the Great War, Vienna's upper classes already had electric lighting in their homes. It had been used in stores since the turn of the century, and also in theater. The Paris Opera introduced electric lights in 1887, and the Swiss stage designer Adolphe Appia published lighting plans for Wagner's operas in 1895 (Beacham 1987). Electric lights were used in Alfred Roller's productions for the Vienna Court Opera in the 1900s. In Vienna, directional spotlighting may have been introduced to exhibitions via the theater. The Viennese exhibition and stage-set designer Frederick Kiesler curated the 1924 International Exhibition of New Theater Technique as part of the Music and Theater festival in Vienna. At this exhibition he used a modular display system, called the L and T system, which incorporated electric spotlights (Staniszewski 1998, p. 4).

Elsewhere, spotlights were used for more spectacular purposes: El Lissitzky's famous and influential design for the Soviet Pavilion at the

Figure 1.1   The Gesellschafts- und Wirtschaftsmuseum in Vienna showing directional lighting. © The University of Reading. Otto and Marie Neurath Isotype Collection, Department of Typography and Graphic Communication, University of Reading.

1928 International Press Exhibition (known as Pressa) in Cologne included a star-shaped construction with spinning globes, lit from beneath by three electric spotlights. The commercial exhibitions and world's fairs had large budgets for their displays, while many museums had very limited exhibition budgets or limited access to technical resources, including electricity. For instance, in 1927–8, Lissitzky constructed his "Abstract Cabinet" for the Hanover Landesmuseum. The walls of the room were covered in vertical metal slats, white on one side and black on the other, so that they changed color as visitors moved through the space. Lissitzky wanted a lighting system that would make this more effective but there was no electricity supply to the exhibition space (Staniszewski 1998, p. 21).

In the case of the GWM, the introduction of spotlighting was not an inevitable step or progression arising from the availability of technologies, nor was it primarily intended as a spectacle of technical achievement. It was tied to a specific social project – that of making legible exhibitions. It shed light not on artworks or artifacts in the strict sense, but on posters, charts, photographs, and models. These were designed to communicate to the working-class population of Vienna, who were the "clients" (as Neurath saw it) for the municipal housing projects, the kindergartens, and other social developments which the museum represented. Neurath developed, with the graphic designer Gerd Arntz, the architect Joseph Frank and Marie Reidemeister (later Marie Neurath), the Isotype system (International System of Typological and Pictorial Education), a visual language of icons or pictograms, used for communicating statistical information. These were exhibited in the GWM in the form of framed posters, in stark black and red. The GWM was associated with the reform programs of the socialist municipal government. As Eve Blau explains, "An important component of all these programs was public dissemination of information about them. In lectures and publications, including newspapers, magazines, books, posters, films, radio broadcasts, exhibitions, and other forms of public presentation, the purposes and methods of the Social Democrats' programs were continually set before the public ..." (Blau 1999, pp. 386–7). For Neurath, part of the point of the museum was to enable visitors to become involved in the civic projects which were reshaping their everyday lives. It was intended to give the people the means to participate in decision-making by enabling them to make comparisons and formulate arguments. For Neurath, exhibitions made possible the practices of comparison and contemplation necessary for critical thought and debate:

> Exhibitions and museums have their characteristics distinguishing them from book illustrations, lantern slides or films. Visitors, for example, can stand around an exhibit, look for longer or shorter times, compare one with another. A filmgoer is presented with a set sequence, a scene appears and goes by quickly, he cannot turn back the pages like the leaves of a book. Museums are free for everybody, groups and individuals can go there, with or without a guide; their discussion could be supported by the visual material itself. (Neurath 1933, p. 238)

Neurath described the origins of the Isotype system in his childhood passion for clarity and simplicity in children's book illustrations and his early fascination with Egyptian wall paintings (Neurath 1946). The Isotype "pictorial language," Egyptian paintings and hieroglyphics, and the museum itself, all worked by combining and arranging multiple elements to enable comparisons. While the Isotype system of symbols gave information a visual, legible form, electrical spotlighting made it visible in the after-dark leisure time of the working population.

Yet directional lighting was already understood as an expressive and dramatic medium in theater. In the theater of the 1880s and 1890s gas and electric lighting had been used to flood the stage, to make vivid every detail (Bergman 1977, pp. 297–8). Some pioneers of electrical stage lighting, including Appia, objected to this. Appia argued for directional use of light, preferring spotlighting over the use of fixed lights, and he saw electric lighting as a means of expression which would enhance the emotional content of Wagnerian opera. There is an element of this in Neurath's choice of spot-lighting to illuminate the Isotype charts in the GWM. According to Neurath the Isotype symbols "should be *living* symbols" (his emphasis), that is, both non-archaic and vivid (Neurath 1946). The Isotypes should be "attractive" and through them, information (such as statistics) which had been previously encoded in inaccessible and extremely dry modes of representation, would come alive. Electric lighting enhanced both the legibility and the vividness of the Isotypes.

The use of spotlighting is, in other words, affective. Brian Massumi describes affect as distinct from emotion and from expression, and in terms of the intensity of sensations. A sad or frightening or joyful experience might be felt at exactly the same level of intensity (Massumi 2002, pp. 26–7). Other writers on affect see less distinction between affect and emotion and emphasize multiple, qualitatively different affects (Sedgwick & Frank 2003, pp. 110–1). In this case, it seems that the exhibition lighting increased the intensity of the viewing experience, without necessarily determining the exact emotional content or meaning of the charts and models.

Neurath's Isotype system is usually seen in terms of standardization, as repetitive, rationalized and modular. Isotypes are associated with Neurath's logical positivist philosophy, his belief in the possibility of objective speech, and of a language in which knowledge becomes information, and "facts" can be transparently presented. Peter Wollen discusses the Isotype system as an example of how Fordism becomes a "world-view" (Wollen 1993, pp. 40, 36). Henry Ford's assembly-line system, combined with F. W. Taylor's methods for rationalizing labour, were models which in the 1920s shaped cultural production as well as industry, in both communist and capitalist states. Rationalization is associated with increased control (Michel Foucault discusses Taylorism in his description of the disciplinary society), and with an emphasis on efficiency at the expense of the sensuous. Yet, though the Isotype system appears rational, functional, even mechanistic, in Isotype exhibitions the techniques and technologies deployed were meant also to be affective.

Multimedia

The greatest intensities of affect were experimented with at the great expositions, especially in the world's fairs of the 1950s and 1960s. The fairground technologies of the ride and the rollercoaster, along with those of cinema and other media, were reconfigured for the purposes of didactic displays of the achievements of industrial modernity (Highmore 2004). To emphasize the bodily appeal and the performativity of the world's fair pavilions is not to downplay their ideological role. Even while these displays might seem carnivalesque in some ways, and offered visitors a sense of bodily liberation, they also, as Ben Highmore argues, gave visitors a taste of what it is like to be "machinic." Multiscreen projections and fairground-style rides gave the sensation of leaving behind bodily limitations and current social relations. The fantasy of technological transcendence was "nailed down" experientially (Highmore 2004, pp. 130–2, 144–5). Theories of discipline and control cannot account for the ideological impact of this affective, multimedia address.

Through working in commercial exhibitions, international and national expositions, early exhibition designers began to realize the great potential of the exhibition medium in its capacity to incorporate other media. Herbert Bayer, whose career began in the 1920s, wrote:

> Exhibition design has evolved as a new discipline, as an apex of all media and powers of communication and of collective efforts and effects. The combined means of visual communication constitute a remarkable complexity: language as visible printing or as sound, pictures as symbols, paintings, and photographs, sculptural media, materials and surfaces, color, light, movement (of the display as well as the visitor), films, diagrams, and charts. The total application of all plastic and psychological means (more than anything else) makes exhibition design an intensified and new language. (Cited in Staniszewski 1998, p. 3)

These designers found in exhibitions a flexibility and range similar to that they found in designing stage sets and department store window displays. In all these contexts, artists could combine new materials and technologies with established ones. Yet it was museums, not exhibitions as such, which provided the conceptual model for the direction in which, it was anticipated, the new mass media would develop, since museums included an exhibitionary function and accumulative and archiving functions. In the late 1920s and early 1930s, while exhibition design was described as the medium to end all others, the museum was often seen as a regressive, bourgeois institution. The avant-garde famously and repeatedly made calls for the destruction of the museum. Yet they coupled this with ambitious and unlikely plans for new kinds of museums. Writing on Le Corbusier's concept of the "museum that contains everything," Beatriz Colomina says, "What makes the museum obsolete as a nineteenth-century accumulative institution is the mass media," for mass media take the contents of the museum and disseminate them into the world and into domestic space (Colomina 1994, p. 213). But reports of the death of the museum are greatly exaggerated. Le Corbusier continued to use the word *musée* to describe projects such as the Mundaneum/World Museum which he worked on with Paul Otlet (on whom more below), and his later notion of a *Musée à croissance illimitée* (Museum of Unlimited Extension). Neurath, too, continued to found museums, even as he described the GWM as "really a permanent exposition" (Survey Graphic 1936, p. 618).

Museums did epitomize, for the avant-garde, both the over-accumulation and imperialist universalism of the Victorian era, and the institutional "death" of art. The way paintings were crammed onto the museum's walls appeared to some writers as a violent battle for the visitors' attention (Marinetti 1909; Valéry 1923). Yet, when they tried to anticipate or describe the directions in which the technologies associated with the mass media would take culture, many writers and artists took the museum as a model. (Later examples would include Walter Benjamin's essay "The Work of Art in the Age of its Technological Reproducibility" (Benjamin 1936) and André Malraux's *Musée Imaginaire* (1947)). For instance, László Moholy-Nagy imagined a "Domestic Pinacoteca" (art gallery) in which pictures would be retrieved using various technical devices, including some which did not, as yet, exist. He mentioned filing systems, color slides, three-dimensional imaging, and a "radio picture service" (Moholy-Nagy 1925, pp. 25–6). Four years later, he produced his "Room one" for the *Film und Photo* exhibition in Berlin. Here he displayed photographic reproductions of various shapes and sizes without accompanying text. In 1930, he exhibited a machine, the *Licht-Raum Modulator* (Light–Space Modulator). This was operated via push-buttons and, through rotating metal plates, projected abstract patterns of light onto walls and ceiling. It has been suggested that the machine was originally designed for use in theater (Staniszewski 1998, pp. 21–2;

Huhtamo 2002, pp. 6–7). In 1926 Frederick Kiesler envisioned a "Tele-museum," in which pictures would be broadcast into domestic interiors through the use of specially sensitized walls. He displayed a version of it the following year (Staniszewski 1998, p. 313). It seems this was basically a darkened room, in which illuminated images of well-known artworks were displayed at the push of a button. In a 1930 book, Kiesler returned to the project, anticipating that, "Through the dials of your Teleset you will share in the ownership of the world's great art treasures" (Kiesler 1930).

The museum was reimagined in terms of new practices of accumulation and display. The museum would extend beyond the walls of the public institution and broadcast itself into the domestic space. According to Neurath, the "Museum of the Future" would rid itself of ritual and the self-serving ambitions of donors and directors, and be oriented toward the visitors. Through a simple device – the electrical switch – exhibition experiments of the late 1920s and 1930s pointed to the possibility of handing over control of the display to the visitors themselves.

Interactivity

Developments in interactivity, which long predate the introduction of computers to museums, were part of a larger "user-orientation" in new exhibition design. The popularity of the GWM and Neurath's traveling exhibitions was perhaps due to the relevance of their content to visitors and to the approach to visitor participation. Some exhibits were explicitly interactive. For instance, in one Vienna branch museum visitors were invited to move a metal ring along a wire; if they accidentally touched the wire, a bell rang. In a 1936 exhibition visitors could make models rotate by pressing a switch (University of Reading 1975, p. 27). These kinds of participatory devices were already beginning to be used in science museums, including at the Deutsches Museum in Munich (1925) and in the Children's Gallery at the Science Museum in London (1931).

In modernist exhibition design, the use of the push-button is part of the appropriation of fairground devices. Bayer used such devices in a 1938–9 exhibition at MoMA, New York, and Kiesler continued to use them into the late 1930s. Journalists were critical, describing Kiesler's use of peepholes at Peggy Guggenheim's *Art of this Century* Gallery as "a kind of artistic Coney Island" and Bayer's use of cut-out footsteps on the floor as a "cheap sidewalk device" (Staniszewski 1998, p. 145; Kachur 2001, p. 201).

These techniques connected the experience of the exhibition with that of the fair, if only synecdochically. That is, rather than being a full-blown attempt at a participatory and affective experience, simple devices such as push-buttons stand in for a larger range of possibilities: for the potential of the media to be controlled by its users, for museums where visitors would organize their own displays, and for the affective possibilities of media (as images appear and disappear into darkness with the press of a button).

The user-orientation of 1920s and 1930s avant-garde exhibition experiments depended on a notion of the "active" visitor which was tied to a socialist vision; it had a meaning which it has lost in our own time. Then, to make the viewer "active" was tightly connected to notions of political agency, jolting people out of the "numb passivity" which resulted from the social and technical arrangements of modernity (Lissitzky 1930, p. 149). Now, interactivity is mainly understood in terms of consumer choice and civic participation. Andrew Barry has written of how interactivity, in science centers especially, is still harnessed for the production of "interested, engaged and informed technological citizens" (Barry 2001, p. 129). Interactivity in these contexts may appear to be a tool to teach scientific facts and principles – the explicit content of the exhibits – but it may also be a training or preparation for the ways in which everyday, sensual experience is configured in relation to certain machinic arrangements. Indeed, we could see many of the present manifestations of interactivity not as increasing agency, but as encouraging acceptance of a new set of machine–body relationships.

The new-media theorist Lev Manovich has argued against seeing interactivity as a defining characteristic of new media. His own distinction between old media and new media relies on a distinction between larger social, economic, and technological developments, between the era of mass standardization (Fordist) versus the information age (also contentiously termed "post-industrial" or "post-Fordist"). Manovich sees the demand for mass standardization as having shaped a "modern desire to externalize the mind." Individual mental processes became understood as standard operations through analogy with the processes of modern media (he mentions Freud's use of photographic analogies). In this way the private and individual become public, shared, and analyzable (Manovich 2001, pp. 60–1). Today, this is taken a step further as computer media produce "a new kind of identification appropriate for the information age of cognitive labor" by asking us to identify with someone else's mental structure, replacing our own mental associations with "pre-programmed objectively existing associations" (Manovich 2001, p. 61). Computer interactivity maps our own thought processes onto those already written into the software. It models certain ways of thinking, or certain ways of understanding our own cognitive practices: to click is to make a choice, to follow a link, to associate one event or piece of information with another. This process of the "externalization" of the mind closes the gap between subjective mental processes and objective, machinic processes. In this sense, like Taylorism, it hooks people and bodies up to machines, making people "thinglike." This argument would suggest that interactivity, which seemed initially to promise agency over "numbed passivity," actually does the opposite, increasing alienation.

The avant-garde, especially in post-revolutionary Russia, embraced industrialization with enthusiasm, even while they recognized the possibility that new materials and technologies would make people "thinglike." For them, becoming "thinglike" was not synonymous with being alienated. In Marxist theory, alienation is a consequence of capitalism, not standardization. It is tied to commodity fetishism – the way in which, under capitalist labour relations, the commodity seems to come "alive." In his essay "Everyday Life and the Culture of the Thing" (1925), Boris Arvatov produced a theory of the socialist thing. Released from the commodity relations of the capitalist system, and redesigned along Constructivist lines, the thing-world of industrial mass production would be beneficial and transformative. Already, modernist things were changing people, shaping "gesticulation, movement and activity." Cognitive and psychological processes were also being changed by the new world of things; as Arvatov claimed, "The psyche also evolved, becoming more and more thinglike in its associative structure" (cited in Kiaer 2004, p. 263). Arvatov believed that the use of materials such as glass, steel and concrete in modernist objects, and the rejection of the decorative casing of the bourgeois object, would lead to a more transparent or legible relationship between a thing, its production, and its use. The modernist reinvention of everyday things, according to Arvatov, might enable the reinvention of consciousness along socialist lines (Kiaer 2004, pp. 265–7).

Exhibition design in the late 1920s presumed that the physical activity of an audience in a space, moving around, pressing buttons and so on, would not just communicate certain content but also induce certain forms of consciousness. To see this in terms of a Fordist world-view, or in terms of the expansion of forms of social control, is to miss how existing technologies and everyday things were perceived as already shaping consciousness, and how the modernist, rationalized thing was seen as the means by which a new political consciousness would be engendered. For 1920s avant-garde exhibition designers and artists, buttons, switches and dials, modular standardized exhibition components, and modern materials stood synecdochally for a whole range of possibilities through which audiences/citizens could realize their own social agency.

Database

The possibilities of visitor participation and affective address, which could be hinted at through the use of buttons, switches, and effects of lighting, were also connected with new ways of imagining the purposes and uses of collection. The over-accumulation and universalism of the turn-of-the-century museum became translated into new kinds of accumulation and universalism associated with modernity. If the large temporary expositions were the greater site for innovation and technical experimentation in display techniques, the museum was the site in which these innovations were put to work in the service of internationalist, universalist, and democratic projects.

One such project was Paul Otlet's World Palace, which attempted to bring together and disseminate knowledge on a global scale. Otlet's work offers an interesting example of the ways in which the museum was being reinvented as a mass medium, and also of how it becomes a model for media more generally. From 1919, at the World Palace in Brussels, he and his colleagues worked on the massive filing system begun two decades earlier. This developed from a device for keeping a record of world literature to a means of cataloguing the world itself. Like Neurath, Otlet used mass reproduction alongside new processes of information retrieval to reinvent the museum, returning to an older convergence of museum, archive and library. Using his Decimal Classification System an archivist could inventory any item by allocating it a number and recording it on an index card. He also worked with Neurath and with Le Corbusier to plan a series of branch museums, called "Mundaneums," intended to be reproduced worldwide. Both Neurath and Otlet were interested in the way museums and exhibitions could develop the potential of mass reproduction and communication technologies to cross national boundaries and create a world culture (Vidler 2001; Vossoughian 2003).

Like Neurath's Isotypes, Otlet's classification and card system has been cited as an example of rationalization and associated with social control. This is due to their connection with policing: police identity cards were introduced in Paris in 1883, by the police bureaucrat Alphonse Bertillon (Sekula 1993, pp. 357–62). Yet index cards were being used by banks and libraries from the 1850s and 1860s. To think of them in relation to this history draws attention to their role in exchange, of information and of money. The filing card replaced linear records (such as the ledger book) because it could be transported from one place to another as necessary. This system allowed for a new mobility and exchangeability of information and artifacts. It liberated things and knowledges from their fixed places. For Otlet it also had the benefit of releasing the museum from its dependence on notions of typicality. Anything can be collected and classified without having to be typical, symptomatic, or exemplary. This makes for a generous and potentially unlimited archive. Denis Hollier compares the index card file to the notion of the "open work" or "open text," pointing to how it

> resists the syntagmatic closure of the sentence by sustaining the openness of the paradigm. It doesn't allow the phrase to gel, to take shape. A filing system is indefinitely expandable, rhizomatic (at any point of time or space, one can always insert a new card); in contradistinction with the sequential irreversibility of the pages of the notebook and of the book, its interior mobility allows for permanent reordering. (Hollier 2005, p. 40)

The filing card system is the antecedent of the computer database, which, according to Lev Manovich, is foundational to new media. For Manovich, one of the things which distinguish new media most sharply from older media is their existence as an interface to a database. Many different interfaces can be founded on and provide access to the same database. This means that new media objects are fundamentally variable, able to "exist in different, potentially infinite variations," rather than the multiple identical copies associated with the mass distribution of older media (Manovich 2001, p. 36).

Because the World Palace realized this potential of the database, Otlet has sometimes been described as one of the forgotten "forefathers" of the internet. However, the World Palace could equally be seen as an antecedent of the breakdown of the distinction between storage and archive, which we find in open-stack systems. In these, the archiving system displaces the museum, or the museum store becomes the exhibit. Open storage display threatens to banish the exhibition as something which frames and stages and re-presents, but in practice, the exhibition becomes the means through which the storage system or archive is navigated. It becomes, in effect, an interface to the storage system, much as Manovich describes the new media object. Wolfgang Ernst has noted this correspondence between contemporary open-stack systems and the structures and processes of new media:

> Today, the idea of providing the final preservation of artifacts, the traditional goal of the museum, is displaced by a practice of intermediary storage, minimizing temporal duration. The electronic inventory systems of commercial companies reduces their storage time virtually to zero by aiming at a real-time access to commodities in the supply–demand relationship, just as electronic random access to computer files turns memory into the omnipresence of data. The museum is no longer the terminal for parcel-post from history, art and culture; instead the institution becomes a flow-through and transformer station. Its demand now is mobilizing, unfreezing the accumulation of objects and images in its repositories, making them accessible to the public by displaying the stacks or recycling them into the exhibition area. (Ernst 2000, pp. 25–6)

Ernst emphasizes mobility and accelerated turnover as an aspect of new display and archival techniques, including open stacks. The parallel between computer RAM and this new kind of "flow-through" museum suggests a new approach to the memory and preservation functions of the museum. The resemblance of these exhibitionary practices to new media is not simply analogous – like the new media object, the new museum is facilitated by computer databases and electronic inventories. Like the worlds of commerce and of communication, it has been rejigged by electronic media.

Ernst proposes a correspondence between new exhibition forms in museums and information "architecture." Data-processing and new media seem to be shaping new exhibition practices. This is not just because new media are being inserted into the exhibitionary context but because the exhibition appears increasingly like new media. It is possible to argue that the exhibitionary forms that Ernst describes are more than just analogous to new media. For the exhibition has become an interface to a database, enabled by automatic searching, even if what is stored is not simply data but also actual things (artworks, artifacts, and specimens).

The resemblance to contemporary new media and information technology leads Ernst to argue that the museum is becoming a medium and to ascribe to it a pedagogic effect: "the task of the post-modern museum is to teach the user how to cope with information" (Ernst 2000, pp. 31, 18).

According to Michael Ames, open-storage displays originated in attempts to "deschool" the museum in the 1970s (Ames 1992, pp. 89–96). "Deschooling" was about establishing a new relationship between the museum and its users. No longer would the museum be a place for straightforward instruction. Instead, the users of museums could – in theory – direct their own learning without the mediation of didactic display. The museum becomes a resource, or, in Ernst's version, "pure register, archive, index … a data bank" (Ernst 2000, p. 26).

Modularity

Another thing which makes some contemporary exhibitions structurally similar to new media is the way in which they are flexible, made of modular parts. Ernst connects modular display systems, such as that at the Museo Gregoriano Profano in Rome, with new media (Ernst 2000, p. 26). New media are characteristically modular, made up of separate parts which can be assembled and disassembled. However, modular display systems predate new media and were pioneered by the exhibition designers I have mentioned. Kiesler's L and T system of 1924 was modular. It was made up of freestanding wooden structures which supported slatted rectangular panels. The T-type structures were cantilevered, so that visitors could adjust pictures to eye height, or reorganize them according to whim, changing their relationship to other exhibited elements. The L and T units were transportable and could be adapted to suit different exhibition spaces. Neurath's exhibitions were also modular, the Isotype charts made up of identical figures pasted onto board, and the display system standardized:

> There were a number of thin walls of wood put together by a sort of hook. In this way it was possible to make smaller rooms of different size which might be changed whenever necessary. On the walls there were two rails of wood at such a distance from one another that pictures a certain number of centimeters high might be put on and taken off without any other apparatus. The normal size of a picture was 126 cm × 126 cm (4 feet × 4 feet),

and the middle-point of a picture was about 150 cm (5 feet) higher than the floor, that is the position of the eye of a normal upright person. Smaller pictures were put together in groups so that every group was 126 feet high .... 90 cm (about 3 feet) of wall-space under every picture was kept clear, so that a table with apparatus, some books or other things on view might be placed there. (Neurath 1936, p. 72)

Neurath, Otlet, and Kiesler transformed the exhibition into a media form made of interchangeable standardized parts. However, Manovich's theory suggests that this sort of modularity can be distinguished from the modularity of new media. The latter allows for customization and is explicitly user-oriented: the readers and users of new media can construct their own media object to some extent. The interchangeable parts of older media and of modernism are viewed by Manovich as corresponding to the logic of mass standardization associated with Fordism (Manovich 2001, p. 30).

The idea of contextualizing media in relation to Fordism derives from the work of the Frankfurt School in the 1930s and 1940s. They analyzed how mass culture addressed an audience whose experience has been qualitatively altered by mechanization, and the permeation of standardization and the rhythms of the assembly line into their everyday working lives. Neurath, Otlet, and Kiesler's displays were all in their various ways explicitly designed to meet the expectations and modes of perception of this new mass audience. The modular interchangeable parts of these early exhibition experiments were primarily intended to be disassembled and reassembled by the authors of the exhibits and could not be customized by individual users to the same extent as some new media. However, they pointed to that possibility through the use of participatory devices such as push-buttons. The exploration of the possibilities of the museum without limits or boundaries, as an open-work or text, suggests an orientation very different from the disciplinary one we now associate with Taylorism and Fordism.

Both new media and museums have been written about in terms of social control and discipline. It is symptomatic, I think, that Bolter and Grusin say that the art museum mediates the experience of art since "the space between viewer and canvas is controlled, institutionalized and policed" (Bolter & Grusin 2000, p. 59). Here, the very notion of mediation seems to imply policing, and the authors echo the critical writing on museums that has analyzed the museum as a disciplinary institution, which polices and regulates visitors (Bennett 1995). Bennett's well-known study of late nineteenth- and early twentieth-century museum discourse revealed its concern with how to police the behavior and appearance of working-class visitors. New display techniques seemed to respond to this anxiety by organizing the walking of visitors, and exhibitions became disciplinary technologies.

However, for the exhibition designers I have mentioned, the mass audience was not conceived negatively or as something to be standardized and controlled. To read these exhibition experiments as disciplinary ones would unnecessarily narrow the terms within which we might understand the remediated museum, then and now. It may lead us to overlook other ways of thinking about the relationships between exhibits and people, and also the impossibility of control via collecting, archives, and systems; that is, the rapidity by which they become uncontrollable, or entropic. For the analysis of museums as disciplinary institutions underplays the madness of museums, the over-accumulation which militates against clarity, sense, and orderliness.

I would also like to hold onto the possibility of recognizing how not-yet-available technologies can shape thinking and practice in a particular social or cultural field. Eve Kokofsky Sedgwick and Adam Frank have made a similar point, writing of the moment between the 1940s and the 1960s, when cyberneticists' understanding of life and the human brain was "marked by the concept, the possibility, the imminence, of powerful computers, but the actual computational muscle of the computers isn't available yet" (Sedgwick & Frank 2003, p. 105). Rather than simply identifying the cyberneticists' understanding of human–machine relations as outdated or disproved, Sedgwick and Frank point to how it allowed for complex differentiations instead of simple binaries, for instance, by treating the analogue and the digital as "interleaved" rather than opposed (Sedgwick & Frank 2003, p. 106).

Similarly, the exhibition experiments of the late 1920s were shaped by the potential of technologies which did not yet exist, and they were informed by an understanding of that potential which was in some ways more supple and rich than present understandings of the significance and social role of both museums and new media. Of course, they were also shaped by what did exist, and some of the examples I have discussed presupposed that new media would be predominantly instruments for the reproduction and dissemination of high art. They also assumed that the single image would still have a power it has mostly conceded to a flow of images now. Yet these early imaginings and experimental exhibitions illuminate existing similarities and shared histories between the museum and new media. They might prove a useful reminder, too, of the possible purposes and aims of deploying new technologies in museums. Although current museum experiments are shaped by ideas about audience, the attractions of interactivity, and the power of new technology, their politics is less explicitly and rigorously understood. New media theory tends to be preoccupied either with the role of media in social control or with its role in forms of personal liberation (via "identity" politics), while museums themselves often deploy new media to attempt to measure visitor response and learning, as well as to enhance popularity and compete with other attractions. In this context the real social, political, and aesthetic potential of new media in museums remains to be explored.

References

Ames, M. M. (1992) *Cannibal Tours and Glass Boxes: The Anthropology of Museums.* Vancouver: UBC Press.

Barry, A. (2001). *Political Machines: Governing a Technological Society.* London and New York: Athlone Press.

Beacham, R. C. (1987) *Adolphe Appia: Theatre Artist.* Cambridge: Cambridge University Press.

Benjamin, W. (2002 [1936]) The work of art in the age of its technological reproducibility, second version. In *Selected Writings. Volume3: 1935–1938*, ed. Howard Eiland and Michael W. Jennings. Cambridge, Mass.: Harvard University Press, pp. 101–33.

Bennett, T. (1995) *The Birth of the Museum: History, Theory, Politics.* London: Routledge.

Bergman, G. (1977) *Lighting in the Theatre.* Stockholm: Almqvist & Wiksell International.

Blau, E. (1999) *The Architecture of Red Vienna 1919–1934.* Cambridge, Mass.: MIT Press.

Bolter, J. D. and Grusin, R. (2000) *Remediation: Understanding New Media.* Cambridge, Mass.: MIT Press.

Colomina, B. (1994) *Privacy and Publicity: Modern Architecture as Mass Media.* Cambridge, Mass.: MIT Press.

Dercon, C. (2000) Still / a novel. In A. W. Balkema and H. Slager (eds.), *Screen-based Art.* Amsterdam and Atlanta, Ga.: Lier and Boog.

Ernst, W. (2000) Archi(ve)textures of museology. In S. A. Crane (ed.), *Museums and Memory.* Stanford, Calif.: Stanford University Press, pp. 17–34.

Graham, B. and Cook, S. (2002) Net works: exhibiting new media. *Art Monthly*, 261: 44–5.

Henning, M. (2006) *Museums, Media and Cultural Theory*. Maidenhead: Open University Press.

Highmore, B. (2004) Machinic magic: IBM at the 1964–1965 New York World's Fair. *New Formations*, 51 (1): 128–48.

Hollier, D. (2005) Notes on the index. In *October*, 112 (1): 35–44.

Huhtamo, E. (2002) On the origins of the virtual museum. Paper presented at the Nobel Symposium *Virtual Museums and Public Understanding of Science and Culture*, Stockholm. http://nobelprize.org/nobel/nobel-foundation/symposia/interdisciplinary/ns120/lectures/huhtamo.pdf (accessed August 2006).

Kachur, L. (2001) *Displaying the Marvelous: Marcel Duchamp, Salvador Dali, and Surrealist Exhibition Installations*. Cambridge, Mass.: MIT Press.

Kiaer, C. (2004) The Russian Constructivist flapper dress. In B. Brown (ed.), *Things*. Chicago: University of Chicago Press, pp. 245–303.

Kiesler, F. (1930) *Contemporary Art Applied to the Store and Its Display*. New York: Brentano's.

Lissitzky, E. (1984 [1930]) *Russia: An Architecture for World Revolution*. Cambridge, Mass.: MIT Press.

Malraux, A. (1967 [1947]) *Museum without Walls*. New York: Doubleday & Company.

Manovich, L. (2001) *The Language of New Media*. Cambridge, Mass.: MIT Press.

Marinetti, F. T. (1973 [1909]) The founding and manifesto of Futurism. In U. Apollonio (ed.), *Futurist Manifestos: An Anthology of the Writings of Futurist Artists*. London: Thames & Hudson, pp. 19–23.

Massumi, B. (2002) *Parables for the Virtual: Movement, Affect, Sensation*. Durham, N.C.: Duke University Press.

Moholy-Nagy, L. (1987 [1925]) *Painting, Photography, Film*. Cambridge, Mass.: MIT Press.

Morris, S. (2001) Museums and new media art: a research report commissioned by the Rockefeller Foundation. www.rockfound.org/Library/Museums_and_New_Media_Art.pdf (accessed August 2006).

Neurath, O. (1946) From hieroglyphs to Isotypes. In *The Crowded Scene*, Future Books no. 3. London: Adprint/Collins, pp. 92–100. Published online at www.fulltable.com/iso/is03.htm (accessed August 2006).

Neurath, O. (1973 [1933]) The museum of the future. In M. Neurath and R. S. Cohen (eds.), *Empiricism and Sociology*. Dordrecht: Reidel.

Neurath, O. (1980 [1936]) *International Picture Language*. Facsimile reprint, University of Reading, Department of Typography and Graphic Communication; originally published London: K. Paul, Trench, Trubner.

Paul, C. (2005) Challenges for a ubiquitous museum: presenting and preserving new media. Paper presented at the Royal Danish Academy of Fine Arts,

Copenhagen,   May   2005.   www.mediaarthistory.org/Programmatic%20key%
20 texts/pdfs/Paul.pdf (accessed August 2006).

Schivelbusch, W. (1995). *Disenchanted Night: The Industrialization of Light in the Nineteenth Century.* Berkeley: University of California Press.

Sedgwick, E. Kokofsky and Frank, A. (2003) Shame in the cybernetic fold: reading Silvan Tomkins. In E. Kokofsky Sedgwick, *Touching Feeling: Affect, Pedagogy, Performativity.* Durham, N.C.: Duke University Press, pp. 93–122.

Sekula, A. (1993) The body and the archive. In R. Bolton (ed.), *The Contest of Meaning: Critical Histories of Photography.* Cambridge, Mass.: MIT Press, pp. 342–88.

Staniszewski, M. A. (1998) *The Power of Display: A History of Exhibition Installations at the Museum of Modern Art.* Cambridge, Mass.: MIT Press.

Survey Graphic (1936) Social showman. *Survey Graphic: Magazine of Social Interpretation,* 25 (11). Published online by the *New Deal Network,* http://new deal.feri.org/survey/36618.htm (accessed August 2006).

University of Reading (1975) Graphic Communication through Isotype. Reading: University of Reading, Department of Typography and Graphic Communication.

Valéry, P. (1960 [1923]) The problem of museums. In *Degas, Manet, Morisot.* Trans. David Paul. New York: Pantheon books.

Vidler, A. (2001) The space of history: modern museums from Patrick Geddes to Le Corbusier. In M. Giebelhausen (ed.), *The Architecture of the Museum: Symbolic Structures, Urban Contexts.* Manchester: Manchester University Press, pp. 160–82.

Vossoughian, N. (2003) The language of the World Museum: Otto Neurath, Paul Otlet, Le Corbusier. *Transnational Associations,* 1–2: 82–93.

Wollen, P. (1993) Modern times: cinema, Americanism, the robot. In *Raiding the Icebox: Reflections on Twentieth-Century Culture.* London and New York: Verso, pp. 35–71.

2

The Labyrinthine Aesthetic in Contemporary Museum Design

Paul Basu

In 1888, in the shadow of the Hawara pyramid, about 80 km south of present-day Cairo, the archaeologist W. M. Flinders Petrie located the site of the legendary labyrinth of Amenemhat III. This famous monument was already of considerable antiquity when Herodotus visited and wrote about it in the fifth century BC. In his *Historia*, Herodotus records that the labyrinth surpassed even the pyramids in magnificence and, significantly, that he found it beyond description, literally "greater than words can say" (MacAulay 1890, p. 185). Through passages going this way and then that, from courts into chambers, from chambers into colonnades, from colonnades into other rooms, Herodotus evokes a vast and bewildering structure, which "afforded endless matter for marvel" (ibid., p. 186).

It wasn't until 1911 that Petrie led an expedition to excavate part of the labyrinth. Alas, he found that it had been "so completely ravaged [in the Roman period] that only a great bed of chips showed its site" (Petrie, Wainwright, & Mackay 1912, p. 28). Nevertheless, fragments of that fragmented monument were collected and distributed to some 32 museums throughout the world, from Cairo to New York to Manchester, and to

Petrie's own collection later to be installed at University College London. More recently, the Petrie Museum and the Centre for Advanced Spatial Analysis at UCL have been experimenting with virtual-reality technologies, extrapolating from such fragments a navigable three-dimensional digital representation of the labyrinth: an experiment, one might say, in the form of the virtual museum (Shiode & Grajetzki 2000).

To remain within the physical space of the Petrie Museum for the moment, however, what is striking as one wanders around its cramped corridors, between display cases crammed with these fragments from antiquity, is the labyrinthine nature of the museum itself – and, of course, the Petrie Museum is not alone in this respect. But whereas the epithet was once invoked as a criticism of poor museum design – in 1882, for instance, Sir John Soane's Museum was described as a "labyrinth stuffed full of fragments," which had a "perplexing and oppressive effect on the spectator" (Adolf Michaelis, quoted in Millenson 1987) – today, as the grand taxonomic schemas and narratives are being contested, the essential ambivalence of this perennial architectural symbol has been mined more constructively. Indeed, to borrow a phrase coined by André Gide, I suggest that the labyrinth has become a *mise en abyme* in museum design: a pattern within a pattern, a self-reflecting mirror of the museum text within the museum text itself. In this essay, then, using the works of Daniel Libeskind as exemplars, I consider the application of the labyrinthine aesthetic as an architectural and narratological experiment in contemporary exhibition and museum design.

The labyrinth, as Ferré and Saward note in an afterword to the English edition of Hermann Kern's monumental study of the form, has experienced a remarkable revival in recent years, becoming, once again, a vibrant concept that pervades many aspects of public consciousness (Kern 2000, p. 314; see also Saward 2002). This popular renaissance of a Renaissance trope is also reflected in a proliferating discourse across numerous academic disciplines in the humanities and social sciences (e.g. Cipolla 1987; Doob 1990; Faris 1988; Snyder 1997; Teski & Climo 1995). While drawing upon its insights, I make no attempt to encompass, let alone synthesize, this diverse literature here. Instead I seek out a path between disciplinary digressions, and my discussion will inevitably take on a somewhat labyrinthine form itself as I pass from detour to detour, pursuing certain corridors of thought, while leaving others unexplored.

Detour 1: The Labyrinth as Embodiment of Paradox

As the embodiment of paradox *par excellence*, I suggest that it is precisely the labyrinth's ability to embrace contradiction that makes it such a potent symbol for our own uncertain and relativistic *Zeitgeist*. The labyrinth thus simultaneously represents order and disorder, clarity and confusion, integration and disintegration, unity and multiplicity, artistry and chaos. This duplicity is deeply perspectival: to the "maze-walker" immersed in the structure's passages, the labyrinth is constricted, fragmented, and confusing, whereas to the "maze-viewer," able to rise above the convoluted chaos and perceive its pattern, the dazzling artistry of the labyrinth is made apparent in all its admirable complexity.

Despite the potential diversity of the labyrinthine aesthetic, there are actually only two paradigms of labyrinth design: the unicursal and the multicursal (figure 2.1). The unicursal maze features a single path, which may twist and turn to the point of desperation, but which entails no dead ends or choices between paths. As Penelope Doob argues in her study of the labyrinth in classical and medieval thought, such mazes are infallible guides to their own secrets, defining precisely the only course to be taken

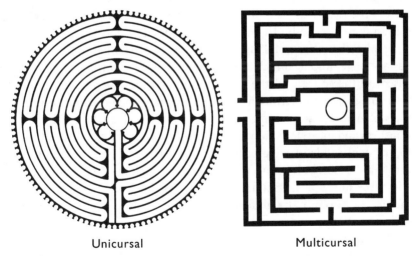

Unicursal · Multicursal

Figure 2.1 The two paradigms of labyrinth design: the unicursal (left) featuring a single path with no dead ends or bifurcations; the multicursal (right) featuring multiple choices between paths, some leading to dead ends. Paul Basu after Gailhabaud (left) and Matthews (right).

(Doob 1990, p. 48). The multicursal maze, on the other hand, features an array of choices between paths and embodies frequent testing and repeated confrontations with uncertainty. Movement through the multicursal maze is thus repetitive, halting, and episodic, with each forking path requiring pause for thought and decision. In contrast to the unicursal maze, the essential experience of the multicursal maze is therefore one of confusion, doubt, and frustration as one ambiguity follows another.

So profound is the difference between unicursal and multicursal labyrinths that many writers, including Kern, recognize only the unicursal form as labyrinths, referring to the multicursal variety as mazes (Kern 2000, p. 23). This "clash of paradigms" arises from distinct representational traditions in the visual arts and in literature. While classical and medieval visual representations of labyrinths often invoke the bewildering *multicursal* "labyrinth-as-building" of classical mythology and literature (most notably the Cretan labyrinth built by Daedalus to imprison the Minotaur), they are virtually all *unicursal* in form. Doob argues, however, that classical and medieval scholars used the same word, *labyrinthus* or *laborintus*, to denote both forms and suggests, therefore, that we engage with the inherent ambiguity of this complex symbol rather than attempt to reduce its complexity by subjecting it to a more recent desire for categorical consistency (Doob 1990, p. 44). Persuaded by Doob's argument, I use the terms "labyrinth" and "maze" interchangeably throughout this essay to refer to both unicursal and multicursal forms.

Despite their structural differences, the two paradigms of labyrinth design share important characteristics. Most fundamentally, both are based on the concept of the path: a journey from a beginning to an at least imagined end. Yet neither model permits straightforward access to this postulated destination. Rather, the journey is characterized by circuitousness and meandering, by detours, delays, and diversions, which serve to fragment and frustrate progress. As a subjective experience, the journey through the labyrinth is thus transformed, through the disorienting twists and turns of the unicursal form as much as the repeated choices of the multicursal, from a straightforward linear progression into a disjointed sequence of movements and perceptions.

This intentional fragmentation of the path reminds us that the labyrinth is above all an exercise in *planned* chaos and that this architectural and metaphorical form has a pedagogic function. In the Middle Ages, the word labyrinth was most commonly spelt *laborintus*, and was believed to be derived etymologically from *labor* and *intus*, meaning "labor within" (ibid., p. 97). If, as Doob suggests, the maze may be understood as representing the laborious journey from, let us say, confusion to understanding, or from ignorance to knowledge, then the unicursal and multicursal models also represent alternative paradigms for progressing from one state to the other. Thus the unicursal maze-walker, having no choice but to pursue a singular, predetermined route, follows a universal and authoritative curriculum, learning by precept; whereas the multicursal maze-wanderer participates more actively in her own education, proceeding by trial and error, learning by dialectic (ibid., p. 57). As "process- and progress-orientated" metaphors, both models imply the possibility of "convertibility" – that is, they both envisage "a perspective-mediated conversion from disorder to order" as the maze-walker discerns the pattern in the chaos and, transcending the maze, effectively becomes a maze-viewer (ibid., p. 52). Whether this envisaged transcendence is finally achievable in practice is another matter and is something to which I shall return later. For now, however, we should at least acknowledge that there is, as de Certeau puts it, a "lust to be a viewpoint," a desire to escape the labyrinth and perceive the whole (1984, p. 92).

Objective pattern and subjective process, singular persistence and pluralistic choice, precept and dialectic, ordered chaos and chaotic order – it is the capacity of the labyrinth to embody such apparent contradictions that makes it such a powerful technology to think with and to engage with the epistemological dilemmas of a late-modern age that has rejected absolute truths.

Detour 2: The Modern and the Postmodern?

Given that both the unicursal and multicursal labyrinth paradigms were apparent to classical and medieval scholars, it may seem foolish to frame their contrariness within more contemporary epistemological debates. As a heuristic aid, however, it is perhaps too tempting not to locate the unicursal maze (and the maze-viewer's perspective) within a modernist aesthetic and the multicursal maze (and the maze-walker's perspective) within a postmodernist aesthetic. Thus, after Hassan (1985), a familiar set of contradistinctions is suggested, which will resonate throughout my discussion.

LABYRINTHINE AESTHETIC

embraces

unicursal paradigm	multicursal paradigm
(maze-viewer)	**(maze-walker)**
modern	*postmodern*
objective	subjective
concept	experience
integration/continuity	disintegration/discontinuity
order/clarity	disorder/confusion
form (conjunctive, closed)	antiform (disjunctive, open)
design	chance
hierarchy	anarchy
artifact/finished work	process/performance
distance	participation
totalization/synthesis	deconstruction/antithesis
presence	absence
determinacy/precept	indeterminacy/dialectic
whole/centered	fragmented/dispersed
root/depth	rhizome/surface
interpretation/reading	against interpretation/misreading
lisible (readerly)	*scriptible* (writerly)
narrative/*grande histoire*	anti-narrative/*petite histoire*

Such binary logic lies behind an often made critique of the modern museum, which contrasts its narrative approach with the supposedly anti-narrative approach of the postmodern museum. Thus Wolfgang Ernst argues that "It should always be clear that the museum visitor is in a kind of archive, in a collection of materialities, not to be confused with the narratives symbolically or imaginarily ... wrapped around them" (2000, p. 33). "The museum", he writes, "should no longer be subjected to the paradigm of historical narrative" and should instead be allowed to display its "proper, archaeological, discontinuous, and modular mode of assembling words and objects" (ibid., p. 18). On the one hand, I agree with this position, that the "expressive value" and semantic potential of material artifacts should not be "hermeneutically controlled" or reduced to serve some didactically predetermined *grande histoire* – for instance, as in the "story-of-a-nation" approach adopted at the recently opened

Museum of Scotland in Edinburgh (Calder 2000). But such a view also displays a somewhat narrow, "unicursal" conceptualization of narrative as a schema for imposing coherence, continuity and order onto the possibly incoherent, discontinuous, and disorderly complex of curiosities in a museum collection. I want to suggest an alternative: that, like the labyrinth, narrative can also be both unicursal and multicursal, both orderly and disorderly, continuous and discontinuous, tending at once toward closure and disclosure.

Detour 3: Drawing a Configuration out of a Succession

This broader, Ricoeurian, conceptualization of narrative reconceives emplotment as an "integrating process" that serves to synthesize a succession of heterogeneous elements, events or incidents into an intelligible whole (Ricoeur 1991, p. 21). Such a conceptualization is rooted in a reading of Husserl's phenomenological theory of time consciousness, which asserts that we can only experience the present against the background of what it succeeds and what we anticipate will succeed it: that events, as we encounter them, are charged with the significance they derive from what Husserl terms our "retention" and "protention" (Carr 1991, p. 163). Like the maze-walker's labored path through the labyrinth, narrative thus becomes a particular sense-making path through the textual landscape: a process through which we wrest an intelligible "configuration" from a spatio-temporal succession of experiences that have no intrinsic meaning in themselves. As Ricoeur stresses, this process of emplotment or configuration occurs not in the "text" itself, nor in the "reader," but is the "common work" of both: a confrontation between the "horizon of expectation" (the reader's world) and the "horizon of experience" (the world of the text) (1991, p. 26).

By considering the exhibition as "text" and the exhibition visitor as "reader," Mieke Bal has applied such narrative theory to the space of the museum. Recognizing the necessarily sequential nature of the museum visit, Bal discusses how the heterogeneous elements of an exhibition become linked through the visitor's itinerary, so that walking through a museum becomes analogous to reading a book (1996, p. 4). Bal reminds us, however, that there is not only a "reader" and a "text" to consider, there is also the "expository agency" of the curator or designer whose discursive strategies often remain invisible in the museum display (ibid., p. 7). Bal's particular concern is therefore to expose this authorial/ authoritative presence that hides behind, yet structures, the seemingly "natural" narrative configurations of the museum text and thus to reveal the constructed nature of its apparently self-evident meanings.

If we accept that narrative can be both "product" and "process," the challenge would seem to be how to use narrative to deconstruct narrative without merely replacing one *grande histoire* with another. And here I return to the notion of the *mise en abyme*, originally a heraldic device in which a particular motif is repeated within itself, but which has been adopted by literary critics to refer to the self-reflecting, labyrinthine plot twists and turns of the *nouveau roman* (Dällenbach 1989). "The *mise en abyme*", writes Gregory Ulmer, "is a reflexive structuration, by means of which a text shows what it is telling ... displays its own making, reflects its own action" (1992, p. 140). Employed as an architectural and narratological technology, I suggest that the labyrinthine aesthetic may be understood as such a reflexive structuration in the museum text. Continually exposing the processes through which its own meanings are made, the labyrinthine exhibition de-centers curatorial authority and disrupts the persuasive "straightforwardness" of the museum's grand narratives and taxonomies through its constant refraction of alternative configurations. Such an organizing principle may be deemed experimental insofar as it reconceives the multiple engagements between people and things, words, sequences and spaces, which constitute an exhibition as a *heuretic* process: a process, which, through creative experimentation, is generative of new understandings rather than merely reproductive of existing, intentionally programmed ones. In this sense, effective exhibition or museum design might be measured according to the degree to which it creates the opportunity for and provokes such inventiveness in the visitor's experience (Ulmer 1994).

Detour 4: Spaces of Encounter: Getting Lost in Libeskind's Labyrinths

Every age, it might be said, has its own Daedalus, and there are grounds for suggesting that the Daedalus of our own age is the celebrated architect Daniel Libeskind. Characterized by their constraining corridors, fragmented paths, acutely angled walls, dead ends, voids, and asymmetries, many of Libeskind's "deconstructivist" museum designs draw explicitly upon a labyrinthine aesthetic. Here I shall be concerned with three examples: the

Felix Nussbaum Haus, Osnabrück (opened in 1998); the Jewish Museum, Berlin (opened in 2001); and the "Spiral" Extension to the Victoria & Albert Museum, London (a controversial project which, having failed to attract public funding, was finally abandoned in 2004). Libeskind is not only an inventive architectural practitioner, but also a prolific writer and theorist: not only a Daedalus, then, but also an Ariadne, leaving a thread of words and drawings that provide an interpretive pathway through these buildings (see especially Libeskind 2001). Libeskind's commentaries are, of course, particularly expressive of authorial intention and it is important to stress that there are other interpretive routes to be explored, opening avenues into differing perceptions and experiences of these spaces. My intention here, however, is to concentrate on Libeskind's experimentation with the labyrinthine aesthetic as a principle of design.

An extension to the Cultural History Museum in the German town of Osnabrück, the Felix Nussbaum Haus was the first of Libeskind's building designs to be completed. The extension was commissioned to house a collection of about 160 works by the German-Jewish painter Felix Nussbaum. Nussbaum was born in Osnabrück in 1904 to a well-respected family and, after studies in Hamburg and Berlin, he achieved early success as an artist, winning a Villa Massimo scholarship in Rome in 1932. After the National Socialists came to power in 1933, Nussbaum went into exile, traveling restlessly throughout Europe and eventually settling in Brussels. In 1940, following the German occupation of Belgium, Nussbaum was arrested as an enemy alien and imprisoned in the internment camp at Saint Cyprien in the south of France. He succeeded in escaping from Saint Cyprien and returned to Brussels, where he went into hiding to avoid further persecution and recapture. In July 1944, however, he was denounced, caught, and transported to Auschwitz, where he was killed. Even in the most constricted of conditions, Nussbaum continued to paint until this final deportation and his paintings chart both his own personal artistic odyssey and the tragic fate of the European Jews in the first half of the twentieth century. Thus the lighter themes of his early work (scenes of family life, tranquil landscapes, Jewish holidays) increasingly descend into dark, claustrophobic visions of alienation, imprisonment, and hopelessness.

Responding to the significance of this particular artist's life and work as emblematic of the abysmal experience of the Holocaust, Libeskind conceived the Osnabrück extension as a "Museum without Exit," in which "every element of the spatial organization, geometry, and programmatic content ... refers to the paradigmatic destiny of Nussbaum":

The museum is the retracing of the fatal elements and dead ends of Nussbaum's life. It is a projection and accessibility to those dead ends as a way of orienting and re-orienting ourselves in the space of the museum and of that history. This architecture opens the space to his paintings, to his experience of what the Shoah meant – without abstraction, without the statistics of six million, but of one human being murdered six million times. (Libeskind 2001, p. 92)

Libeskind achieves this dialectic between "spatial organization" and "programmatic content" by drawing upon a labyrinthine aesthetic, structuring the museum as a series of interlinked galleries, corridors, ramps, and bridges, which shape one's experience of the exhibited artworks without interpreting them according to some reductive script. Those works painted, for example, while Nussbaum was hiding out in a small attic room in Brussels are placed within the dimly lit "Nussbaum Gang," a narrow corridor "that does not allow for aesthetic distancing, but rather allows for a context that communicates the claustrophobic and dimming environment in which they were painted" (ibid., p. 96). While the architecture is expressive in this way, bringing one closer to Nussbaum's experience, it is also alienating, creating, through its angular walls and intersections, a sense of fragmentation and disorientation. Encountering blank walls, dead ends, and dark corners, instead of explication, we are forced to consider the limits of expressibility: to ask ourselves what is paintable and what unpaintable.

The labyrinthine character of the Felix Nussbaum Haus is heightened by the pathway-like structure of its galleries, which meet with sudden breaks and unpredictable intersections. This disjunctive quality is described by Thorsten Rodiek in his architectural monograph on the museum:

The paths, the alternation of narrow and wider spaces, the contrast in the materials, the diagonal arrangement in the external facades or the lighting covers, the cracks in the ceilings and floors and the aggressive, acute angles – all this ultimately means that the architecture is experienced as a fragmented unity, whose main characteristics are dynamics, expressiveness, emotionality and richness of metaphor. In this architecture there is no standing still. (1999, p. 67)

Indeed, the museum's architecture unsettles in many ways. Here, Rodiek argues, a physically discernible "making uncertain" of the visitor is taking place (ibid., p. 28). This is, then, a troubling space that disturbs one's habitual perspective. A space in which, as one follows the unicursal path of Nussbaum's destiny, one can easily become disoriented. It is a demanding space in which the visitor is forced to meet the "challenge" of the architecture, not through abstracted contemplation (it resists straightforward visual comprehension), but through the physical act of walking, through exertion (ibid., p. 21). Approaching Nussbaum's last known painting, "Triumph of Death" (1944), the floor literally gives way beneath one's feet and one is suspended precariously by a metal grille above the galleries below. Arriving at this vertiginous aporia in the "Museum without Exit," the sensation is of having undergone an ordeal, and as one gazes at Nussbaum's Brueghelesque portrayal of the *danse macabre* – its grotesque cadavers reeling over the ruins of Europe's supposed civilization – one is reminded of the choreographic function of the classical labyrinth, the "Truia" or "dance floor" that Daedalus "cunningly wrought" for Ariadne (*The Iliad* 18.592, cited in Kern 2000, p. 25). And, of course, one realizes that there *was* an exit to the labyrinthine prison that Nussbaum's life had become and that the artist's own triumph was in being able to confront it with such satire.

Libeskind states that the intention of his design for the Felix Nussbaum Haus was to rebel "against the idea that a museum is appearance, stasis or icon rather than substance and dynamic" (2001, p. 92). Employing a labyrinthine aesthetic, Libeskind succeeds in making vulnerable the biography and oeuvre of Felix Nussbaum, unsettling any settled meaning and opening up a "space of encounter" in which the visitor is called upon to play an active role. In effect, Libeskind creates a *mise en abyme*, constructing a frame around the frames of Nussbaum's life and works. Into this befittingly disjointed frame the visitor must enter and so become "part of the picture." If, as Libeskind writes, the Felix Nussbaum Haus "is about the placing and displacing of memory" (ibid.), then the visitor, too, is placed within that house of memory: placed in a position, that is, of reconsidering his own position in relation to the history of the Holocaust.

Detour 5: Unfolding the Spiral of Discovery

Although it now seems unlikely that Libeskind's controversial extension to the Victoria & Albert Museum (the V&A) in London will ever be built, I include a discussion of it here since, of all his museum designs, it draws most explicitly upon a labyrinthine aesthetic. Indeed, by calling the proposed extension "The Spiral," Libeskind invokes a geometric form that shares many characteristics of the unicursal labyrinth and is often incorporated into labyrinth design (Purce 1974). The proposal for the extension was not, however, "conceived as an a priori form or 'ready made' artifact" imposed upon the V&A site, but emerged as a response to the tortuous complex of buildings and galleries that comprise the existing museum (Libeskind 2001, p. 154). Many acquainted with the museum will recognize their own experiences in Libeskind's speculation that more than ninety percent of visitors to the V&A are lost within five minutes of entering its fifteen kilometers of gallery spaces (ibid.). Rather than considering this a design flaw to be "straightened out" in his pro- posals, Libeskind regards this as an appropriate, if accidental, metaphor for the late-modern condition in which the positivist paradigms of rationalism and certainty have given way to a contemporary *Zeitgeist* predicated on uncertainty and perspectival contingency.

> The twenty-first century will not be about finding ourselves, but losing ourselves much deeper in the history that created the future. So I did not try to make a box that gives everybody clear, easy routes to the Raphael cartoons, to the Greek collections, to the Cast Courts, to the Constables, to the Frank Lloyd Wright rooms – I followed the labyrinthic collection into the innermost recesses of the spiral of the V&A itself. (Ibid., p. 151)

Like many of Libeskind's museum designs, the proposed Spiral extension gives architectural form to this contemporary epistemological crisis. Indeed, through such designs, Libeskind uses architectural form to delib- erately confront the visitor with uncertainty, provoking a crisis in the visitor by refusing to satisfy her desire to readily grasp the principle or position that structures the museum's text and reassuringly establishes its meaning. Libeskind's museums withhold such reassurance. Such a strategy draws attention to the problematized nature of positionality in an age which, Libeskind maintains, has denied all principles: "What does it really mean to have a principle?" he asks. "On what is the principle based, and who is to guarantee and legitimate any principle today?" (ibid., p. 145). Thus the Spiral is not conceived as a "stage" for the V&A's collections (the "white cube" approach), but as "a thinking about how and what a museum does" (ibid., p. 151). To these ends, Libeskind argues, "the architecture is very strongly responsible for giving vectors for how a Museum operates in the future" (ibid.).

Although, technically, the proposed V&A extension takes the form of a continuous spiral, for the visitor – the maze-walker – this spiral is not evident, there being no privileged position from which to view its pattern. There is therefore no possibility of transcending the spiral and assuming the maze-viewer's perspective: no totalizing vision is permitted. Furthermore, since this is not a "traditional spiral" with a single center and axis, but a "contemporary spiral" with multiple centers and multiple axes, it opens in a plurality of directions along many trajectories, and provides an array of unexpected routes, spaces, and ambiances to be experienced by the visitor (ibid., p. 157) (figure 2.2). The unicursal form of the spiral is thus disrupted to create a multicursal maze or, as Libeskind puts it, a "labyrinth of discovery":

> This image of the labyrinth is not only a symbolic device, but a reinforcement and intensification of the unique qualities of the V&A. This emblem of a heterogeneous and open system of organization for the artifacts and exhibitions provides a diversity of experiences woven into a net of similarities and differences – an aggregate of traces about unexpected topics still to be explored. (Ibid.)

Figure 2.2 Architect's model of the interior of the proposed "Spiral" extension of the Victoria & Albert Museum, London. Courtesy of Studio Daniel Libeskind.

The visitor's journey through the spiral is not intended, therefore, to unfold in a linear fashion like a unicursal narrative leading the visitor to a particular conclusion, but is transformed into an exploratory process along multiple paths: an open-ended experiment in meaning-making.

We should, however, also recognize the paradoxical nature of Libeskind's experiment. To assert, for example, the impossibility of having a position is, surely, a position in itself. And, while no exterior, omniscient perspective is permitted in the architectural form of the Spiral, its architectural space is nevertheless situated in a wider discursive field – Libeskind's writings and drawings, for instance – in which the artistry of the architectural artifact is made apparent. Similarly, even though the design disrupts the telling of a predetermined, linear narrative, the visitor passing even randomly from object to object and gallery to gallery is engaged in an unfolding narrative process as he makes associations between the objects and spaces encountered. In Barthesian terms, the museum is thus transformed from a "readerly" (*lisible*) text to a "writerly" (*scriptible*) one, in which, as Libeskind insists, the visitor becomes "engaged in the work not as a voyeur but as a participant" (ibid., p. 151; cf. Barthes 1979). Positional and antipositional, artifactual and processual, continuous and discontinuous, Libeskind's proposed Spiral extension, in common with his other museum projects, embodies contradiction in a manner entirely consistent with the labyrinthine aesthetic.

Fragmenting the museum text into its composite *lexias* or "reading units" in a manner akin to Barthes's *S/Z* (1990), such a multi-lineal approach to museum design destabilizes the traditional roles of reader and writer, visitor and curator, redistributing authorial/curatorial power. The museum thus becomes a "site of activity," involving the visitor in a metonymic labor with and within – *labor intus* – the museum text, in which the visitor is called to (re-)establish meaningful relationships between the purposefully "dis-integrated" parts of an imagined whole.

Detour 6: Reading between the Lines

The most labyrinthine of Libeskind's museum designs is also his most celebrated. Although the Jewish Museum, Berlin underwent numerous name changes during its convoluted evolution, Libeskind's preferred title for the project has remained "Between the Lines." Libeskind describes his concept as being about "two lines of thinking, organization, and relationship. One is a straight line, but broken into many fragments; the other is a tortuous line, but continuing indefinitely" (2001, p. 23).

Although Libeskind does not explicitly refer to the labyrinthine aesthetic, these two organizing principles are, of course, precisely equivalent to the two paradigms of labyrinth design discussed earlier: the multicursal and the unicursal. It is, however, Libeskind's desire to embrace the contradictory and irreconcilable character of these paradigms in a single form – and to use this paradoxical form to engage with an irreconcilable history – that makes the Jewish Museum truly labyrinthine.

These two lineal principles are expressed throughout the museum and are fundamental to the architectural structure of the building. Thus, seen in plan or from above, the museum appears in the shape of a zigzag or lightning bolt (actually a dislocated Star of David). The zigzag is suggestive of the continuous, if tortuous, line of the unicursal labyrinth, and it also evokes the transcendent maze-viewer's perspective, which alone is able to perceive the shape. True to form, however, this is an unattainable perspective in the Jewish Museum, since, as Libeskind remarks, the zigzag design is not in fact apparent to the visitor and is "surely an image only seen by an angel" (ibid., p. 25). Cutting through the continuous zigzag of the museum is the discontinuous straight line of what Libeskind terms "the void." This void, suggestive of the fragmented path of the multicursal labyrinth, is an impenetrable cavity formed in raw concrete, which bisects the museum both horizontally and vertically. Contrasting with the exhibition areas, this void forms a "negative space" that penetrates the whole museum and which the visitor must continually cross via a multitude of bridging corridors as she moves around the building. According to Libeskind, this void refers to "that which can never be exhibited in the museum": it is an "embodiment of absence," reflecting the greater absence left in the wake of the Holocaust (ibid., p. 28). As the unicursal form of the museum is disrupted by the negative space of the void it effectively becomes a multicursal form, and the visitor's abstract appreciation must be abandoned as he is forced to inhabit the embodied experience of the maze-walker. "As you walk through the building", suggests Libeskind, "the walls, exhibition spaces, and the building's organization generate an understanding of the scale of disrupted tradition" (ibid., p. 26).

The Jewish Museum was envisaged by its commissioners as an extension to the baroque Collegienhaus on Lindenstrasse, home to the Berlin Museum since 1969. Libeskind's response, however, was to create what appears to be an entirely separate building, but one that can only be entered through a subterranean passage leading from the older building. On the surface, Libeskind thus preserves what he regards as "the contradictory autonomy" of the two buildings, while, contrary to appearances, the two buildings are in fact bound together "in the depth of time and space" (ibid., p. 27). Through such means Libeskind materializes programmatic resonances in architectural form: an assertion, then, of the inextricability of German and Jewish culture, but also a recognition that such connections have been systematically denied, made invisible, driven underground. This incongruence between the visible and invisible, between that which can be shown and that which is beyond representation, is also made apparent when examining the floor plans of the museum, where it is revealed that the underground floor has an entirely different shape to that of the building above (figure 2.3).

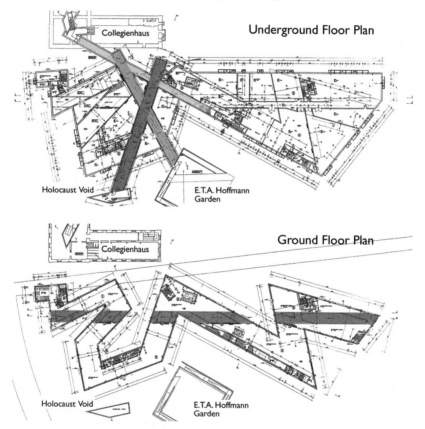

Figure 2.3   Underground and ground floor plans of the Jewish Museum, Berlin. The underground floor plan showing the subterranean passage from the Collegienhaus and the three axes (of continuity, exile and Holocaust); the ground floor plan showing the discontinuous straight line of the "void," which bisects and fragments the continuous zigzag of the museum. Courtesy of Studio Daniel Libeskind, annotated and shaded by Paul Basu.

The visitor to the Jewish Museum emerges from the subterranean corridor that leads from the Collegienhaus into a labyrinth of sloping passages, which comprise the underground level of the building. The intersecting structure of these passages is accentuated by the clear lines of the lighting design, the starkness of the slate floors, and the straight, white walls, pierced only by occasional angular recesses. In fact there are only three main "roads" in this labyrinth, each providing a trajectory toward a particular destination, each narrating a different historical destiny for Berlin's Jewish population. The first and longest road is called the "Axis of Continuity." This ends at a staircase that leads, metaphorically, "to the continuation of Berlin's history" and hence up to the main exhibition spaces on the upper floors of the museum. The second road, the steeper "Axis of Exile," leads to a glass door through which one can exit to the so-called "E. T. A. Hoffmann Garden." This garden, signifying the escape of exile and emigration, is itself a labyrinthine form, comprised of a tilted grid of 49 seven-meter-high concrete columns into which are planted willow oaks whose foliage tangles into a overarching canopy. As Bernhard Schneider notes, this "field of columns" evokes a range of associations: not least the labyrinthine "street grid between the skyscrapers of the New World" (1999, p. 50).

The third and final "axis" ends at the "Holocaust Void": a stark 27-meter-high concrete tower, accessed through a heavy door. This tall, chill, acutely angled chamber is illuminated by a needle of daylight passing through an aperture high in one wall and is connected to the museum building only by the underground "Axis of Holocaust": above ground, it stands isolate, a brutal and impenetrable form. Prosaically, an interpretation panel informs the visitor that "this tower commemorates the many millions of Holocaust victims." More emotively, Libeskind writes that "the Holocaust Void is a place that has to be experienced as an end, which will forever remain a dead end. For they will not return" (2001, p. 27). The dead ends of the labyrinth are thus given an all too literal meaning.

The unresolved tension between the two principles that structure the architecture of the Jewish Museum is also manifest in the display of the museum's collections in the upper floors. It is sometimes argued that the monumentality of Libeskind's architectural vision for the museum is incommensurable with its curatorial vision (see, for example, Fleming 2005, p. 57). The building, as James E. Young muses, seems to forbid showing much else besides itself and is therefore in danger of becoming its own content (2000, p. 13) – a rather less generative employment of the *mise en abyme.* Libeskind's intention, however, is to use the expressiveness of the architectural form to provoke a different relationship between audience and exhibit. In his entry to the architectural competition for the project, Libeskind argues that the "museum form itself must be rethought in order to transcend the passive involvement of the viewer" (2001, p. 29). To these ends, Libeskind explains that "standard exhibition rooms and traditional public spaces have been dissolved and disseminated along a myriad of complex trajectories in, on, and above the ground," and that "linear structures interact to create an irregular and decisively accentuated set of displacements, providing an active path and distancing the viewer in the investigation of the exhibits" (ibid.).

In his subtle analysis of the Jewish Museum, Young draws upon Anthony Vidler's (1992) conceptualization of the "architectural uncanny" to explore this "distancing" process. "Instead of merely housing the collection", Young writes, "this building seeks to estrange it from the viewers' own preconceptions" (2000, p. 17). The museum's disconcerting geometry thus subverts the "stabilizing function of architecture" and ensures that the museum never domesticates the events it engages with, "never makes us at home with them, never brings them into the reassuring house of redemptory meaning" (ibid., pp. 2–3). The museum thus disrupts the continuity of its own exhibitions and instead draws attention to the gaps and absences of Jewish history in Berlin.

Detour 7: Walking in the Museum

In February 2003, Libeskind's "Memory Foundations" proposal was selected as the preferred design for the redevelopment of the former World Trade Center site in Manhattan. Writing many years before "9/11," de Certeau describes the serene sense of being "lifted out of the city's grasp" as he gazes down upon New York from the summit of Yamasaki's original "twin towers": "An Icarus flying above these waters, [one] can ignore the devices of Daedalus in mobile and endless labyrinths far below" (1984, p. 92).

There is, de Certeau concedes, an undeniable pleasure in "seeing the whole": it satisfies a "scopic drive" that has long been associated in Western tradition with a "gnostic drive" – to be "all-seeing" is to be "all-knowing." Seeming to make possible such a celestial perspective, de Certeau writes that the view from the World Trade Center's 110th floor "transforms the bewitching world by which one was 'possessed' into a text that lies before one's eyes. It allows one to read it" (ibid.). He argues, however, that the knowledge permitted by this vantage point is merely a "theoretical" simulacrum, a "facsimile" little different from the architect's drawings or the urban planner's charts. The panoramic "totalizing view," which makes the complexity of the city comprehensible, is in fact quite blind to the "murky intertwining daily behaviours" that constitute the lived reality of the city (ibid.). The "readable city" is thus illusory, and the monumental figure of the "tower" plays no small part in the orchestration of the fiction. Predicting – poignantly, as it happens – an "Icarian fall," de Certeau proposes a return to the "opaque mobility" of the city-labyrinth and to the everyday spatial practices of the city's walkers "whose bodies follow the thicks and thins of an urban 'text' they write without being able to read it" (ibid., p. 93).

De Certeau's rereading of the city as a multitude of "migrational" processes rather than a "space of visual, panoptic, or theoretical constructions" has much relevance for the study of the museum (ibid.). If we shift the site of de Certeau's critique from the city to the museum, we are provoked into questioning the nature of the knowledge produced through those expository conventions employed to make readable the complexity of the museum's collections. In place of the "imaginary totalizations" of classificatory schemas and organizing narratives, we might consider the more opaque networks of the museum-walker's movements as corporeal enactments of Ricoeurian narrative processes: kinetic configurations, which "compose a manifold story that has neither author nor spectator" (ibid.; cf. Ricoeur 1991). To paraphrase de Certeau, we might say that the spatial order of the museum organizes an ensemble of narratological possibilities and interdictions, and that the museum-walker "actualizes" some of these possibilities, bringing them into being (1984, p. 98). But the visitor also brings into being other, unanticipated possibilities as the various improvisations that constitute the practice of walking privilege and transform certain elements, while abandoning others. Through such "pedestrian speech acts" the museum visitor appropriates the topographical system of the museum, opening up meanings and directions according to an itinerary that is only partly determined by its curator's or designer's intentions.

Such an analysis may be applied to any museum: the more complex the museum's topography, the larger the ensemble of spatial possibilities and interdictions, and hence the more opportunity for the museum-walker to improvise. But the labyrinthine museum is not merely a complicated space, it is also a complicating space. Young describes Libeskind's designs for the Jewish Museum, Berlin as "the spatial enactment of a philosophical problem" (2000, p. 10). Indeed, I suggest that Libeskind enacts architecturally the same problem that de Certeau explores in writing. While this critique of the production of absolute knowledge extends far beyond the museum's walls and beyond the concerns of architecture, Libeskind's achievement is to recognize in the labyrinth a formal expression of this epistemological crisis and to express this form in the architecture of the museum. Experimenting with the labyrinthine aesthetic, Libeskind thus "performs" what might be described as an architectural paradox, critiquing the concept of the museum through the medium of the museum itself. Here, again, is the reflexive structuration of the *mise en abyme*.

As Young notes, Libeskind's drawings for the Jewish Museum seem "more like the sketches of the museum's ruins" than proposals for a new museum building (ibid.). And, indeed, the ruins of the modernist paradigm are evoked beside the Felix Nussbaum Haus in a tumbled pile of neoclassical columns (figure 2.4). In galleries fragmented by empty voids, in shards of a shattered whole, in the twisted logic of a non-spiral spiral,

Figure 2.4 Evoking the museum's ruins. Exterior, Felix Nussbaum Haus, Osnabrück. Photograph by Paul Basu.

and, most literally, in a heap of antique masonry, the visitor to Libeskind's museums continually stumbles upon the ruins of an ideology that still haunts the institution of the museum. Frustrating expectations, these museums play with the visitor's scopic/gnostic drive, but refuse to satisfy it. Rather than fulfilling the promise of rendering their obscure texts readable, providing a straightforward pathway from ignorance to knowledge, these labyrinthine museums provoke the visitor's own Icarian fall, thrusting her back into the troubling realms of partial truths and uncertainties. In this way, Libeskind's museums are truly expressive of the labyrinthine paradox in which both maze-viewer's and maze-walker's perspectives coexist, each implied in the other. Thus, even as we recognize that we remain forever maze-walkers, mired in the contingencies of our own subjectivity, the "idea" of the maze-viewer's transcendent objectivity haunts the imagination and motivates our onward journey.

Detour 8: To Arrive at Where I Started

Commenting on his designs, Libeskind repeatedly expresses a belief that the institution of the museum must be rethought in order to disrupt the passive voyeurism of its visitors. Libeskind's experiments with the museum form are not the results of such rethinking, they are materializations of the very process of rethinking. Drawing upon the process-oriented metaphor of the labyrinth, Libeskind creates of the museum's corridors and galleries an "active path," which not only invites the active participation of its walkers, but insists on it. As Doob writes of the labyrinth, so we might say of the labyrinthine museum: that, here, "means dominate ends, process obscures product, and the wanderer must continue, choose, or retreat with no sure knowledge of the consequences" (1990, p. 57).

The museum's active path is thus labyrinthine in another sense, since it is also demanding of its walker's labors – the labor, for instance, of reconfiguring the syntagmatic relationships between exhibits that have been dissociated from each other. There is, after all, no grand, unicursal narrative to follow here. Instead, the museum must be regarded as a space of narrative potential: a space that is potentially generative of a diversity of paths and stories, but which is reliant upon the enunciative spatial practices of each visitor to bring them into being. If the visitor is not inspired to such "labors within" the museum's walls, it may be legitimate to claim that the experiment fails. This is surely a dangerous policy for public institutions devoted to widening participation and opening access. But the decentering of curatorial control also widens participation and opens access in other ways, and, indeed, the remarkable popularity of museums such as the Jewish Museum, Berlin would seem to suggest that Libeskind's disorienting architecture is not also an alienating one. On the contrary, we are intrigued by the puzzle of the maze and provoked by its complicating narratives, which cause us to question the procedures through which we routinely make simple sense of a complex world.

To enter the labyrinthine museum is to be called to find a passage of associations through the multicursal maze of its text: a passage of associations, which, if it could be traced – as Ariadne's thread, for instance – would paradoxically take a unicursal form. In other words, our movement through the nonlinear discursive space of the labyrinthine museum is necessarily a linear one, in which we reorder its disorderly displays according to our own interests and sensibilities, constructing our own narratives from the narrative potential implicit within its walls.

While, through our labors, we may discern a story – perhaps many stories – within the museum text, we are never left in doubt that the "whole story" is always beyond: that there are corridors as yet unexplored and undiscovered, that there is always an *excess* of meaning. Made conscious of the partialness of our knowledge and explication, we may be reminded of Herodotus marveling at the labyrinth of Amenemhat III: that no matter how eloquent the enunciator, the greater part remains "greater than words can say."

References

Bal, M. (1996) *Double Exposures*. London: Routledge.

Barthes, R. (1979 [1971]) *From Work to Text*. Trans. R. Miller. New York: Hill & Wang.

Barthes, R. (1990 [1973]) *S/Z*. Trans. R. Miller. Oxford: Blackwell.

Calder, J. (2000) From artefacts to audience: strategy for display and interpretation. In J. M. Fladmark (ed.), *Heritage and Museums: Shaping National Identity*. Shaftesbury: Donhead, pp. 41–52.

Carr, D. (1991) Discussion: Ricoeur on narrative. In D. Wood (ed.), *On Paul Ricoeur: Narrative and Interpretation*. London: Routledge, pp. 160–74.

Cipolla, G. (1987) *Labyrinth: Studies on an Archetype*. New York: Legas.

Dällenbach, L. (1989 [1977]) *The Mirror in the Text*. Trans. J. Whiteley and E. Hughes. Cambridge: Polity Press.

de Certeau, M. (1984 [1980]) *The Practice of Everyday Life.* Trans. S. Rendall. Berkeley: California University Press.

Doob, P. R. (1990) *The Idea of the Labyrinth from Classical Antiquity through the Middle Ages.* Ithaca, N.Y.: Cornell University Press.

Ernst, W. (2000) Archi(ve)textures of museology. In S. A. Crane (ed.), *Museums and Memory.* Stanford, Calif.: Stanford University Press, pp. 17–34.

Faris, W. B. (1988) *Labyrinths of Language: Symbolic Landscape and Narrative Design in Modern Fiction.* Baltimore: Johns Hopkins University Press.

Fleming, D. (2005) Creative space. In S. MacLeod (ed.), *Reshaping Museum Space: Architecture, Design, Exhibitions.* London: Routledge, pp. 53–61.

Hassan, I. (1985) The culture of postmodernism. *Theory, Culture and Society,* 2 (3): 119–31.

Gailhabaud, J. (1858) *L'Architecture du Vme au XVIIme siecle,* vol. 2. Paris: Gide.

Kern, H. (2000 [1982]) *Through the Labyrinth* (R. Ferré and J. Saward, eds.). Munich: Prestel.

Libeskind, D. (2001) *The Space of Encounter.* London: Thames & Hudson.

MacAulay, G. C. (1890) *The History of Herodotus.* London: Macmillan.

Matthews, W. H. (1922) *Mazes and Labyrinths: A General Account of Their History and Developments.* London: Longmans, Green & Co.

Millenson, S. F. (1987) *Sir John Soane's Museum.* Ann Arbor, Mich.: UMI Research Press.

Petrie, W. M. F., Wainwright, G. A., and Mackay, E. (1912) *The Labyrinth, Gerzeh and Mazghuneh.* London: Bernard Quaritch.

Purce, J. (1974) *The Mystic Spiral.* London: Thames & Hudson.

Ricoeur, P. (1991) Life in quest of narrative. In D. Wood (ed.), *On Paul Ricoeur: Narrative and Interpretation.* London: Routledge, pp. 20–33.

Rodiek, T. (1999) *Daniel Libeskind: Museum ohne Ausgang.* Tübingen: Ernst Wasmuth.

Saward, J. (2002) *Magical Paths: Labyrinths and Mazes in the 21st Century.* London: Mitchell Beazley.

Schneider, B. (1999) *Daniel Libeskind: Jewish Museum Berlin.* Munich: Prestel.

Shiode, N. and Grajetzki, W. (2000) A virtual exploration of the lost labyrinth: developing a reconstructive model of Hawara Labyrinth pyramid complex. CASA Working Papers 29. University College London, Centre for Advanced Spatial Analysis.

Snyder, I. (1997) *Hypertext: The Electronic Labyrinth.* New York: New York University Press.

Teski, M. C. and Climo, J. J. (eds.) (1995) *The Labyrinth of Memory: Ethnographic Journeys.* Westport, Conn.: Bergin & Garvey.

Ulmer, G. L. (1992) Grammatology (in the stacks) of hypermedia. In M. C. Tuman (ed.), *Literacy Online.* Pittsburgh, Pa.: University of Pittsburgh Press, pp. 139–64.

Ulmer, G. L. (1994) *Heuretics: The Logic of Invention.* Baltimore: Johns Hopkins University Press.

Vidler, A. (1992) *The Architectural Uncanny: Essays in the Modern Unhomely.* Cambridge, Mass.: MIT Press.

Young, J. E. (2000) Daniel Libeskind's Jewish Museum in Berlin: the uncanny arts of memorial architecture. *Jewish Social Studies,* 6 (2): 1–23.

3

Exhibition as Film

Mieke Bal

Photography as Storyboard, Exhibition as Film

Exhibitions, if taken at all seriously either as art form or as predominantly visual discourse, are often interpreted or framed in terms borrowed from other art practices. This transfer between disciplines and practices is useful: it helps museologists to conceive of their practice, while providing critics with conceptual tools to analyze exhibitions. For example, in my book *Double Exposures* (1996), I critically examined some famous museum exhibitions. The key metaphor in my analysis was narrative, conceived as a meaning-producing sequentiality, emerging from the viewer's walk through an exhibition. Putting one thing next to another, in other words, produced a time-bound relationship between the two, one that moved from the first to the second.

Instead of using metaphors to criticize exhibition practices, I would here like to discuss various metaphors as tools for enhancing the aesthetic and political efficacy of exhibitions. Theater, narrative, poetry, and cinema: these genres, I contend, help us understand how exhibitions, not the particular artworks in them, work, how they produce effects that imprint themselves on us and make us leave the galleries transformed by the experience. I will theorize these models by means of close analysis of actual displays in one exhibition, *Partners*. This award-winning exhibition curated by Canadian art collector and curator Ydessa Hendeles, is the best – most effective, gripping, and powerful – exhibition I have ever seen.

As the title of the exhibition, *Partners*, intimates, it establishes long-repressed, albeit ambivalent, links forged by histories between the Jewish and the German peoples, as well as between the two sides of the Atlantic. This political efficacy is wrought by means of a profoundly effective, indeed thrilling, aesthetic in which, far from being opposite or even distinct domains, politics and aesthetics operate together, in an inextricable merging that strengthens both.

This aesthetic, I argue, is intimately bound up with the predominant medium of the exhibition – photography, aligned with sculpture and video. Whereas exhibitions, by virtue of the spectator's movement through the space and the temporal sequentiality involved in the visit, are always to some extent narrative, the medium of photography in exhibitions tends to take on cinematic effects. This effect has been enhanced in *Partners*, so much so that a tension between photography and film is the primary aesthetic at play. In this respect, *Partners* can be said to be a meta-exhibition – an exhibition exploring the nature of exhibiting.

To understand the artistic work performed by this exhibition, then, the most productive metaphor to deploy is film. Specifically, since many of the works exhibited here are, or are derived from, photography, *Partners* invites us to consider photography – the medium, the art – as a storyboard or visual scenario for a cinematic vision of art presentation. This cinematic element moreover intensifies the inextricable bond between aesthetics and politics this exhibition examines and performs. This relationship between art and politics is introduced according to an aesthetic vision that ties the contemplation of art to a repositioning of the subject in relation to the world. This works as follows. The thrust of the cinematic vision at work in this exhibition is to establish, or at least to encourage, an affective relationship, not only between the art and the viewer but also between the artworks themselves. These relationships between the artworks constitute the exhibition's syntax, which is affective in nature. Between a perception that troubles us and an action we hesitate about, affect emerges. Photography, the key element in *Partners*, projects this relationship of affect as the possibility of translating heterogeneous emotions into each other. The common foundation on which such translation works is the notion that through art, it is possible to identify with other people's pasts as they lived them; in other words, to "have" other people's memories, to produce world memories.

Exhibition as... Competing Models

Partners occupied fourteen exhibition rooms in the Haus der Kunst in Munich: thirteen medium or small ones, around one large central space.

The rooms are devoted to objects ranging from early photographs to contemporary sculpture. Neither strictly sequential nor circular, the exhibition had a single entrance, leading into an exhibit of three very different objects, none of which belong to canonical art: an early self-portrait of Diane Arbus, made before she became an artist and for a private purpose; an antique toy of a Minnie Mouse figure carrying Felix the Cat in a suitcase; and a studio photograph of a group of bandits. After this small entrance room, the exhibition offered several possible itineraries (see figure 3.1).

Already on this very basic level of the floor plan, the exhibition raises the question of conceptual metaphors. Most frequently, one speaks of exhibitions in terms of either theater or narrative. Theater recalls the *mise-en-scène* all exhibitions imply, whereas narrative invokes the walking tour the visitor makes, moving through the exhibition. The relevance of the conceptual metaphor of theater as a frame of reference is easy to grasp. Exhibiting a number of artworks under the best possible viewing conditions, curators need to develop a scenography. They arrange objects in a

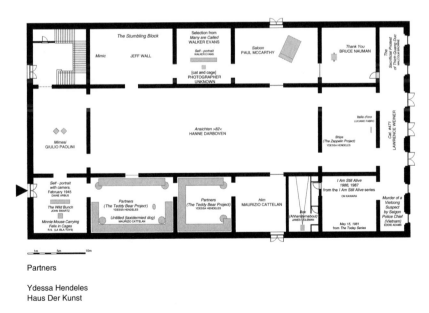

Partners

Ydessa Hendeles
Haus Der Kunst

Figure 3.1 Floor plan of the exhibition *Partners* by Ydessa Hendeles.

space that, by virtue of the status of those objects as art, becomes more or less fictional. The gallery suspends everyday concerns and isolates the viewer with the art.

But the gallery space also isolates the viewer from the art. The objects can be approached, but only to a limited degree, and most often without being touched. This turns the gallery space into a stage separated from the spectator sitting in the dark. To make a convincing exhibition, the curator arranges the objects like still life, as a tableau vivant. The distancing this entails constitutes the limit of the usefulness of the metaphor of theater. While *Partners* deploys this metaphor, it is not limited to it.

To be sure, an exhibition is necessarily the result of a *mise-en-scène*, and *Partners* is no exception. But what does this mean? In theater, *mise-en-scène* is: the materialization of text (word and score) in a form accessible for public, collective reception; a mediation between a play and each individual in the public; an artistic organization of the space in which the play is set; and an arrangement of a limited and delimited section of real time and space. As a result of all this arranging, a differently delimited section of fictional time and space accommodates the fictional activities of the actors, who perform their roles in order to build a plot. In the case of exhibitions, it is important to realize that the role of actor is not limited to the objects on display; both the visitors and the objects are the actors, and it is the interaction between them that constitutes the play.

The subject of this activity – the (stage) director – makes a work of art. Her tools are time, space, actors, props, and light. Her activities comprise: the projection of dramatic and musical writing into a particular time-space, or chronotopos, specifically spatial coordination; the highlighting of some meanings over others; and the keying of text and score in between performers and public. The ensuing work is sometimes "totalizing," and always, to use a term I prefer, *mise-en-pièce(s)* (Pavis 1998, pp. 361–8; Bal 2002).

Adapting Hans-Thiess Lehmann's notion, *mise-en-scène* is a mediation from logos to landscape (Lehmann 1997, pp. 55–60; Bal 2002). The activity of *mise-en-scène* makes for an intervention that turns words leading to the formation of abstract meanings – in the case of exhibitions, the conceptual understanding by the curator of the artworks – into a spectacle receptive to the turmoil of liberated meanings variously attached to concrete, visible, and audible phenomena and signs. Borrowed from theater, *mise-en-scène* indicates the overall artistic activity whose results will shelter and foster the performance of the concrete realization of the art. In its mobility, and in the change over time it entails, *mise-en-scène* fits nicely as a metaphor for the experience of an exhibition, because theatrical *mise-en-scène* creates an affective relationship with the spectators, on the basis of, among other things, spatial arrangements. It is also a metaphor that theater shares with film.

The narrative conception of exhibitions is discussed in the catalogue to *Partners* – explicitly by Ernst van Alphen in his essay "Exhibition as Narrative Work of Art" (2003), and implicitly by Ydessa Hendeles in her "Notes on the exhibition" (2003). This idea is based on the visitor's journey through the exhibition as a series of events constituting a "plot." Narrative and theater share the element of plot, but there is also a major difference between them. Instead of standing still in front of an imaginary stage, reminiscent of a theater, the viewer now walks through a forest of objects. And instead of being a spectator of the play, she is a co-narrator, fulfilling in her own way the script that predetermines the parameters within which the story can be told. This temporal dimension of exhibitions is the guiding principle of narratological analysis. Like reading a novel, when the reader accumulates an understanding of and affective relationship with the events and characters, walking through an exhibition creates, in the experience of the visitor, an accumulative relationship with the art on display.

In the catalogue, Van Alphen offers a narrative model for exhibitions as an alternative to the three traditional principles of coherence, derived from (1) the centrality of the individual artist, (2) a chronological unfolding of an artist's or a group of artists' "development," and (3) thematic unification. These principles are unsurprising, hence unchallenging. In contrast, a narrative exhibition asks of the viewer that she establishes connections as she moves through the exhibition, building up a "story," which has, as its outcome, or dénouement, an effect. This effect binds together the different experiences evolving from the confrontation with the artworks.

Such shows need not have the typical coherence of traditional exhibitions. On the contrary, since they activate the viewer, compelling her to create rather than consume the exhibition-as-narrative, such shows can harbor heterogeneous objects that only cohere because of the narrative constantly "under construction." *Partners* brings this art of storytelling, by means of a particular installation of objects, to a new level of intensity.

In Van Alphen's analysis of this exhibition, the narrativity is conceptualized primarily through Peter Brooks's theory of plot and repetition. Harking back to a structuralist model, according to which a plot is constructed from building-blocks arranged in a tension between similarity and difference or in an ongoing transformation, Brooks sees narrative as a constant postponement that frustrates but also maintains a desire for the ending. This desire is the basis of the activity of the reader, who performs what Brooks calls "reading for the plot" (1984).

But, like novels, exhibition narrative also achieves this effect by means of a specifically narrative rhetoric. This brings it closer to poetry. In her straightforward, ostensibly descriptive "Notes" in the catalogue, Hendeles hints at some particular poetical figures that articulate this narrative in *Partners*. It is in these figures that the unique effectivity of this exhibition can be perceived. One such figure is contrast. This figure is at work, for example, between the quietness of the room in which are installed On Kawara's date work from the *Today* series (1966–present) and elements from his *I Am Still Alive* series (1969–present), and the loud, pounding sounds of the adjacent room where James Coleman's *Box* (Ahhareturnabout) from 1977 is staged (Hendeles 2003, p. 223). The contrast is effective because the soundproof door between the two rooms turns the loudness of *Box* into an unexpected shock.

Hendeles also hints at subtle counterpoints, such as between the themes of murder and suicide found in Darboven's *Ansichten >82<*, reiterated in the photojournalist narratives of Malcolm Browne and Eddie Adams (Hendeles 2003, p. 220), on display at opposite ends of the long, narrow room. But after Darboven's work, these two embedded themes are no longer clear opposites. Rather, they are complex entanglements with the real world, in which perpetrator and victim positions are not always in clear opposition, partly because the individual does not act alone. But, whereas the contrast between Kawara and Coleman proceeds in a forward movement of linear time, the resonance between Darboven's work and the two photojournalistic series emerges retrospectively. This difference – between prospective and retrospective resonance – is of a narratological nature (Bal 1997; Genette 1972).

A third poetic figure is reiteration. This is at work, for example, in the continuation of a duality proposed in a room preceding *Partners (The Teddy Bear Project)*. The duality between comfort and danger, affection and hostility, established as early as the entrance gallery by the toy called Minnie Mouse Carrying Felix in Cages, continues in the later, overwhelming installation of thousands of pictures of teddy bears (an artwork that the curator-collector has herself contributed as an artist; see figure 3.2), establishing a version of what Dutch curator Rudi Fuchs has

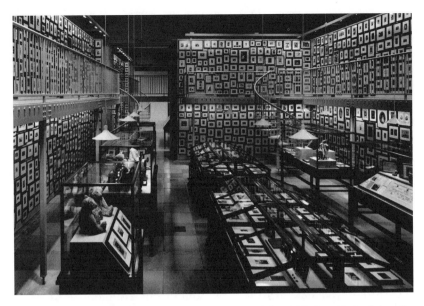

Figure 3.2   Overview of Ydessa Hendeles' *Partners (The Teddy Bear Project)*, installation 2002. Photograph by Robert Keziere, 2004.

called couplets – often unexpected analogies and resonances produced by means of juxtapositions.

Exhibition as Film, After Photography

All three models, of theater, narrative, and poetry, were operative in a transformative way in *Partners*. What makes the exhibition exceptionally effective though is the overarching model of cinema. Cinema is specifically relevant for three reasons. First, it encompasses all three models, binding them together: film requires *mise-en-scène*, unfolds narratives, and deploys poetic strategies to enforce its affective impact, slowing down the forward thrust of the plot. Second, cinema is the art of the masses, and as such an effective tool for political activism. Eisenstein's use of a montage of dialectical contrast effected a Soviet politics, whereas Griffith's early Hollywood organicist montage of oppositions produced its own politics. Third, and most importantly here, this new medium of the beginning of the twentieth century is not simply a continuation of photography. Instead, cinema responds to photography, critically and ambivalently. This response concerns not only movement and time but also, more subtly, the insistence on the limits of visibility inherent in time, which cinema inscribes in the black intervals in and between frames (Doane 2002).

Cinema, then, takes off where photography reaches its literal limits: in the frame. Photography serves as cinema's scenario or storyboard, and cinema is photography's commentary: a meta-photography. This is emphatically – though not exclusively – the case in *Partners*. With photography as its storyboard, this exhibition animates the visual scenario by means of cinematic strategies. These strategies include the obvious ones, such as: the construction of a space that is proper to the exhibition and that offers connections to the outside world without coinciding with it; the tension between movement and time, each possessed by its own rhythm; and the deployment of stylistic figures that thicken the narrative and change its pace, such as those of montage (e.g. dissolves) and framing (e.g. close-ups). The cinematic – the soul of this exhibition – comes to operate most powerfully at a few key junctures.

One such moment or juncture is the transition between the entrance gallery and *Partners (The Teddy Bear Project)*. This immense photo archive of thousands of snapshots, studio pictures and other inconspicuous forms of photography, all uniformly matted and framed, is the heart of the exhibition, next to the entrance gallery if one elects to move ahead instead of turning left. Here, the collector has ordered the wall-covering photographs according to taxonomies that repeat, and thus mock, nineteenth-century models of exhibiting, in the process slowing down the narrative to the extreme. All photographs have one element in common whose importance the artist – as I must now call Hendeles – has not found but created by her collecting acts: in each a teddy bear is visible.

The categories established here center on these toys. One child, two children, twins with teddy bears; soldiers, sailors, hunters with teddy bears; women, dressed or naked, with teddy bears; children aiming sometimes adult-size rifles at small teddy bears. Bears in strollers or baby-carriages, group portraits with a teddy bear, or babies competing with teddy bears in size and cuteness. These two galleries, covered from ceiling to floor, confine and hold the visitor in a necessarily time-consuming act of voyeurism, an intimacy with unknown people, most but not all of whom must be dead by now. After these two crowded galleries, a near-empty fourth one beckons.

This next room contains a single sculpture: a young adolescent boy kneeling in a pose of prayer. It turns its back to those who exit the photo galleries. Slowed down by the time-consuming, indeed, time-halting photo galleries, one is not too rushed to see the boy's face. The moment of total shock occurs when one walks through that third gallery to see the boy's face. The face is Hitler's. The sculpture (figure 3.3), made by Maurizio Cattelan, is called *Him* (2001).

Indeed, it is when Cattelan's sculpture *Him* enters the picture that, for me, the narrative model suddenly yields to the altogether different cinematic one. We encounter this sculpture when exiting the two crowded rooms of *Partners (The Teddy Bear Project).* The contrast between the

Figure 3.3   Maurizio Cattelan, *Him*, 2001. Photograph by Robert Keziere, 2004.

intimate installation of the photo archive, which invites us to dwell, explore, and remain in this installation-within-the-installation, and the lone figure seen from the back in an otherwise empty gallery, produces the estranging sense of a sharp cut between one episode and the next, set in a completely different space. The visual contrast is comparable to the auditory contrast between the quiet Kawara and the loud Coleman installations. The contrast between quiet and loud is here one between multitude and singularity, between overwhelming and meditative, between welcoming warmth and cold loneliness. The lone figure kneeling on the cold stone floor is cut out – literally.

This contrast sets up an expectation of contrast on the level of content as well. Indeed, a sometimes convincing, sometimes deceptive sense of comfort and safety is created in the Teddy-Bear galleries by means of an old-fashioned, homey living-room, illuminated by domestic lamps and overwritten by the even more old-fashioned, nineteenth-century museum of natural history theme, with its odd classificatory drive and crowded showcases. This cozy ambiance contrasts with the danger to which this child-size kneeling doll seems to be exposed. But the doll turns its back to us. This has the effect of pulling us closer, compelling us to approach, to walk to the other side, to see its face, bend over. The movement performed by the viewer is the kinetic equivalent of a zoom-in, from a long shot to a close-up. And, after we turn around and zoom in, the face we finally come to see – against the backdrop of the Teddy-Bear galleries that continue to beckon us – destroys any sense of safety, warmth, or comfort that may linger.

The tension between expecting a face we do not know and seeing one we do – one that more than half a century of tabooing has taught us not to look straight into the face – creates a gripping sense of fear, if only for a split second. This face, so low that we have to mentally or even physically crouch down to look it in the eyes, is cinematic, both symbolically and physically, in that it is an isolated close-up. I see it as a close-up indeed, but one abstracted from the Teddy-Bear photo installation where it was visually absent, but constantly if implicitly evoked. It thus stands for cinema as a commentary on photography. Close-ups exaggerate photography, pushing realism to its limits, and sometimes beyond, when the view comes so close that the image becomes illegible, where the grain of the photograph and the grain of the skin become one, whereby the object recedes behind its representation.

As I will explain below, *Him*, in its function as cinematic close-up, isolates us from itself and from the history that precedes us, a history embodied in the Teddy-Bear installation. The close-up in cinema re-becomes photography but "beyond" cinema: it stops time, undermining the linearity of temporality that the cinematic had just installed. This is the primary function of the close-up in film. It imposes a qualitative leap indifferent to linear time. And, since time and space are imbricated in the same move, close-ups undermine spatial continuity as well. They are not aggrandizements of a segment of the image. Rather, they are abstractions, isolating the object from the time-space coordinates in which we were moving as if "naturally." A close-up immediately cancels the whole that precedes it, leaving us alone, thrown out of linear time, alone with a relationship to the image that is pure affect.[1]

Exhibition as Film "Before" Photography

In its function as cinematic close-up, Cattelan's sculpture *Him*, technically not a photograph, does three things to the relationship between photography and cinema and to the complementary relationship between the exhibition space and the outside world. First, it instills the sense that, incredibly, this excessively realistic sculpture is more photographic than all of the thousands of photographs in the gallery just left behind: it is more precise, more readable, because larger in scale. At the same time, and secondly, the object of the photo-realistic representation is shocking enough to stop us in our tracks: physical and psychic stopping coincide, aggrandizing each other's effect. Finally, echoing Diane Arbus's tiny self-portrait that opens the show and programs our mode of being in it, the eyes can be looked into, but they don't look back. If Arbus's miniature is a model for the kind of photographic look that this show mobilizes, then Hitler's glassy eyes are mercifully out of reach. Instead, his large eyes – looking, but not at us – must be looking into a mirror; the mirror of history we just left. This sculpture can be said to be "mirroring evil."[2]

Since close-ups are cinematic images that counter the linearity of time, the deployment of this form to (re?)present a figure who, historically, orchestrated the greatest catastrophe ever, is a way of protesting against a certain conception of nation, history and time. Exhibited as it is after *Partners (The Teddy Bear Project)*, this sculpture militates against the historical conception that construes time as inevitably linear, unstoppable, and that simultaneously relegates the past to a distance. Producing a close-up of Hitler is a way of bringing him, and everything he stands for, into the present tense.

Hence, the relation between photography and cinema as its successor and commentator changes gear, to become a relationship of pre-posterous reversal, where photography comments on cinema as its (surviving) successor. From the retrospective vantage point of the present tense the temporality of the thousands of photographs in *Partners (The Teddy Bear Project)* receives its multilayered density, a density that is, I contend, the aesthetic point of this "affective syntax." We look back, and the coziness becomes impenetrable. In actually going back, I became sensitized to the way this exhibition counters narrative linearity, while remaining a multi-layered narrative. Compared to Hitler's overly readable face, the snapshots, already caught in the long shot of multitude, are even harder to read yet in greater need of reading: I spent more time with them on this second visit, despite the frustration that reading them is both impossible and pointless.

The sheer number of photographs had the same uncanny effect mass graves can have. "After" Hitler, I wanted to know if and when they died, how many survived "Him." After Hitler, I see them through the face that over-layers them in the equivalent of a cinematic dissolve: a superposition of two images – one singular, one massively multiple – creating memory space. In form, it is no different from Leni Riefenstahl's dissolve in *Triumph des Willens* (1935), where an image of a crowd of soldiers melts into an image of Hitler speaking, thus "creating a third image where Hitler is made up of all the small men that represent Germany," a composite image that quotes "the depiction of power and the 'body of society' in the cover illustration of Leviathan by Thomas Hobbes from 1651" (Iversen 2003).[3]

In the flashback constructed by the contrast between *Him* and *Partners (The Teddy Bear Project)*, which all but imposes a return through *Him* – is an implicit commentary on the political visions "imaged" by both Hobbes and Riefenstahl. This compels us to reflect from within on a tension inherent in *Partners (The Teddy Bear Project)*: the tension between safety, comfort, and childhood innocence, on the one hand, and the dangers of conformism and its bond with commerce, on the other, as well as the serious, formative potential of play, fantasy, and fiction.

This is compounded with the tension on which this work thrives – between the value of each singular person, a value embodied in some elaborate wall labels, and the absorption of each person in multitudes, the multitude of Hitler's soldiers, who went along with his soothing discourse until the Hobbesian social body was formed, so that the multitude of victims could arise. And through the transitional object of the teddy bear, the question of emotional complicity peeps in from around the corner.

Since the dissolve specifically involves a close-up and a long shot, it produces a memory space that binds both the past to the present, and this exhibition-visit to tragedy. For each of us visitors, that past tense has different connotations, inflections, but the affect of it cannot be held at bay. And for each of us, the memories which that affect yields are composite – not our own, but translated through innumerable stories and images. They are, as film theorist Kaja Silverman (1996) has argued, heteropathic memories, that is, the memories of others, felt in a strong affect-image, as a gift to those who perished.

The current exhibition space, in the former Haus der Deutschen Kunst, which Hitler commissioned to host purely German art away from the "degenerate art," enables a translation of all those emotions into world memories. Through its displacements, the *Partners* exhibition is no longer the *mise-en-scène* of a fictional, fabulous space, but the arrangement of a segment of the world that is itself syntactically linked to other places it has affected and touched in the past, and which it continues to touch in the present.

But the worldwide provenance of the snapshots comes about in other ways as well. In her "Notes," Hendeles mentions the many countries from where the photographs came. The act of clutching a teddy bear is presented as a worldwide act of conforming to that awkward partnership between Germany and North America. The history of the teddy bear itself, with its dual, staggered "invention" and implementation as a globally popular toy, testifies to that ambiguity. Like Karl May's American Indian, the toy was invented, copyrighted, mass-produced and sold, named and cherished, in an episodic history where first Germany, then the USA, took the leading role.

After, with, and through Cattalan's Him ... wherever we rest our gaze in the return to *Partners (The Teddy Bear Project)*, the innumerable memories – each of which is individual, irretrievable but for this single snapshot – imprint themselves in our present tense.

Exhibition as Film "During" Cinema

At this point, in order to give more substance to the conceptual metaphor of cinema as a way of understanding the power of this exhibition, let me describe a number of cinematic devices that respond to photography.

(1) The recomposition of movement out of instants. In this, cinema is most rigorously meta-photography. The fact that the teddy bear pictures are often posed photographs makes them stand in opposition to cinema's movement-images, turning photography inevitably into a meta-cinema. At the same time, their installation itself is still cinematic. Cinema, according to the French philosopher Gilles Deleuze, is essentially dependent not on photography in general but rather on the snapshot that freezes the instant (1983, p. 14). As a "post-photographic" form of photography, cinema decomposes and recomposes movement in relation to equidistant instants (see also Marrati 2003).

As a commentary on photography, then, *Partners (The Teddy Bear Project)* makes two interventions. First, the posed production quality of many of the photographs recedes in favor of their informal, amateurish use quality, which delimits the pose in time and inscribes its brief duration: they become snapshots in Deleuze's sense of *instantanés*. The ambiguous category here is the posed snapshot. Second, the uniform matting and framing along with the equidistant hanging (metaphorically?) reintroduce the equidistant instants of cinema's recomposition of movement. Closely in line with Deleuze's view of cinema, the installation offers a precarious and provisional stability that is, as Henri Bergson would have it, "a slice of becoming." Thus, the installation of *Partners (The Teddy Bear Project)* harks back to photography, its "storyboard" made from the vantage point of cinema.

(2) Pro-spective folding. After experiencing so many photographs, the encounter with the non-photographic – here represented by some of the sculptures – is photographically "incurved." With this verb, I point not only to the tight bond between affect and action, but, specifically, to a baroque conception of point of view derived from another of Deleuze's works, according to which point of view enfolds the viewer rather than allowing him to take in a spectacle at a distance (1993). The point of view of "the fold" compels the viewer to enter the fabulation of the artwork, to travel inside and out again, and emerge transformed by the experience. This principle, one might say, is literalized and aggrandized in the intimate rooms of *Partners (The Teddy Bear Project)*, where immersion, not linear perspective, reigns supreme.

(3) Play with the "mechanical reproducibility" of the photograph. An example of this device is the effect of the photo installation on Paolini's sculpture *Mimesi* from 1975–6 (figure 3.4), exhibited in the gallery one enters after the confrontation with *Him*. This dual copy of a classical

Figure 3.4   Giulio Paolini, *Mimesi*, 1975–6. Photograph by Robert Keziere, 2004.

sculpture similarly appeals to the enfolded look I just mentioned. Standing for classical beauty – celebrated as the ultimate confusion between art and sex, between aesthetic and erotic attraction – the Medici Venus, flagrantly copied here as one of innumerable copies, is photographic not only in its resemblance to the alleged original, but also in its doubling, in its multiplication *in situ*, which entices us to look at this sculpture differently. The two figures do not offer their bodies, nor do they confront our gaze. Instead, narcissistically gazing into the mirror, they flaunt their indifference, denying us both close-ups of their faces and their supposedly attractive bodies. Suddenly, the fake modesty of the pudica gesture comes back to life as "real": their modestly covered genitals are now "really" out of visible reach.

How, then, is *Mimesi* cinematic? Decomposed, doubled, and recomposed as one image of two equidistant instants, this sculpture brings the Venus to a life – of movement and becoming – it never had. But, in the sequence of the film, as an alternative to Him, the snow-white, larger-than-life-size double form confronts us with the issue of beauty in history, the perverted aesthetic of ethical indifference. This is the exhibit's antagonist, evoked, by contrast, every time the tight bond between aesthetics and politics is foregrounded.

(4) Framing. The frame determines the whole of what can be seen at any given moment. By delimiting what is present, the frame also stipulates what is absent. With montage, framing is a fundamental element in cinema, an element it shares with its predecessor and partner, photography. The frame can be either saturated – as it is in the long shots pulled up close in *Partners (The Teddy Bear Project)* – or rarefied, as in the framing rooms of *Him* and *Mimesi*. With the former, we saw how the depth of the frame reintroduced the saturated background of the photo-installation, enabling it to reclaim its status as principal scene. In the case of *Mimesi*, precisely because of its isolated, venerated position both in the history of art and in this gallery, where it stands alone, the self-duplicating simulacrum of art flaunts its own framed position. The compelling desire to see makes us walk around the sculpture, surrounding it, as in an inversion of the panoptical gaze of surveillance. Thus, we enact cinema, we play the starring role, caught up in a scopophilic system of double exposure.

(5) Continuous color-montage. The example, here, is Hanne Darboven's installation *Ansichten >82<* from 1982, installed in the large central gallery of the exhibition. While the harsh white still saturates our retinas, the romantic soft focus, the starry-eyed black-and-white sailor, the orange ship, and the rhythmic repetition of Hanne Darboven's installation quite suddenly reverse our physical position. After walking around the sculpture, we are now inside it. Indeed, Derboven's *Ansichten >82<* presents itself like the inside of a gigantic sculpture. Unlike *Partners (The Teddy Bear Project)*, this work, in its imposing hall – with, again, equidistant tableaux – is at first so cold that the ship's orange color beckons with its warmth. Temperature alone suffices to establish a connection between Darboven's ballad of suicide and murder and two tableaux by Jeff Wall, also using orange (*Wall* (1991) and *Mimic* (1982)). By extension, the themes of suicide and murder, toned down in these works as they are set in the mood of comedy, remain present as threats, and taint the falling woman in *The Stumbling Block* and the bullying street guy in *Mimic* with

the same duality of potential violence. Our "film" takes on a decidedly postmodern incongruity here. It is for all these reasons that I contend that this exhibition exemplifies an aspect of exhibition practice that may well be inherent to it: its fundamentally pre-posterous temporality. In *Partners*, this aspect is more strongly present because it is overdetermined by the reversal of roles between cinema and photography.

But the continuity remains cinematic. Enough, at any rate, to allow, in the next room on the right, readings of Walker Evans's self-portrait as potentially murderous, and of his confined subway-riders displayed on the opposite wall as locked up in the tragedy of history. And so we arrive at the back gallery, where suicide and murder are literally, photographically, represented before our eyes, as action-images, in the two facing series of journalistic photography. Malcolm Browne, *The Sacrificial Protest of Thich Quang Duc, June 11, 1963*, and Eddie Adams's *Murder of a Vietcong Suspect, February 1, 1968* are the twin emblems of that other war. With new wars raging today, cinema and other visual arrangements have a renewed responsibility.

The Affect-Image of World Memory

This exhibition then translates emotions into instances of world memory. This term entails more than the sheer provenance of the collection from all over the world. I mean acts of memory that do not encompass the whole world, which would be both impossible and pointless, but that go out into the world, address it, and link up with it on its own terms (Bal, Crewe, & Spitzer 1999). Before I elaborate further, I need to explain why another concept, affect, is so central, both to the very possibility of world memory and to the deployment of the cinematic in exhibition practices. To understand affect without resorting to psychology, our best resource is Deleuze (1983). He puts Bergson's vision of perception – a selection of what, from the universe of visuality, is "usable" in our lives – to work in his own theory of cinema (Bergson 1997, p. 29. See also Bergson 1998).

Perception makes visible the usable "face" of things. This is why perception is bound up with framing: cinema as well as exhibitions makes selections for us, proposing a particular perception. Such a selective perception prepares the possibility for action. "Action-images," as Deleuze calls them, show us how to act upon what we perceive. Deleuze uses the verb "incurver": to "incurve" the visible universe is to measure a virtual relationship of action, between us and the things we see. Mutuality is key here: images can act on us as much as we can act on them. As I wrote earlier, between a perception that troubles us and an action we hesitate about, affect emerges. "Affect-images" present a temporarily congealed relationship between perception and the action that coincides with subjectivity. In other words, the viewer sees (what is within the frame), and hesitates about what to do; she is thus trapped in affect. Affect-images are important because, like the close-ups whose form they often take, they arrest linear time.

The specific receptivity that such images entail connects them to aesthetic effect. Hendeles's filmic exhibition is made mainly out of art, that is, objects becoming art in this exhibition. For instance, the teddy bears of *Partners (The Teddy Bear Project)*, as well as the snapshots there that were not originally intended as art, are treated and displayed like art, and hence, turned into artworks. "Art preserves," wrote Gilles Deleuze and Félix Guattari (1994), and these objects of preservation are like "blocs of sensations," that is to say, a compound of percepts and affects. These blocs exist independently of the subjects experiencing them. After closing hours, the gripping documentary photographs of suicide and murder, the romantic face of Derboven's sailor, and Wall's freeze-framed cinematic image of an act of bullying continue to exist. They exist in the dark as blocs of sensations, percepts, and affects, and, as syntax: a syntax that "ascends irresistibly into his [the writer's] work and passes into sensation." But, even if they endure, they do not, themselves, have a memory (Silverman 1996, pp. 163–4).

The relationship of complementary contrast between photography and memory is key to an understanding of the contribution to this cinematic exhibition of photographs as artworks and of objects that, in the wake of photography, take on its primary characteristics. Kaja Silverman formulated this relationship thus: "Whereas photography performs its memorial function by lifting an object out of time and immortalizing it forever in a particular form, memory is all about temporality and change" (1996, p. 157). The cinematic cut from *Partners (The Teddy Bear Project)* to *Him*, the zoom-in to a close-up, the flashback that ensues once the close-up has stalled linear time, and the resulting dissolve, all constitute a particular instance of a montage that stitches together photography and memory. As a result – and this is, here, what "art preserves" – the visitor is able to let the installation "introduce the 'not me' into [her] memory reserve" (Silverman 1996, p. 185).

Hence the world memory this exhibition produces through its many cinematic devices is not inherent in the art objects themselves. The syntax is there thanks to the installation, which juxtaposes works to form a sequence, readable by means of the rhetorical figures mentioned earlier, so as to create narratives. But the heteropathic memories that contribute to creating an affective discourse in the present tense are virtual, not actual, so long as visitors do not "perform" the film. Once they do, induced by this montage, world memory becomes activated and can become actual – in the present tense, which is not inherent in the image but is one of its potential modes. This process is what makes this exhibition, with all its historical objects, utterly contemporary.

Meditating on the contemporary is the contribution of the silent, meditative gallery that houses Kawara's date painting and box, and his press clipping with its appeal to a media consciousness. In her "Notes" in the catalogue, Hendeles rightly opposes the notion that the date paintings might be history paintings. The latter genre, like photography, seeks to commemorate historical events. Memory, instead, responds to the images of events that circulate, and thus constructs these as memorable events. Hendeles writes that, instead of commemorating events, Kawara attempts in his work to locate himself in history. In view of Deleuze's concept of the affect-image, one might say that he produces just that: a temporarily congealed hesitation in the face of the images that frame the event for him, hesitant about if and how to act, but already stretching out, as it were, beyond the selective perception alone. In this sense, Kawara's work as installed here is a particularly revealing instance of how photography can be, so to speak, curated beyond itself, to encompass heteropathic – or world – memory. Without being photography – it only includes a weak instance of it, in the faded and vulgar press clipping – Kawara's installation becomes a cinematic image that comments on photography.

Exhibiting Photography as Meta-Cinema

In view of my interpretation of exhibition as meta-cinema, it is necessary to speculate on why photography is so prominent in Hendeles's exhibition and in her collection. And why, specifically, is the combination of historical and contemporary photography so effective? At first sight, the common denominator of the works in this exhibition is that they are cinematic because they are also photographic. However, the relationship between photography and cinema is not only one of historical development but also "pre-posterous." With that term, already used but not fully explained, I wish to usher in my conclusion, which turns the relationship upside down and seeks to understand photography, in Hendeles's hands, as a critical commentary on cinema.

Pre-posteriority is the temporal reversal that inhabits all exhibitions: situated in the present, they rewrite the past, revising our relation to it but also its meanings as such (Bal 1999). It is as we stand in front of the two most clearly cinematic sets of photographs – the press photos of the suicide captured by Browne and the murder displayed for Adams's camera – that we almost fall back into the most standard Hollywood action movie. Almost, but not quite. For these two mutually rhyming sequences are reigned in from their potential Hollywood status by Lawrence Weiner's words. It is in this gallery that Weiner's word-picture *Vis inertiae (cat. #471)* from 1980, on the materiality of slowing down in temporal close-up, spells out how physical, transformative, and perhaps decisive the affect of affect-images is. The picture says:

> A change in inherent quality
> (vis inertiae)
>
> La réaction d'un objet au
> Contact suffisant à entraîner
> Un changement de qualité
> Inhérente (vis inertiae)

The two series of photojournalism, Browne's and Adams's – recalling, through their generic background, America's nationalistic hubris in Vietnam, the presence of words in newspapers, and the way they connect individuals to the world – inaugurate a reading of this exhibition that, pre-posterously, turns it into commentary on cinema from the vantage point of photography.

Let me explain this. Press photographs, like action movies, come and go. They pass quickly, and their visual overload hampers rather than promotes our connection with the world. These two series, like the novel *Uncle Tom's Cabin* in its time, seem to turn these action-images into affect-images. Integrating them with other images of violence, in this space, here, now, not only recalls the events, the changes in the course of the Vietnam War resulting from them, but, beyond that specific historical world-memory, puts also into an affect-image the very power of images: that is, if we allow them – harbored in an exhibition that does not lock out the world, in a space that is world history – to exercise that power to make us hesitate just long enough to be transformed by them.

Our present has embarked upon, and is entangled in, a new episode of that perpetual war of which the Vietnam War was an earlier episode. No nation seems to be able to disentangle itself from this long war. In this present, an exhibition that thinks through cinema with the help of a photography that is able to critique its successor from "before" can be seen as deeply political, precisely because it is so profoundly and transformatively aesthetic. I find this aesthetic to be a major contribution to a cultural philosophic that attempts to heal the severance between art and the melancholic powerlessness before, or the insidious complicity with, the politics that threatens both art and all our lives. This politics is powerful and complex – too complex, multiple, and subtle to discuss at length in this context. If, for example, I have refrained from even mentioning the gender politics that clearly run through this show, from the Wild Bunch photo of bandits in the first room to Saloon, and back to that group portrait of bandits looking like nice guys, it was so that I could invite my readers – now, at the end – to return to the beginning and start all over again. But that will have to be another essay.

Meanwhile, this volume offers fresh thoughts about how endeavors such as Hendeles's Partnership with history can help museums experiment and find new ways to engage viewers. Exhibition-makers can, thanks to the paradigm of *Partners*, deploy modes of exhibiting in which the political and aesthetic are inextricably, and effectively, linked. As the primary task of exhibitions, I contend, they ought to encourage visitors to stop, suspend action, let affect invade us, and then, quietly, in temporary respite, think.

Notes

1 Susan Buck-Morss (1994) points to the fear of early cinema spectators when confronted with close-ups. Sometimes they clamored to see evidence that the figure whose head was the only visible part of the body had not been beheaded.

2 I am referring to the exhibition *Mirroring Evil* held at the New York Jewish Museum, curated by Norman Kleeblatt. It is no coincidence that Cattelan's sculpture diminishes the figure of Hitler to the size of a preadolescent boy,

thus bringing it close to the toys that were so prominent in Kleeblatt's exhibition. See Van Alphen (2002) for a critical study of the use of toys in relation to historical trauma.

3   Strikingly, Angès Varda's 2004 film on *Partners (The Teddy Bear Project)* interprets the installation cinematically in precisely this way. In her film, the face of Hitler is superimposed retrospectively on the photographs, coloring them a sickly green.

References

Alphen, E. van (2002) Playing the holocaust. In N. Kleeblatt (ed.), *Mirroring Evil: Nazi Imagery / Recent Art*. New York: Jewish Museum, pp. 66–83.

Alphen, E. van (2003) Die Ausstellung als narratives Kunstwerk / Exhibition as a narrative work of art. In Y. Hendeles, C. Dercon, and T. Weski (eds.), *Partners*. Munich: Haus der Kunst, and Cologne: Verlag der Buchhandlung Walther König, pp. 143–85.

Baer, U. (2002) *Spectral Evidence: The Photography of Trauma*. Cambridge, Mass.: MIT Press.

Bal, M. (1996) *Double Exposures: The Subject of Cultural Analysis*. New York: Routledge.

Bal, M. (1997) *Narratology: Introduction to the Theory of Narrative*. Toronto: University of Toronto Press.

Bal, M. (1999) *Quoting Caravaggio: Contemporary Art, Preposterous History*. Chicago: University of Chicago Press.

Bal, M. (2002) *Travelling Concepts in the Humanities*. Toronto: University of Toronto Press.

Bal, M., Crewe, J., and Spitzer, L. (eds.) (1999) *Acts of Memory: Cultural Recall in the Present*. Hanover: University Press of New England.

Bergson, H. (1997 [1896]) *Matière et mémoire*. Paris: Presses Universitaires de France.

Bergson, H. (1998 [1907]) *L'Evolution créatrice*. Paris: Presses Universitaires de France.

Brooks, P. (1984) *Reading for the Plot: Design and Intention in Narrative*. New York: Alfred A. Knopf.

Buck-Morss, S. (1994) The cinema screen as prosthesis of perception: A historical account. In C. Nadia Seremetakis (ed.), *The Senses Still: Perception and Memory as Material Culture in Modernity*. Chicago: University of Chicago Press, pp. 45–62.

Deleuze, G. (1983) *Cinéma I: L'Image-mouvement* [Cinema I: the movement-image]. Paris: Editions de Minuit.

Deleuze, G. (1993) *The Fold: Leibniz and the Baroque*. Trans. T. Conley. Minneapolis: University of Minnesota Press.

Deleuze, G. and Guattari, F. (1994) *What is Philosophy?* Trans. H. Tomlinson and G. Burchill. London: Verso.

Doane, M. A. (2002) *The Emergence of Cinematic Time: Modernity, Contingency, the Archive.* Cambridge, Mass.: Harvard University Press.

Genette, G. (1972) *Figures III: Discours du récit* [Narrative discourse: an essay in method]. Paris: Editions du Seuil.

Hendeles, Y. (2003) Anmerkungen zur Ausstellung / Notes on the exhibition. In Y. Hendeles, C. Dercon, and T. Weski (eds.), *Partners.* Munich: Haus der Kunst, and Cologne: Verlag der Buchhandlung Walther König, pp. 187–229.

Iversen, G. (2003) Dissolving views: style, memory and space. Paper delivered at the Modes of Seeing conference, University of Trondheim, 6–8 November.

Lehmann, H.-T. (1997) From logos to landscape: Text in contemporary dramaturgy. *Performance Research,* 2 (1): 55–60.

Marrati, P. (2003) *Gilles Deleuze: Cinéma et Philosophie.* Paris: Presses Universitaires de France.

Pavis, P. (1998) *Dictionary of the Theatre: Terms, Concepts and Analysis.* Toronto: University of Toronto Press.

Silverman, K. (1996) *The Threshold of the Visible World.* New York: Routledge.

Varda, A. (2004) *Ydessa, les Ours, et etc.* French documentary, 45 mins., by Photovardaciné, co-produced by the Musée de Paume, Paris.

4

Experimenting with Representation: *Iconoclash* and *Making Things Public*

Peter Weibel and Bruno Latour

A museum exhibition is deeply unrealistic: it is a highly artificial assemblage of objects, installations, people and arguments, which could not reasonably be gathered anywhere else. In an exhibition the usual constraints of time, space, and realism are suspended. This means that it is an ideal medium for experimentation; and especially for addressing the current crises of representation, as we discuss below.

A key feature of an experiment is that it can fail. Indeed, we argue that exhibition experiments should ideally be set up according to very precise principles in order to explore contradictory outcomes. Too often, exhibitions are not used in this way but act merely as a site for manifesting the autonomy of preformed curatorial tastes. As we show through examples below, however, exhibitions can be used to think how an assembly of totally improbable elements can be gathered to raise a question that can be proven wrong or right. The success of such exhibition experiments depends on careful planning and debriefing.

Such exhibition experiments cannot, of course, be accomplished without long preparation and an intense collaboration between the curators and the "experimentalists" (a term we prefer to "artists"). The main point is that neither artists, nor academics, nor curators are putting their sacrosanct autonomy first. Rather, in the experimental exhibition process, everyone submits to the risks and interests of *heteronomy.*

Exhibition Experiments at ZKM

In this chapter we discuss two examples of experimental exhibitions that we have curated at the Zentrum für Kunst und Medientechnologie (ZKM), the Center for Art and Media, in Karlsruhe, Germany. The first, *Iconoclash*, was staged between May and September 2002, the second, *Making Things Public*, between March and October 2005.

ZKM opened in 1997 with the objective of integrating the arts and new media. The Center continually analyzes the theory and practice of new media in order to be able to react to the fast developments of information technology and its social influences. ZKM considers itself a forum for bringing together the sciences, the arts, and politics. As a platform for experimentation and discussion, its goal is to be actively involved in working for the future, since the question of how to use technologies in a meaningful way is constantly redefined and asked anew.

ZKM comprises various museums and institutes, including the Media Museum, the Museum for Contemporary Art, the Media Library, the Media Theatre, the Institute for Visual Media, the Institute for Music and Acoustics, the Institute for Basic Research, and the Institute for Media and Economics. Together, these enable the Center to develop interdisciplinary projects and international collaborations. This model differs considerably from traditional museums, since it creates room for research and experimentation, and is concerned equally with classical art and new media. Unlike other museums that focus on collection and presentation, ZKM accommodates all the essential stages of new media art production: research, production, presentation, and collection, as well as publication and archiving.

Iconoclash[1]

Iconoclash explored the question: Is there a way to suspend the iconoclastic gesture in order to interrogate it instead of extending it further? In other words, could iconoclasm (so important in the histories of religion, art, politics, science, and literature) be turned from an unquestioned resource into an interesting and problematic topic? Once this abstract question is raised, the only way to experiment with it is by conducting a real experiment with real images brought into the imaginary and unrealistic space of a museum, in this case the marvellous set-up of ZKM. But the conditions of the experiment also dictate what should be gathered for the experiment in order to be able to falsify or confirm the hypothesis. If we had assembled only contemporary art objects and installations, we would have obtained only one set of attitudes and reactions. The same would have been true if we had shifted our interest to art history or religious studies only. So, instead, we brought these together (figure 4.1).

Figure 4.1   View of the exhibition *Iconoclash: Beyond the Image Wars in Science, Religion, and Art*, ZKM, 2002. In the foreground is Elaine Sturtevant's "Duchamp Bicycle Wheel" (1969–73); in the middle replicas of Marcel Duchamp's "La boîte-en-valise" (1966, original 1936/1941) and "Bottle Rack" (1964, original 1914); in the background, from left to right, Kasimir Malevich's "Black Circle" (c. 1923), Alan McCollum's "30 Plaster Surrogates" (1982–90) and Kasimir Malevich's "Black Square" (c. 1923). Photography: ONUK, Bernhard Schmitt, Karlsruhe.

The exhibition aimed to display, in a systematic confrontation, three great clashes about representation – about its necessity, sanctity, and power – in the domains of science, art, and religion. Image wars are everywhere, from the Taliban destruction of the Bamiyan Buddhas, to the controversy over the Danish cartoons of Mohammed, to doubts about scientific imagery. By linking the three domains of theology, art, and science all at once, the aim was not to increase the critical mood or to reinforce disbelief and irony. On the contrary, it was to transform iconoclasm from being an indisputable resource into a topic to be systematically interrogated.

Instead of mocking once more those who produce images or simply being furious with those who destroy them, the show aimed at placing the viewer in a quandary: "We cannot do without representation. If only we could do without representation." Monotheist religions, scientific theories, contemporary arts, not to forget political theories, have all struggled with this contradictory urge of producing and also destroying representations, images and emblems of all sorts. Through many works of ancient, modern, and contemporary arts, and through many scientific instruments, the show explored that quandary – a quandary which has been so important for the self-understanding of the Western world. It aimed at moving beyond the image wars by showing that behind this dramatic history of the destruction of images, something else has always been going on: a cascade of image production, which was made visible throughout the exhibition, in traditional Christian images as well as in scientific laboratories and in various experiments of contemporary art, music, cinema, and architecture. While the great struggles of iconoclasts against icon-worshippers were going on, another history of iconophilia has always been at work. This alternative history of the Western obsession with image worship and destruction allows the establishment of less biased comparisons with other cultures influential in the rest of the world, where images may play a very different role.

Neither an art show, nor a science and art show, nor a history of art show, *Iconoclash* offered a bewildering display of experiments on how to suspend the iconoclastic gesture and how to renew the movement of images against any freeze-framing. With numerous documents, scientific objects, religious idols and artworks, the exhibition made clear that the word "image" includes all sorts of representations and mediations. The show became experimental only when it was decided to gather entirely different repertoires of images that had never been juxtaposed before: in contemporary arts, reformation, and science. It became even more so once it was resolved to let visitors decide whether they were being faced with copies or originals from these various sources. And it became more experimental still when it was decided to involve not one or two curators, as is usual in exhibition-making, but seven, who would meet regularly for three years, visit other exhibits together, and work collectively not to come to an agreement but to settle on the best ways to produce what could be called interference patterns between all those segments of iconoclastic histories.

It is not for us to decide whether the experiment failed or succeeded as a show, but it is clear that it was neither a traditional show nor simply a *mêlée* of disjointed elements. We had proven that iconoclasm, which until then was considered the unquestionable basis for any advanced critique, itself deserved to be suspended, examined, and transformed into a topic (cf. Besancon 2001).

Making Things Public [2]

Making Things Public aimed at pushing exhibition experimentation even further, this time by creating a really impossible space by making an installation of installations created entirely for the purpose of the experiment. The topic was apt: a parliament of parliaments, an assembly of assemblies, an exploration into the techniques of representation. The idea once again was to explore crises of representation, this time not by probing the reasons for the iconoclastic urge, but by taking stock of the very results of the *Iconoclash* experiment. If, as the subtitle of that show indicated, we could move "beyond the image wars in science, religion and art," then an obvious consequence was to explore the implications of this for politics.

Without a doubt, this was an unusual exhibition. It aspired to nothing less than a renewal of what constitutes an art show as well as of ways of thinking about politics and methods of establishing new forms of collaboration between artists and academics. The reason for such an undertaking was that we live in rather discouraging times as far as political life is concerned. Just the right moment, then, to make a fresh start by bringing together three modes of representation more usually kept apart: How to represent people? Politics. How to represent objects? Science. How to represent their collective gathering? Art.

The main idea behind this show was that politics is all about *things*. It's not a sphere, a profession, or a mere occupation; it essentially involves a concern for affairs that are brought to the attention of a *public*. The public is not cast in stone for all time. We're not talking here about the people as represented by their elected officials. The public has to be created for each new issue, for each new matter of concern. So the question we explored was: "What would happen if politics were made to revolve around disputed states of affairs?" This is why the show began with a section entitled NO POLITICS PLEASE, which introduced visitors to other types of assemblies in several different cultures. Politics is not universal and nor is democracy, but collecting people and things undoubtedly is. This issue of collection was crucial to the next sections, THE PUZZLE OF COMPOSITE BODIES and GOOD AND BAD GOVERNMENT. At the end of the first part the question has become: WHICH COSMOS FOR WHICH COSMOPOLITICS?

It turns out that the oldest meaning of the English and German word for "thing" concerns an assembly brought together to discuss disputed matters of concern. Hence the choice of the slogan "From Realpolitik to *Dingpolitik*," a neologism invented for the show. This major shift was reflected in the aesthetic of the show, in the ways in which its one hundred-plus installations and works of art were presented, and in the general physical and virtual architecture. What we attempted to do was to compare modernist with non-modern attitudes to objects: a move FROM OBJECTS TO THINGS.

The next section, the ASSEMBLY OF ASSEMBLIES, showed the visitor that there are many other types of gatherings which are not political in the custom-ary sense, but which bring a public together around things: scientific laboratories, technical projects, supermarkets, financial arenas – THE MAR-KET PLACE IS A PARLIAMENT, TOO – churches, as well as around the disputed issues of natural resources like rivers, landscapes, animals, temperature, and air – THE PARLIAMENTS OF NATURE. All these phenomena have devised a bewildering set of techniques of representation that have created the real political landscape in which we live, breathe, and argue. Hence, the question that can be raised in respect of all of them is: They may be assemblages, but can they be turned into real *assemblies*?

The next sections making up the third part of the show conveyed that PARLIAMENTS, TOO, ARE COMPLEX TECHNOLOGIES. Instead of saying that voting, talking, arguing, and deciding are quaint pieces of machinery, the visitor is prompted to consider them with great respect because of their delicate set of fragile mediations. Instead of looking for democracy only in the official "sphere" of professional politics, this section drew attention to the new technical conditions enabling things to be *made* public. NO MEDIATION, NO REPRESENTATION.

The next logical step was to imagine what representative assemblies could become if only they could benefit from all the techniques of mediation considered earlier. Hence, the fourth and last part of the show is concerned with imagining the future of politics by developing A NEW ELOQUENCE and NEW POLITICAL PASSIONS.

The exhibition made clear that the repertoire of attitudes and passions usually associated with taking a political stand is much too narrow. There are many other ways of reacting politically in non-Western traditions, in the old political philosophies, in most contemporary science and technology, in the new web-based spaces, and in the instruments of representation, of which parliaments are only a part. So why not try an "OBJECT-ORIENTED democracy" and "get back to things"?

Making the public

During a visit, without fully realizing it, you as a visitor will have become at once an actor in, and the screen of, an invisible work of art that has tried to put flesh on the bones of the new body politic. Collectively exploring the unintended and unexpected consequences of our actions was the only way, in the words of the great American philosopher, John Dewey, "for the Public to come into being" (1927). This is precisely what we tried to do with the visitors to this show: to reassemble them and make them part of a totally new *Thing*, a new assembly.

We know from Walter Lippmann's concept of "the phantom public" (1925) that the public sphere and the general public are not a biological body that remains the same forever, but something that is threatened with extinction if we do not constantly reactivate it. The issue of what constitutes public interest and the general public, or specific things and public opinion, is very broad. We could even paraphrase the title of Dewey's *The Public and its Problems* (1927) and say: the problem of the public is the public itself, because the latter is something that is made, made of countless other issues that are initially made public. For this reason, everyone – the mass media, the cultural institutions, politics – is busy hunting for the phantom that is the public. The question: "How are things made public?" is therefore a multiple question: How are things made? How is the public sphere made? How is the public made? How are things made public?

Once upon a time, the belief prevailed that reason ruled the public domain – a Kantian ideal for the public sphere. On the free market, the new public space of the eighteenth century, the free exchange of opinions ensued, an intellectual marketplace. This free market for opinions was the expression of a liberal democracy and was used by the citizens as a weapon against the monopoly on opinion formation held by the aristocracy and the church. Sovereign citizens commit to rational consensual debates on matters of public concern in public spaces. In principle, the state was accountable to the citizens in public space. In the twentieth century, with public and private interests permeated by both the mass media and the government, this public sphere ceased to exist. As of 1920 the state bureaucracy and the market start to use the media to steer opinion. The public is transformed from a "reasoning cultural public into a culture-consuming public," as Habermas (1962) puts it, from active sovereign into passive consumer. Lippmann (1925), however, showed that the "omnicompetent, sovereign citizen," on whom the ideal of representative democracy is based, no longer existed. No citizen had access any longer to all the information and arguments necessary to make an informed judgment such as keeps the mechanisms of representative democracy in motion and justifies their existence. This raises the question of whether the notion of representative democracy had become illusory.

In the 1993 anthology edited by Bruce Robbins, entitled *The Phantom Public Sphere*, the authors argue that the ideal of the omniscient citizen was only drawn up in order to be able to denounce it as a phantom and phantasm, and thus relativize the very ideal of democracy. For this reason, they distance themselves from proposing general solutions to social problems and prefer instead to offer solutions to actual problems on the basis of human rights. The fleeting nature of the public and of public space – its phantom quality meaning that the public cannot be pinned down as a thing – is actually what constitutes its democratic character. Hence, the idea that the public is a phantom, a powerful intellectual concept which shifts the definition of politics from a *substance*, which is always there no matter what we do, to a *movement* that can be interrupted at any moment if we fail to carry it further. The changing "Public Phantom" or "Phantom Public" is thus an expression of democracy. In democracy all power emanates from the people, but they cannot be pinned down as an entity and identified, although they are likewise not an amorphous mass. Thus, the power actually belongs to no one but has to be reconstituted and legitimized each time anew. You cannot speak of democracy without speaking of the public sphere and the general public. Nevertheless, this public sphere is not lost, as some sociologists bemoan; its absence is only a matter of a change in representation. If the bourgeois public sphere has perhaps been lost, then this does not also mean that the public sphere as a whole has been lost; it only means that we can no longer find it where we are accustomed to seeing it and must therefore hunt for it in another shape and another place, or even perhaps on the move as Derrida (1991) has suggested. Moreover, even if the public sphere is no longer a universal entity valid for all members of society, it may exist in many sub-spheres (such as "the proletarian public sphere" outlined by Negt and Kluge (1972)). The task of democracy today, then, is no longer to speak of minorities and majorities, of dominant opinion and deviant, but to respect the multiplicity of opinions in multiple public spheres (Warner 2002).

Since it is in the mass media, in particular television, that an extremely anti-democratic impulse prevails (Bourdieu 1996), new forms of and forums for the public sphere, ranging from interactive media art to the virtual laboratory, are the places that now occupy the role once reserved for coffeehouses, clubs, debating societies, and leagues in the early days of the public sphere. This makes them immensely important for the new democracy. If constitutional democracy seems about to collapse along with the welfare state and what Alfred Müller-Armack branded the "social market economy," then confidence in democracy will disappear along with it. This makes it all the more important to restimulate the idea of the democratic.

The Phantom

To try to explore such ideas, we invited digital artists Michel Jaffrennou and Thierry Coduys to design an exhibit. Their brief was to convey to visitors the idea of a mobile, changing public sphere in which individuals both are caught up in the consequences of others' actions and may themselves trigger (often unintended) effects. The result was "a quasi-invisible work of art" (Jaffrenou & Coduys 2005, p. 218) called the *Phantom Public.* Rather than being an exhibit located in a specific area of the exhibition, the *Phantom Public* involved a set of audio-visual effects distributed throughout *Making Things Public* (figure 4.2). Thus, the workings of the *Phantom Public* were evidenced by alterations in lighting and sound effects, and by particular exhibits in different areas of the exhibition being switched on or off (sometimes in patterned sequences).

Each visitor to the exhibition was given an individual Radio Frequency Identification on their ticket. This made it possible to track visitor

Figure 4.2 View of the exhibition *Making Things Public: Atmospheres of Democracy,* ZKM, 2005. Featuring Michel Jaffrennou and Thierry Coduys's *The Phantom Public* installation: interactive, virtual, variable scenography, based on the behavior of the visitors of the exhibition. Photography by Franz Wamhof.

movements and build information – such as visitor numbers and distribution – into the complex software governing the behaviour of the *Phantom Public.* The *Phantom Public's* behavior was also shaped by a number of other factors, such as "the climate in Karlsruhe, the time of the day and the 'mood' of the *Phantom Public*" (Jaffrenou & Coduys 2005, p. 220), as well as in some cases by visitors pressing particular buttons within the exhibition. The idea was to give visitors a vague and uneasy feeling that "something happens" for which they were at least sometimes responsible – sometimes in a direct way, but mostly in ways not directly traceable – just as politics passes through people as a rather mysterious flow. In this way, not only did visitors shape the exhibition that they visited – no two visitors or visits being at all likely to be the same – they were also the screen onto which the workings of the Phantom were projected. In other words, the artwork purposely eschewed a strategy such as showing the collective behavior of visitors on a monitor or screen, but left each visitor to experience individually the effects generated.

Whereas Hobbes's *Leviathan* represented on its frontispiece a body represented in turn by a multitude of bodies, the frontispiece of a contemporary book on democratic society would show Jaffrenou and Coduys's *Phantom Public*. For here the public is not represented but is itself part of the system that it observes. The whole exhibition is an interactive participatory artwork that is what it shows: an assembly of assemblies, a parliament of parliaments, a new type of political gathering. The entire exhibition responds to the visitors' behavior. The visitors act as representatives of the public sphere and they construct the public sphere.

Object-oriented democracy

The exhibition itself was a real commonwealth and the model for a commonwealth that arises from the relationship between "things." It showed that implicitly any exhibition is an assembly – an assembly with a political character. It also showed dramatically and transparently what essentially constitutes every public assembly that is "thing"-based: a complex set of technologies, interfaces, platforms, networks, media, and "things," which gave rise to a public sphere. Precisely in this way, the exhibition itself becomes the model of an "object-oriented democracy": a "gathering," a "thing" in itself. The visitors' behavior triggers influences, responses, and changes at every moment, repeatedly creating new public spheres.

To this extent, the exhibition and its design were not only the image of an "object-oriented" democracy and not only the model of *res publica* but themselves constituted a democratic "gathering." Precisely by virtue of being not some giant body consisting of many small bodies but a Phantom, composed of many things and a diversity of mobile and variable visitors who move through the space, the exhibition visualized the exact opposite of the historical, political body, the massive crowned giant Leviathan, hierarchically composed of many bodies. The democratic public sphere is not a "body" or an organism made up of bodies. Democracy is a phantom of bodies, a deceptive illusion of bodies, a dynamic network of moving and acting subjects. The art of democracy at the pinnacle of democracy is no longer an anatomical image of the body but the behavior of subjects as kindled by an emerging system. The focus of the show was thus not on representing the enchanting spirit of democracy through images or on captivating beholders but on *enacting democracy* (Weibel 1999). Democracy cannot be represented, it can only be "enacted." The same is true of democratic art, as the *Phantom Public* shows.

At the same time, the visitor no longer enjoys the privilege of being a special visitor. No visitor is a sovereign. Yet each visitor's behavior influences the surroundings and thus the perception of the other visitors. Here, visitors are indeed equals. In other words, this exhibition presents a counter-image of a "state without a state," precisely because this is one of the features of global society today: the fact that the state is no longer that artificial being invented in order to protect and defend natural persons, as Hobbes once thought, for the modern state itself may become the enemy of man (Neumann 1942). Today it seems that the state exposes people to the powers of the market, rather than protecting them from it.

To show the difference between the myth of the state and democracy, another metaphor helps: that of the blind leading the blind. Pieter Breughel's *Parable of the Blind Man* (1568) refers to the Bible: "Let them alone: they be blind leaders of the blind. And if the blind lead the blind, both shall fall into the ditch" (Matthew 15: 14). The painting shows a chain of blind men, each with his hand on the next man's shoulder, following a blind man leading them toward an abyss. The customary reading would have it that whosoever is not part of the Christian faith will be blinded to the truth and fall into the abyss. Yet it is not only an iconography of belief but a political iconography, in which we see how people are blinded by the absolute power of the state. The blind leading the blind: there is no better image for totalitarian systems, and yet the recognition that no superior power is able to see better and farther than the common folk is also what allows democracy to thrive. This painting poses the question of competence. For this reason, what is needed is a democratization of politics in the service of competence. We are all blind, legally incompetent persons, but we can help each other to become competent, to become seeing with the help of new tools and media. We wish to advance the very tools of democracy, to expand the laboratory of democracy to include artistic and scientific tools, techniques, devices, apparatuses, and methods, in other words to achieve a surplus of parliamentarianism, but less by representation and more by new technologies and interfaces to the parliamentary. So the crisis of political representation is a complementary phenomenon to the crisis of representation in art. The crisis of democracy today is a crisis of competence.

The Power of the Performative

Why should museums be used to stage such exhibition experiments? Is this not the role of social science and political philosophy? And if the question is to stage politics, how can a show be more than a mock-up of real political "demonstration" in the street? If it is not able to do politics for good, can a show of the sort we have outlined be anything but a boring demonstration of some *a priori* ideas? This is where the notion of experiment should be taken seriously. There is no other way to test an idea in advance of its realization than by means of a simulated space such as that we attempted to create in *Making Things Public*. But did our experiment succeed or fail? Was this assembly of assemblies a realistic anticipation of things to come – *the Parliament of Things* – or a mere mumbo-jumbo of accumulated junk? We did not gather visitor feedback ourselves, but what we did do was to stage a final experiment in which visitors could put our exhibition on test for themselves. The key question of the show was the ability of artists, politicians, philosophers, scientists, and the visitors themselves to shift from the aesthetics of objects to the aesthetics of things. Perhaps it will be initially puzzling to learn that the two final walls of the show were occupied by Otto Neurath Isotypes – an archetypically modernist combination of philosophy of science (logical positivism), and politics (the socialism of Red Vienna), and aesthetics (Bauhaus) brought together in the statistical data form of the Isotype (see also Henning, this volume). Well, here is a good case of how you can stage a *falsifiable* exhibition experiment. If the visitor who quits *Making Things Public* concludes that Neurath's modernist solution to the quandary of our age is much more efficient, rational, pleasing, and politically correct than what is presented in the show – in other words, that objectivity is much more forward-looking than "thingness" – then our show has failed. If, on the other hand, the visitor looks at the final Isotype section with a bit of nostalgia for the modernist style but grasps that the quandaries of our age can no longer be tackled by such a philosophy, politics, and design, then our experiment has succeeded. If so, visitors have hopefully been stimulated to inquire into how to assemble, through whatever means, the parliament of parliaments, the assembly of assemblies, that we have anticipated in this exhibition experiment.

The aesthetic object of Modernity was a closed object. Modernity itself was the response of art to the machine-based Industrial Revolution. The Postmodern is art's response to the post-industrial computer-assisted information revolution. In the information society, not only does the aesthetic object become Eco's "open artwork" (1962) but the work as such disappears and is replaced by instructions for enactment, for communicative action, and for options for action. Open fields of enactment mean new alliances arise between author, work, and observer, in which new actants such as machines, programs, multiple users, and visitors operate on the same level.

Contemporary avant-garde artists respond sensitively to social changes by changing the structure of their approach to their work and entering into new alliances with new forms of enactments. Forms of enactment for sculpture, images, texts, and music define their practices, and we can therefore speak of a "performative turn." The technical arts, the computing arts, play the pivotal role here. In the interactive artwork, the viewer becomes another actant in the field of enactment, and has the same rights as all others. The artwork is no longer the dream of autonomy, of the absolute, and of sovereignty, but a practice of service.

The aesthetic object thus collapses, and its place is taken by the field of enactment, which, of course, does not consist solely of linguistic instructions or performative acts, for the things themselves are also actors *for action.* The object options and object fields serve as the medium for actions. Art as a social construct helps to construct the social. The aesthetic product is replaced by an artistic practice that can be object-based or object-free but nevertheless expands the scope for enactment. Therefore this complete, interactive, physically visitor-dependent exhibition mirrors our concept of an "object-oriented democracy." It is an exhibition experiment that is what it shows: performative democracy, for the first time in history.

Notes

1 http://www.iconoclash.de/ (accessed August 2006).
2 http://makingthingspublic.zkm.de/ (accessed August 2006).

References

Besancon, A. (2001) *The Forbidden Image: An Intellectual History of Iconoclasm.* Chicago: University of Chicago Press.

Bourdieu, P. (1996) *Sur la télévision.* Raisons d'Agir. Paris: Liber.

Derrida, J. (1991) *La Démocratie ajournée.* Paris: Minuit.

Dewey, J. (1927) *The Public and its Problems.* Chicago: Swallow Press.

Eco, U. (1962) *Opera Aperta.* Milan: Bompiani.

Habermas, J. (1962) *The Structural Transformation of the Public Sphere.* Trans. T. Burger with F. Lawrence. Cambridge: Polity Press.

Jaffrennou, M. and Coduys, T. (2005) Mission impossible: giving flesh to the phantom public. In B. Latour and P. Weibel (eds.), *Making Things Public: Atmospheres of Democracy.* Karlsruhe: Zentrum für Kunst und Medientechnologie, and Cambridge, Mass.: MIT Press, pp. 218–23.

Lippmann, W. (1925) *The Phantom Public.* New York: Harcourt Brace & Co.

Negt, O. and Kluge, A. (1972) *Öffentlichkeit und Erfahrung. Zur Organisationsanalyse von bürgerlicher und proletarischer Öffentlichkeit.* Frankfurt: Suhrkamp.

Neumann, F. L. (1942) *Behemoth: The Structure and Practice of National Socialism.* New York: Oxford University Press.

Robbins, B. (ed.) (1993) *The Phantom Public Sphere.* Cultural Politics, 5. Minneapolis: University of Minnesota Press.

Warner, M. (2002) *Publics and Counterpublics.* Durham, N.C.: Duke University Press.

Weibel, P. (1999) *Offene Handlungsfelder.* Cologne: DuMont.

5

Walking on a Storyboard, Performing Shared Incompetence: Exhibiting "Science" in the Public Realm

Xperiment! – Bernd Kraeftner, Judith Kroell, and Isabel Warner

The exhibition hall of the national museum of a small country in Western Europe. A big piece of canvas covers the floor of the hall, which resembles the nave of a neo-Gothic church. The white canvas is stained with various colors dominated by green, red, orange, and yellow. Some people are strolling on the canvas. Their gaze is bent down. Looking from above we can recognize a pattern: records, jottings, scribbles, interview transcripts and excerpts, sketches, paintings, and people. They circle like satellites around one slowly moving person; thus the group drifts as a whole from one end of the canvas to the other. Low voices, words, fragments of sentences reach my ears.

Field note by member of Xperiment!, January 2002 (see figure 5.1)

We are Xperiment!, a small Vienna-based group of "researchers in the wild" (Callon, Lascoumes, & Barthe 2001) whose aim is to experiment with the communication of science in the public realm. In this chapter

Figure 5.1 Navigating on the map/storyboard, Swiss National Museum, Zurich, 2002
© Swiss National Museum, Zurich, COL-14866.

we describe an exhibition experiment called *Good Bye Tomato – Good Morning Rice*, which we staged in Vienna and Zurich in 2001–2. This exhibition was the unanticipated outcome of a project that had begun two years earlier, the objective of which was to explore solutions to the problem of how to present to the public a particular scientific research program concerned with the genetic modification of rice. In the course of the experiment we found ourselves conducting a form of ethnographic fieldwork, spending weeks "in conversation" with the public, discussing and exchanging stories about scientific innovation. It is important to say that, with diverse professional biographies and loose affiliations with academic and art institutions, we ourselves are scientific outsiders, and the exhibition caused us to reflect on our own position in relation to the issues and organizations with which we were engaging.[1]

By telling our stories – for whom or for what do we become spokespersons? Do we speak on behalf of the rice project or for those it is intended to benefit? Or for the methods and theories developed by science and technology studies? Do we speak on behalf of our own project, or of science in general? (Field note by member of Xperiment!, January 2002)

In our description of *Good Bye Tomato – Good Morning Rice*, we retain the spirit of the sometimes "fuzzy knowledge navigations" that took place in our encounters with scientific insiders and scientific outsiders – with experts and non-experts. We use this notion of "fuzzy knowledge navigations" as a kind of shorthand to refer to the ephemeral and volatile everyday conversations between speakers and listeners who belong to various worlds of relevance in a situation of shared activity. These navigations also include breakdowns where no mutual understanding is necessarily reached and where "misunderstanding" may even be deliberately produced. They include the spoken and the unspoken, the enacted and the not enacted, the listening and the unpredictable patterns of knowledge creation. For this reason we try to avoid reproducing an academic master narrative, preferring instead to continue our open-ended and pluralistic approach to narrating versions of this scientific innovation in a manner characteristic of our approach to the exhibition experiment itself.

A Point of Departure: A "Realistic" Account of the Scientific Project

The experiment began with our search to find a suitable scientific research program that would enable us to engage fully in the debate between scientific insiders and outsiders. Our title, *Good Bye Tomato – Good Morning Rice*, reflects the process through which we came to settle on the so-called "Golden Rice" project. An earlier "project of desire" was concerned with genetically modified tomatoes, but this research project proved to be unsuccessful (see Harvey 1999; Martineau 2001), and since that particular debate had cooled down, we continued looking for alternatives.

When we finally came across the Golden Rice project, this is what we learnt. Rice is a staple food for over four billion people worldwide. Since it is such an essential foodstuff, its nutritional quality has great significance. In order to stop rice turning rancid when stored, an oil-rich layer is removed from the kernel. In this process β-carotene, a precursor of Vitamin A, and other important nutrients are also eliminated. During the 1980s research demonstrated that Vitamin A deficiency, a problem that is widespread among populations in developing countries, results not only in blindness, but also in high rates of child mortality. It is estimated that improved nutritional intake could prevent 1–2 million child deaths annually. Worldwide, various relief organizations are conducting supplementation, fortification, and education programs to fight the symptoms of Vitamin A deficiency disorders.

In 2000 two scientists, Ingo Potrykus, a plant specialist, and Peter Beyer, an expert in cell biology, made a breakthrough in rice technology that was published in the well-known journal *Science* (Ye, Al-Babili, Klöti, Zhang, Lucca, Beyer, and Potrykus 2000). This breakthrough was the culmination of an eight-year project funded by the Rockefeller Foundation, the Swiss Federal Institute of Technology, and the European Commission. The innovation entailed introducing the entire β-carotene "biosynthetic pathway" into the normally carotenoid-free rice endosperm.[2] In other words, by genetically modifying the rice, Potrykus and Beyer sought to retain the nutritional value of the rice normally lost during processing. Their goal was (and is) to develop a strain of rice that could combat Vitamin A deficiency syndromes in the developing world. By looking at the images in the article in *Science*, even with our inexpert eyes, we could see that the yellow color of the genetically modified rice kernels indicated the presence of the carotenoids. Indeed, this color gave the laboratory-produced rice strain the name Golden Rice.

One could say that on July 31, 2000 Golden Rice went public. On this date, it was the leading story in the American issue of *Time* magazine, the front cover of which showed Ingo Potrykus pictured between rice plants under the headline, "This rice could save a million kids a year" (Nash 2000). But how and at what cost, we might ask, will the rice reach these "kids"? Potrykus and Beyer own a patent for their invention, but in order to create the Golden Rice it was of course necessary for them to work with technologies and gene constructs already patented by other researchers and organizations. Indeed, to reach freedom to operate, the inventors had to negotiate with no fewer than 32 owners of 70 patents: a challenging prospect for such laboratory-based researchers. In order to achieve their goal, the two scientists struck a deal with a UK-based company,

Zeneca Agrochemicals, which holds an exclusive license to one of the genes used. In exchange for commercial marketing rights in the US and other affluent markets, Zeneca lent its financial resources and legal expertise to support the inventors' ambitions to provide the Golden Rice free of charge to poor farmers in developing countries. This part of the Golden Rice project became known as the "Humanitarian Project."[3]

At the time of writing, the outcome of the Golden Rice project remains uncertain. Whether it should be regarded as a success story or a failure is not easy to ascertain: since it is an ongoing project, you will get different responses depending on whom you ask. Either way, the project certainly introduced new dimensions (particularly ethical ones) to the heated debate concerning genetically modified organisms (GMOs). For us – the members of Xperiment! – the question was not so much whether or not the researchers or other stakeholders achieved their goal, but rather how to describe this scientific project in the public realm.

"Performing Shared Incompetence": A Transdisciplinary Intervention Strategy

The accumulation of scientific knowledge is inevitably linked with the growth of ignorance and uncertainty. But despite this uncertainty and the fact that ignorance has no limits, decisions that affect us all must nevertheless be made. Our strategy of "performing shared incompetence" (Xperiment! 2005) asks how these decisions come into being. An approach of this sort requires a public domain such as the museum mentioned in the opening quotation taken from our field notes. We designate this public territory "a research center of shared incompetence," a space with doors wide open to everybody. In this space emphasis is put not so much on academic ranks and disciplines but on matters of concern, observations, skills, abilities, curiosity, self-reflection and, last but not least, on uncertainty.

Our method differs from the approach commonly known as the "Public Understanding of Science," which attempts to decrease the knowledge discrepancies between experts and laypeople by explaining or providing so-called scientific information to the party on the other side of the knowledge gap. Performing shared incompetence follows a different direction by trying to avoid this asymmetrical approach. It entails a "trans-disciplinary" endeavor, during the course of which we leave our familiar areas of competence and enter into an unknown territory of incompetence where we will meet with others – coming from different practices – in order to elaborate common goals. As a result of our moving around in this foreign territory – in our case, the scientific-technological innovation called Golden Rice – many unforeseen and delicate situations and associations may occur.

Entering the Realm of Incompetence

The problems entering this difficult territory are exemplified in the following comments from an interviewee and in an excerpt from our field notes.

> "I am not asking you for the source of your project financing because I am questioning your independency as such. But in my opinion, you possibly did not take into account the highly polarized public debate on this subject matter that I basically refer to as 'green technology' – i.e. the application of gene technology to agriculture. And as a matter of fact, this example, the Golden Rice, serves as a showcase project for the companies using genetic engineering and, of course, for the researchers affiliated to these companies. Therefore from my very biased point of view, I consider it partisanship that you have chosen this project. I am not saying at all that you did this on purpose. On the contrary, it was maybe even unpleasant for you that this project is not neutral." (Interview with head of the Swiss campaign against gene engineering, Greenpeace Headquarters Switzerland, Zurich, January 2002)

> The telephone rings. A member of Xperiment! takes the phone. A female person says that she is writing an article on human nutrition and global food safety for a well-known weekly magazine published in Austria. And that she is doing research on rice because the majority of the human population on our planet lives to a great extent on this staple food. As it turns out she came across the Golden Rice project and called P. Beyer, one of the inventors, to ask him for more details. In return, P. Beyer told her to contact Xperiment! since the group is about to elaborate a "kind of exhibition," that will be shown in Vienna. She is not interested in our work at all but in our role as informants for her story on nutrition. (Field note by member of Xperiment!, December 2001)

Isn't the Swiss Greenpeace campaigner right? Haven't we been exploited by the industry and/or the researchers? Doesn't the fact that Beyer, a scientific insider and expert in cell biology and microbiology, forwards a journalist's request for more insider information to an outsider group like Xperiment! perfectly affirm the activist's suspicion? How should we handle the confidence that one of the inventors seems to put in us, which at the same time foments the distrust and suspicion of the activist?

On the other hand, might it not be conceivable that members of our group "transmit" to the journalist a distorted or technically inaccurate picture of the scientific methods and experiments applied to enrich the rice strain with β-carotene? Furthermore, isn't it possible that we could tell various stories or versions of the project that deliberately diverge from the public relations agenda of the scientists? But then, which version to choose? Even if we do want to speak on behalf of the scientists, the question immediately arises, which one? The microbiologists, plant scientists, breeders, nutritionists, and epidemiologists involved in the project all disagree in many respects.

What does it mean to stay independent? How to assess the "neutrality" or otherwise of a given scientific-technological innovation? We ask ourselves, should we act as spokespersons for Vitamin A or the pro-Vitamin A β-carotene? As spokespersons for Greenpeace? For the malnourished children, for subsistence farmers in developing countries, for multinational companies, or for agencies such as FAO (Food and Agriculture Organization) or WHO (World Health Organization)? Indeed, are we actually qualified to speak at all? We have to recognize our incompetence. At the time we have no answers. Have we been transformed, betrayed, manipulated?

How to "Describe" the Various Interlinked Versions of the Project?

What is meant by the word "describing"? Does it mean, first, to correctly interpret and understand the predetermined "good" or "bad" of a scientific project or technological innovation? And, second, to find aesthetically satisfying solutions to represent and depict the corresponding facts and values? Following Bruno Latour we came to the conclusion that describing a scientific project is not a question of using old or new media to depict scientific facts. For us, in fact, it is important to decide if a scientific project should be described, for instance, as "realistic" (i.e., to say "how it is" and to rely on the scientist's account). Or, alternatively, to give a fictional account by saying "how it could be." Furthermore, one could opt for a science-fictional account: "The project could be that way, taking into consideration the present scientific knowledge." Additionally, one could choose a journalistic account, popularizing its science or exposing its politics: "It is not as it seems to be." Last but not least, there remains the option of a sociological account: a method that sometimes puts the hard sciences in question by treating the soft ones as a dogma (Latour 1996).

Although our approach probably uses knowledge, instruments, and methods from all of these accounts, we tried to steer away from propaganda or denunciation, from trivialization or demonization of science. By avoiding the tendency to treat scientific facts as black boxes and ethical values as pre-given we tried to enter into a kind of "dramatic rehearsal" (Keulartz, Schermer, Korthals, & Swierstra 2004) of the various narrations of a scientific innovation *cum* and *coram publico*. But at that time, of course, we did not know how to tackle this endeavor.

Starting out Performing Shared Incompetence

Potrykus and Beyer are scientific insiders. We are scientific outsiders. By saying this we "enact" a demarcation (Mol 2002; Varela & Dupuy 1992). We enact it simply by defining two categories: people who work with plants, E. coli, mass spectrometers and such like, and people who do not. The fact that none of us in Xperiment! is a plant scientist or microbiologist makes it self-evident that we had to describe the Golden Rice project from an outsider's position.

According to our own definition of "performing shared incompetence," we then had to move around: we had to enter a new territory of incompetence. We had to go and meet the scientists and observe how they do research. And that is how we started *our* research. We entered the territory of plant science, microbiology and genetics armed with computers, database, telephone, video and sound equipment, and the determination not to get caught in a student–teacher relationship that would eventually convert us into "experts lite." Over the course of two years we tried to follow the protagonists in their efforts to make their scientific idea into a reality. We talked to them, read newspaper articles, surfed the web, interviewed opponents, collaborators, managers. We audio-visually taped our work. We started to make field notes, to shoot photographs, to paint, to draw, to connect, to trace actors that we encountered and subsequently considered important.

We had to be very careful in enacting two categories and thus creating a line of demarcation, which follows the well-established divide between "experts" and "non-experts," "scientists" and "laypeople," "Science" and "Public." This divide is dangerous because it tends to make us think that only one side has to move: in our case the non-experts, the laypeople, "the" public. The attempt to educate the public and to increase its scientific literacy is based on this divide and a so-called "deficit model" (non-experts being deficient in scientific knowledge). Therefore, if we were really interested in a "politics of what" (to do) instead of a "politics of who" (is entitled to speak) (Mol 2002), we were obliged to focus on "cooperation" rather than "division" to defrost the frozen relationships between experts and non-experts. We would have to make the experts move as well and create symmetric and equal starting positions to set off a process that creates – at least temporarily – a common reality between experts and non-experts.

A Progress Report, or How we Stumbled into an Exhibition Experiment

At the end of 2000 we were confronted with the request of our sponsor, Austria's Federal Ministry for Education, Science, and Culture, to deliver a progress report. We felt uncomfortable writing only a conventional text-based report since we wanted to experiment with new ways of communicating our experiences: how to handle the multiplicity, the ontic diversity of interdependent enacted project entities? By molding this into dichotomized categories of pro and con perspectives, by freezing it into a static text version of what we did and what the project was all about, without showing the dynamic and intricate practices of research and our own reasoning, we would mislead people into thinking that we know what the Golden Rice project *is.*

Another problem arose. Through our preoccupation with work conducted in the field of Science and Technology Studies, we were at risk of constructing a progress report that dealt with the "Public Understanding of Science and Technology Studies" instead of creating a space for experimentation with the accessibility of scientific technical innovations. Thus, we were in danger of establishing the very divide between experts and non-experts that we sought to avoid. We therefore wanted to produce a publicly accessible progress report. Our intention was to organize a small-scale presentation (for friends and their friends) in order to experiment with the description of the Golden Rice project in the public realm.

A Fictional Account

How did we realize our report? We could tell you now the following story. After listening to the major protagonists of the Golden Rice project and after one year of research in order to recontextualize the project, historically, scientifically, socio-economically, financially, and politically, we decided to draw a "map" of the project. This map would be made accessible to the so-called public. Before we ventured into what was for us an unknown territory of experimentation, we tried to strengthen our resolve with some theoretical considerations that were inspired by two contradictory expressions we came across. The first was: "The map is not the territory" (Korzybski 1941, p. 58), quoted in a book called *Maps are Territories* (Turnbull 1989, p. 3). This thin book offered us a rich "gallery" of historic and current examples of maps elaborated in the Western and non-Western traditions. We liked the book and in particular the chapter called "Maps and Theories," from which we learned that maps are selective, that they do not, and cannot, display all there is to know about any given place in the environment. And if they are to be maps at all they must directly represent at least some aspect of the landscape.

We could continue our fictional account by asserting that we went straightforwardly from reasoning and reading to deciding on how we could outline a plan to organize our materials (texts, audiovisual footage, drawings, and paintings) and, finally, proceeded to the map-making, a map that shows what this project *is*. Unfortunately, or luckily, at that time we had not even read the book from which we are quoting here. Nor were we able to "pin down" *the* project, since we were permanently confronted with numerous accounts and narrations about what the project actually was, and we thus seemed to be confronted with not one but many projects. So, which one to choose? Which one to represent? Which one to map?

How to Map a Scientific Controversy?

To facilitate our alternative progress report a large space in a car park garage was put at our disposal. Our basic idea was to paint the report on a piece of canvas measuring 250 m^2. So, off we started, using the term "map" for our endeavor (figure 5.2). As pointed out before, at that time, we did not know very much about maps. And soon the first difficulties arose: Should we depict the project via an iconic representation; that is, should we directly portray certain visual aspects of the human and non-human actors involved? Or should we opt for a symbolic represen-tation and utilize conventional signs, numbers, letters, and graphics? Then, how could we map an ongoing, vibrant Golden Rice project com-prised of many actors (per)forming more or less stable entities and alliances? And how could we avoid the map becoming a mere picture?

We soon recognized that, as a means of orientation in this ample landscape, we were urgently in need of a method. Hence, it was no surprise that an article entitled "A Note on Socio-Technical Graphs" (Latour, Mauguin, & Teil 1992) attracted our attention. There we read

Figure 5.2 Map/storyboard, Vienna 2001 © Xperiment!

the words: "to map the development of a scientific controversy or a technical innovation" (p. 33). The paper explains a procedure that helps to describe the dynamics of a scientific controversy and we utilized this outline as our point of departure for the construction of our own "progress report map."

Further, we borrowed some ideas from "actor-network theory," a method developed in the field of science and technology studies (Law & Hassard 1999). This method helped us decide how to select from the abundance of accumulated material and how to depict some aspects of the scientific technological innovation called Golden Rice. One of the main advantages of this approach is that it makes facts tangible and negotiable. Scientific researchers or experts usually present their results not as preliminary and experimental, as work in progress or as issues of controversy, but as finished products or facts untouchable to us laypeople or non-experts. The traditional way to refer to scientific facts is that they are pure, objective, and true, not in need of any legitimation within political discourse. Actor-network theory departs from this well-trodden path and makes it possible to reintroduce those facts into the public realm.

One aspect of this theory/method supported our aim in particular: its attempt to keep all players, both human and non-human, in the game and on the same level, with no pyramids of hierarchies, no fixed role attributions, no authorities *per se*. It encouraged us to identify and to present on the map all the actors and artifacts involved. You can find them all together on our map: depictions and descriptions of researchers, rice plants, risk factors, cells, health organizations, test kits, recommended daily allowances for β-carotene, supplementation programs, and so forth, including depictions of ourselves in the role of scientific outsiders. The actor-network theory enabled us to create a territory to show part of the trajectory of the project's evolution beyond so-called "old" debates that remain locked in a "for" and "against" pattern.

The Transformation of a Map into a Storyboard

At the end of the production process of our "socio-technical graph" or "progress report map," we were exhausted, happy and sobered all at the same time. It was evident that something was missing, and we realized that there were many more stories or versions of the Golden Rice project than we could ever show on our map. We were, after all, trying to use a static map to describe a dynamic project. And thus we felt that we had to create a space where the scientific endeavor could be experienced again as a dynamic process with all its facets and intricacies.

After pondering this for a while, we started to offer "guided tours" to our visitors and guests to tell them more about the Golden Rice project(s). By walking with our guests on this graphic territory we became more or less actors ourselves, and soon we began to accept our role as performers and storytellers. We were not so much interested in the question of whether our guests supported the "real" project or if they learned something about gene technology or not. We were interested in the question of whether or not we would be successful in entering into a commitment with our guests to create a mutual understanding of the world surrounding us. Step by step, the map became our "storyboard," a process that for us is precisely reflected in John Law's discussion of *performing* actor-network theory:

> we are in the business of creating links, of making them, of bringing them more or less successfully into being. Which means in turn that we are no longer trying to find good ways of narrating and describing something that was already there. Instead, or in addition, we are in the business of ontology. We are in the business of making our objects of study, of making realities that we describe. Of trying to find good ways of interacting with our objects, ways that are sustainable ways that make it possible to link with them. (Law 1997, p. 9)

Finally, we began to understand what was happening both to this piece of canvas and to us. We started out as observers plotting a diagram. Then we became cartographers who tried to craft a map. Instead, we created a storyboard and became storytellers. We became researchers who were explaining an experiment, but not the one conducted by the Golden Rice researchers, as may at first appear. No, we were now explaining our own experiment. We welcomed visitors on our storyboard, and using our index fingers we pointed toward various "inscriptions" on the storyboard (figure 5.3). We emphasized, explained and meticulously tried to preserve the chain of references. We talked about who we were, by whom we were funded, where we came from, why we were doing this, what travels we had undertaken, how we had gathered our material, which contingencies had guided us to find the project, why we made this selection, and what methods we applied. In addition we told our visitors and guests that we were telling stories that were told to us. Thus, we became spokespersons for our own inscription. We strove to create the conditions that would allow us, together with our guests, to perform shared incompetence.

Opportunistic Compromise or Cunning Reason?

Thus, the project *Good Bye Tomato – Good Morning Rice* was originally planned as a progress report for our funding institution and it was realized as a small-scale presentation. It was an independent production by the group Xperiment! made publicly accessible in a car park garage far away from any institutional constraints.

Alas, we could not convince our sponsors to accept the 250 m² map/storyboard as an official progress report and our failure to submit an acceptable report would endanger future financing. This threat and the fact that the extraordinary format could not be incorporated into the ministerial archives compelled us to write an additional, more conventional report. Even so, we succeeded in leaving behind the classical format

Figure 5.3   Index finger pointing at an inscription, Swiss National Museum, Zurich 2002 © Xperiment!

of an academic report and instead wrote a dramatized script that would serve us as a rehearsing tool for our guided tours. The sponsors finally accepted this "script" before we made our map accessible to the public in June 2001.

Actors and Interactions: Walking on a Storyboard

It was then that we were invited to the Swiss National Museum in Zurich to present our storyboard in the exhibition hall mentioned at the beginning of this essay. The museum is a venerable and slightly dated institution. Inside we find an extensive and eclectic collection, ranging from prehistory through ancient times, from the Middle Ages to the twentieth century. Nevertheless, the institution was eager to add "the displaying of science" to its portfolio and to test new exhibition concepts.

Our storyboard opened to the public in Zurich in January 2002 and, in the space of a few weeks, we had conversations with nearly every one of over a thousand guests who visited. Our guided tours lasted approximately one hour each and during these we discussed the project with all kinds of people, some who came seeking education, others who looked for entertainment and distraction. We encountered young people who enjoyed navigating on the map and looking at the comic strip; older people who wanted to learn the "true" and "final" argument that could guide them through the GMO debate. We met with students, teachers, professors, experts, non-experts, journalists, artists, science communicators, public relations persons, and social scientists from the local science and technology studies community. We also discussed our approach with curious curators from the museum and other members of the museum staff. Finally, we could introduce our perspective on the project to the major protagonists involved in the "real" project itself: the researchers, the business partners, technology-transfer specialists, activists from Greenpeace.

Visitors were not exactly sure how to categorize us. Time and again they tried to classify us: could it be that we were researchers from the hard or the soft sciences? Were we artists or green activists? Or were we in the very act of selling science in the name of gene-tech companies, the government or the nearby university? Every now and then the visitors paused for a moment during our conversations, navigations, and walking-tours and asked us probing questions: "Who are you?" "Where do you come from?"

"Who paid for the presentation?" "Why are you doing this?" "Who was responsible for the content creation?" and, of course, if we were "for" or "against" gene technology and the Golden Rice project. At this stage of the tours our narrations were put to the test.

It was of decisive importance that we were able to give comprehensible and credible answers. The fact that we as scientific outsiders undertook the task of describing the making of a scientific-technical innovation and the fact that we did not represent any of the aforementioned institutions was frequently judged to be unorthodox and idealistic. If indeed we were successful in offering a rationale for our endeavor, this created an atmosphere of relief and a readiness to enter into a mood of trust, enabling passionate, engaged, and sometimes humorous conversations.

When a Difference Makes a Difference

> It seems to me that the central activity of telling a story is not necessarily the mediation and communication of content or information. Maybe it is more about interaction and trust building. It is surprising to see that during our conversations the skeptical, reserved, and sometimes even hostile facial features of our guests start to relax and gain expressiveness. In my opinion this is due to the fact that we try to create some space for their thoughts, worries, and anecdotes, and not primarily because of the content of our story – yes, this is a hypothesis. (Field note by member of Xperiment!, January 2002)

All of our visitors were encouraged to express their impressions, opinions, emotions and criticisms in guest books that we had provided. Alongside our own observations and discussions they became an additional source for us to learn more about what we accomplished and ignited with our experiment. Without overemphasizing the significance of the entries, we find one observation especially interesting. In approximately 200 entries in our guest books we cannot find the word "information" even once, whereas we find the word "exciting" frequently.

No healthy person permanently and exclusively screens scientific papers, journals, or magazines for scientific propositions. From the perspective of non-scientists and scientific outsiders (and, of course, the majority of scientific insiders as well) most scientific propositions simply do not exist. For the majority of us there exists no obvious reason to be concerned or interested – we feel no obligations or commitments.

An experimental proposition concerning the amount of β-carotene in a laboratory rice strain or the phenotypical variation of a genetically modified plant model does not include any proof or explanatory potential that would allow us to draw conclusions about its significance and acceptance outside the laboratory. A scientific or experimental proposition holds a negative authority: in fact it has acquired the means to prove *not* to be fictional (as the publication on the "introduction of the entire β-carotene biosynthetic pathway into rice endosperm" in the magazine *Science*, 287, 2000 shows). But with regard to its positive consequences or significance, it remains silent: the experimental event creates a difference, but it does not reveal for whom this difference might be relevant (Stengers 1993).

For fellow researchers and colleagues from the same discipline a particular experimental event and the respective proposition in general will perhaps make a difference. They will accept the challenge of the experimental laboratory arrangement since they are interested and concerned. For scientific researchers this interest means being associated with somebody or something and entering into a commitment (Fleck 1979).

However, in the exceptional case when a proposition does arrive in the "realm of scientific outsiders," it does not represent "information" in the sense of a "difference which makes a difference" (Bateson 1980). It rarely attracts public interest since it does not relate to daily concerns and at best it is part of the daily informational background noise. So, for us, it is interesting to know whether we merely contributed to that noise. This would not be surprising given the large amount of information presented on our storyboard and in our narrations concerning the subject of plant science and genetics. Furthermore, the "depth of information" was also considerable: one could, for instance, find details of the carotinoid pathway engineering in a copy of the patent application as it is filed at the European Patent Office or gain insight into gut physiology and the problem of bioavailability of carotinoids (a topic that is controversially discussed by nutritionists).

However, in our guest books, we find no indication or complaint that could tell us whether we featured amounts of information that were either too large or too intricate. We got the impression that this issue simply was not important for our guests. Rather, the use of the term "exciting" catches our attention. In our visitors' entries we frequently find this word, and judging from their comments, it appears that the Golden Rice story is indeed an exciting one. They even want us to follow up the "real" project, to continue our research and to tell our stories. We are tempted to say that our visitors even wanted us to experience the course of the project on their behalf.

Maybe we avoided reducing the "landscape of practices" (Stengers 1993), the activities and passions, to one global instance or principle that exerts an exclusive explanatory authority. This kept us from proclaiming slogans "in the name of science," and from the use of a reductionist rhetoric. Instead we gave accounts of risky experimental constructions and the proliferation of scientific experimental propositions.

Thus, we believe that we understand the reason for the frequent use of the term "exciting." Many of our visitors gave us the impression that they were surprised – even overwhelmed. They were surprised by our narrations, by our storyboard, by the unusual perspective on a scientific discipline: they experienced something unexpected. Perhaps all this appears to be a trivial process, but, as we pointed out before, the interesting point is that neither in our encounters on the storyboard nor in our field notes is the issue of "information transfer" mentioned explicitly. The entire process – this performing of shared incompetence – remains implicit and embodied in the interactions. The process is not about learning facts and figures as is the case in a student–teacher relationship, or about understanding and accepting scientific propositions. It is about the question of whether or not we, the scientific outsiders, are ready and willing to interlink with the intricacies of the Golden Rice project – to create a new version of the Golden Rice project and articulate it with our own interests. This is not to say that no "information transfer" took place. On the contrary, we think that the setting enabled many participants to create meaning.

A Peculiar Plasticity of "Public" Opinions

It is not easy to grasp the meaning of the term and concept of "the public." John Dewey points out that "the" public does not exist *per se*. In fact, we can observe the co-evolution of a public with a specific "problem." A problem can be understood as the violation of the interests of one group by the activities of another group. As soon as the problem is resolved, the specific public disappears. This is the reason why participation cannot be prescribed or regulated: participation and engagement are associated with dispersion, and with the varying interests and concerns of different actors in our societies. Dewey asserts that "the essential need . . . is the improvement of the methods and conditions of debate, discussion and persuasion. That is the problem of the public" (Dewey 1927, p. 208).

In contrast to the meaning of Dewey's public, when we talk about "the public" in everyday life, by and large we equate it with "public opinion." We are accustomed to the habit that "public opinion" manifests itself in the form of large numbers. As a rule, these numbers come into existence by procedures of statistical aggregation and they signal consent or dissent on a given topic. Such public opinion-poll techniques assume that individuals have a predetermined personal opinion that can thus be queried by matching this public opinion with prefabricated questions (Callon, Lascoumes, & Barthe 2001). Alternatively, public opinion can be seen as a "medium"; that is, as a set of loosely coupled elements that are available to take on various forms or shapes. It can be seen as a mental potential for awareness, as a contribution to issues of social communication. As a prerequisite for such communications, the pertinent topics/issues have to be known (Luhmann 1997).

This is probably the reason why public discussions so often follow the depleted formula of "pro" and "contra" debates around scientific-technical innovations such as genetic modified organisms. Advocates and opponents and their particular interests shape communication in the mass media. Usually, in general the arguments for or against are known only very roughly. The complex daily routine of a scientific project disappears behind slogans of progressive euphoria or scenarios of disaster. There are almost no public spaces where new questions and identities can be formed, articulated, and reconfigured first-hand. As soon as we look at public opinion as a "medium," as loosely coupled elements that are available for the shaping of forms, it follows that a multitude of forms can be created – depending on how complexly and intensely dialogues, debates, or controversies are realized.

Thus, it is not surprising that in our discussions with our visitors we did not come across any singular public opinion. We had the impression that in these discussions combinations of communications crystallized and dissolved again, temporarily stabilized and destabilized. Rarely could we find a rigid expression or articulation of opinions. Probably the inter-action between the persons present – including ourselves – created these phenomena. "Therefore, it belongs to the self-regulation of the system of interaction that all parties owe each other consideration and furthermore can count on a mutual respect for each other's roles" (Luhmann 1997, p. 815, translated by the authors).

Navigating on the Storyboard

The interactions on our storyboard were not characterized by the exchange of static assumptions, standpoints, or convictions on either side. A peculiar plasticity of opinions and a shifting of positions shaped these interactions. Our stories did not and could not give the ultimate answers, solutions, and proven facts that might provide a basis for "educated" decision-making. We could not fulfill the need of some visitors to find relief in delegating this responsibility to "the scientific truth" or "the experts." Nevertheless, our attempt to avoid the presentation of scientific facts and figures as untouchable and beyond debate introduced unexpected dynamics into our fuzzy knowledge navigations.

Alongside our more or less *ad hoc* presentations of this messy narrative, the storyboard itself, with its combination of handwritten texts and quotations, its depictions of scientists, green activists, managers, and technology transfer specialists as comic-strip characters, and its images of gene guns, red stink bugs, rice plants, a tattered patent application, etc., created a fertile terrain for these dynamics. This environment created the conditions for what we might describe as a temporary loosening of mutual role attributions. Here, we do not understand "role" as a disguise for an invariable core identity (Goffman 1971). Instead, we understand "role attribution" as something proffered in interaction, which may or may not be accepted, and which may change the "ontological drift" of the actors involved. This phenomenon might also be referred to as a "shifting between modes of reference" (Limoges 1993; Dodier 1998).

It was interesting to watch this unfold on the storyboard. As we shifted between modes of reference according to the roles that were attributed to us (for example, the roles of experts, laypeople, idealists, salespersons, artists, and activists), so the visitors also started to shift between roles and modes of reference. This gave rise to a dynamic that, at least temporarily, disrupted the static attribution of roles that takes place between experts and non-experts, between representatives of "the" science and "the" public, between supporters and opponents of gene technology.

Schoolchildren in the "learning mode" gave up the attempt to study "chaotically" represented facts for their biology class. Such visitors shifted into the "entertainment and discussion mode" when they got caught by a more exciting and messy Golden Rice story. Students from the renowned university nearby, who used the map to deepen their understanding of biosynthetic pathway engineering, finally stopped their study of "hard facts" and started to listen to our uncertain narratives with all their bio-socio-economic dimensions. Some students who refused any information from non-experts like us nevertheless spent an hour navigating on the map. Trained natural scientists entered into the narrative of a complex story and kept silent. Environmental activists facing particular quotations on the map shifted from the "mode of protest" into the "mode of scientific experts." One of the inventors entered the "mode of an activist" when confronted by protesters. A senior manager of one of the biotech companies involved brought his family and oscillated between "private" and "PR" modes. The second inventor breathed a sigh of relief when he realized that he was not being presented as a "science hero." The curators of the museum were not sure if they could agree with what they saw in their own house.

Experimenting is Exhibiting – Exhibiting is Experimenting?

Through working on *Good Bye Tomato – Good Morning Rice* we learned that there is a strong demand for the description and presentation of scientific projects in museums. These institutions are in general considered to be "neutral" places for public debate. But scientific projects are not simple to grasp: they change constantly, are discussed controversially, and provide ambiguous and intrinsically uncertain results. Even as we exhibited and experimented with the communication of uncertainty, the danger of becoming an "expert" was almost unavoidable. We had to strive to retain our own incompetence and resist the temptation to provide a "God's-eye view" on the project.

The weeks we spent walking and talking with our visitors on a piece of canvas in the Swiss National Museum clearly demonstrate that a museum can be much more than a territory that represents facts, that a museum can also be a territory of interaction and experience, an environment that generates various kinds of communications that consistently produce in the participants "a difference which makes a difference."

Our strategy of performing shared incompetence provides a method for us to include the opinions of those who are not interested in science and who might wish to preserve their legitimate indifference in a manner which nevertheless keeps them from putting the whole responsibility on the shoulders of experts. At the same time, it provides scientists and experts with the opportunity of entering the political arena. There, their observations can be treated with respect in a context which does not necessarily couple this respect with political acceptance. In this arena, where the comedy of errors and the tragedy of decisions are constantly enacted, perhaps we do not need to resort to "nature," "society," or "culture" as final arbiters to decide how we want to live. Here we may create a context in which we are able to share uncertainty, elaborate shared hopes, and accept shared risks and responsibilities.

Notes

1   Our research project was supported by the Austrian Federal Ministry for Education, Science, and Culture.
2   A biosynthetic pathway describes, we are told, "a series of chemical reactions occurring within a cell, catalyzed by enzymes, that yield various – intermediate – products" (P. Beyer, pers. comm.).
3   In 2000 Zeneca Agrochemicals merged with the agribusiness of the Swiss company Novartis and formed a new company called Syngenta, which now holds the respective licenses. In 2004 Syngenta withdrew from the commercial project and now only the public-sector project focusing on the humanitarian aim remains.

References

Bateson, G. (1980) *Mind and Nature: A Necessary Unity.* New York: Bantam Books.
Callon, M., Lascoumes, P., and Barthe, Y. (2001) *Agir dans un monde incertain: essai sur la démocratie technique* [Acting in a world of uncertainty: an essay on technical democracy]. Paris: Editions du Seuil.
Dewey, J. (1927) *The Public and its Problems.* Athens, Ohio: Swallow Press.
Dodier, N. (1998) Clinical practice and procedures in occupational medicine: a study of the framing of individuals. In M. Berg and A. Mol (eds.), *Differences in Medicine: Unraveling Practices, Techniques, and Bodies.* Durham, N.C., and London: Duke University Press, pp. 53–85.
Fleck, L. (1979 [1935]) *The Genesis and Development of a Scientific Fact.* Chicago: University of Chicago Press.
Goffman, E. (1971 [1959]) *The Presentation of Self in Everyday Life.* Harmondsworth: Penguin.
Harvey, M. (1999) *Genetic Modification as a Bio-Socio-Economic Process: One Case of Tomato Purée.* Manchester: Centre for Research on Innovation and Competition, University of Manchester.
Keulartz, J., Schermer, M., Korthals, M., and Swierstra, T. (2004) Ethics in technological culture: a programmatic proposal for a pragmatist approach. *Science, Technology, & Human Values,* 29 (1): 3–29.

Korzybski, A. (1941) *Science and Sanity*, 2nd ed. Lancaster, Pa.: International Non-Aristotelian Library Publishing Co.

Kräftner, B., Kroell, J., and Warner, I. (2002) "Good bye tomato – good morning rice!": Über die Darstellbarkeit eines wissenschaftlichen Projekts für Nicht-Interessierte ["Good bye tomato – good morning rice!": how to present a scientific project for the uninterested]. Report for the Federal Ministry for Education, Science, and Culture, Austria.

Latour, B. (1987) *Science in Action: How to Follow Scientists and Engineers through Society*. Cambridge, Mass.: Harvard University Press.

Latour, B. (1996) *Aramis, or the Love of Technology*. Cambridge, Mass.: Harvard University Press.

Latour, B., Mauguin, P., and Teil, G. (1992) A note on socio-technical graphs. *Social Studies of Science*, 22: 33–58.

Law, J. (1997) "Traduction/Trahison: Notes on ANT," Centre for Science Studies, Lancaster University. www.lancs.ac.uk/fss/sociology/papers/ law-traduction-trahison.pdf (accessed August 2006).

Law, J. and Hassard, J. (eds.) (1999) *Actor Network Theory and After*. Oxford: Blackwell.

Limoges, C. (1993) Expert knowledge and decision-making in controversy contexts. *Public Understanding of Science*, 2: 417–26.

Luhmann, N. (1997) *Die Gesellschaft der Gesellschaft* [The society of the society]. Frankfurt am Main: Suhrkamp.

Martineau, B. (2001) *First Fruit: The Creation of the Flavr Savr Tomato and the Birth of Biotech Food*. New York: McGraw Hill.

Mol, A. (2002) *The Body Multiple: Ontology in Medical Practice*. Durham, N.C., and London: Duke University Press.

Nash, J. M. (2000) Grains of hope. *Time*, 156 (5), July 31.

Stengers, I. (1993) *L'Invention des sciences modernes* [The invention of modern sciences]. Paris: Editions La Découverte.

Turnbull, D. (1989) *Maps are Territories: Science is an Atlas: a Portfolio of Exhibits*. Chicago: University of Chicago Press.

Varela, F. J. and Dupuy, J.-P. (1992) *Understanding Origins: Contemporary Views on the Origin of Life, Mind, and Society*. Boston Studies in the Philosophy of Science, vol. 130. Dordrecht: Kluwer Academic Publishers.

Xperiment! (2005) What is a body/a person? topography of the possible. In B. Latour and P. Weibel (eds.), *Making Things Public: Atmospheres of Democracy*. Cambridge, Mass.: MIT Press.

Ye X., Al-Babili, S., Klöti, A., Zhang J., Lucca, P., Beyer, P., and Potrykus, I. (2000) Engineering the provitamin A (β-carotene) biosynthetic pathway into (carotenoid-free) rice endosperm. *Science* 287 (5451) (January 14): 303–5.

6

From *Capital* to *Enthusiasm*: an Exhibitionary Practice

Neil Cummings and Marysia Lewandowska

As artists we have been collaborating together since 1995, and have worked with many curators, academics, historians, archivists, gallerists, people with technical expertise, enthusiasts, collectors, and many, many others. During this time, we have moved away from the habitual aesthetic appearance of art and its exhibition – and even from the production of autonomous objects as art[1] – and closer to a collaborative, research-driven practice. Echoing wider cultural shifts, we have turned our attention from sites of art production – the studio – to the spaces of distribution and consumption – the gallery and the museum.

We have been interested in thinking about and working alongside many of the organizations that choreograph the exchange of values between art and its publics. We have worked with various galleries (both public and private), museums, art schools, publishers, and broadcasters. When you work with these institutions and their exhibitionary technologies – technologies which include: the means of collection, installation, and display; the production of publications, catalogues, and promotional material; educational projects; the writing of wall texts, object-labels, audio tours, and gallery guides, and so on – you become aware that these technologies can be turned upon any object, image, artist, maker, experience, city, country, or nation.[2] These powerful exhibitionary technologies are the means of producing, presenting, and disseminating the work of the work of art.

The exhibitionary technologies of art are also diffusing into wider economies of display;[3] economies animated by the movement of images, information, knowledge, value, people, goodwill, loyalty, and trust. These forces, which have traditionally been recognized as within the realm of culture, are now central to our "new" financial economies convened around the slippery exchanges of creativity, knowledge, intellectual property regimes, and capital. So we have also been interested in the spaces where art, through exhibition, dissolves into public policy and social management, into promotion, sponsorship, and investment, into products, advertising, and lifestyle choices; this has encouraged us to initiate projects with department stores, advertising agencies, archives, independent commissioning agencies, and corporations.

Each project has resulted in a range of different outcomes appropriate to the project's location. For example, we have made exhibitions such as *Free Trade* (2003) at the Manchester Art Gallery, using collections of paintings, sculpture, fine furniture, ceramics, and miscellaneous objects, which enabled us to explore the entanglements of art and emerging nineteenth-century capitalism through our rediscovery of the Beatson Blair Bequest; or *Use Value* (2002) at the Victoria and Albert Museum, an installation replaying sounds of the social exchanges, the uses of things – eating, cooking, drinking, and the like – within the pin-drop quiet of one of the largest exhibitions of ceramics in the world. We have researched and produced books such as *The Value of Things* (Cummings & Lewandowska 2001a), which explored, via the British Museum and Selfridges, the parallel ideological and exhibitionary history of the public museum and the department store. And we have built collections and exhibitions – often with amateur material previously excluded from "official" cultural institutions – like *Not Hansard* (2000) and *Enthusiasts* (2004).

In our exhibitionary practice, we have tried to engage with many of the technologies that cultural institutions use to designate and mediate art to their public. In particular, we have explored the conventions of exhibition, and attempted to experiment with these conventions rather than be subject to them – as a consequence these conventions become our media.

To this end we increasingly use research as a means of identifying the location of our *artwork* as well as any potential exhibitionary form this *artwork* might take. For us, research or fieldwork has replaced "site specificity" as a means of designating our engagement as artists. Research incorporates the recognition that the "exhibition" itself often consists of interlocking yet distributed fields of aesthetics, knowledge, promotion, social practices, and economic forces. The exhibition is discursively formed through our act of engagement; it does not pre-exist as an "empty" location waiting to be filled. We have sought to vividly reanimate the practice of exhibition, so that our artworks are no longer viewed as points of origin, founded on "individual" creativity, or of termination, housed in museums and galleries or their stores, but as nodes in networks of social exchange. What we have been interested in developing is a heightened sensitivity to the idea of an *exhibitionary context* in which the work of the work of art is activated, and the material and immaterial conditions in which our practice as artists is engaged and made legible.

Capital

As a more concrete example, we'll recount a project that became known as *Capital*, developed at Tate Modern in London and exhibited from May to October 2001 (Cummings & Lewandowska 2001b). We were commissioned by senior curator Francis Morris to propose a pre-opening project, which meant that we started researching eighteen months before Tate Modern opened in 2000. We were invited to think about the Tate and its immediate environment; its geographical location, and its social and cultural environment in Southwark, in the City, and in London more generally.

The more we researched the Tate and the more we learned about its ambition and power, its various departments and components (including Tate St. Ives, Tate Liverpool, Tate Britain, and Tate Modern), its vast stores in high-security but nondescript industrial buildings in south London, the archive of the artworld that it is buying from artists and from galleries and other institutions, its art library (the best in Britain), its vast conservation and art-handling departments, its aggressive publicity division, and its huge educational ambition (from working with teachers and schools, to conferences with internationally renowned academics, writers, historians, theorists, and artists). We learned that the practice of exhibition, the most public face of the Tate, is a mere sliver of its activities. With its huge cultural ambition and image in the public consciousness, we began to consider the Tate as, in some ways, a central bank: a central bank in a different kind of economy – a *symbolic economy.* Something, perhaps, like the Bank of England.

The Bank

Over a year before the project was due to open, we approached the Bank of England with a vague idea about some sort of collaboration with the Tate through us. Shocked at our own ignorance about finance and the practices of money, we began to research what the Bank of England does, and a little of the history of banking.

The Bank of England is the banker to the whole British financial system and also plays a major role in structuring global monetary relations. This role is essentially as the "lender of last resort," which means that the Bank may decide to rescue an ailing financial institution if its economists fear a systemic collapse or a catastrophic loss of confidence in the whole British or world financial system. Its role as "lender of last resort" gives the Bank the authority to guarantee the necessary trust and confidence to secure the various interlocking domestic and foreign commodity and financial markets. To cut a very long and complicated story short, the Bank regulates or distributes trust and confidence through these various economies by managing the availability and price of debt. Effectively, by raising or lowering interest rates, it adjusts the cost of borrowing to accelerate or decelerate the flow of capital debt into the markets. This debt, this black hole, this lack that the Bank manages the price of, is principally that of the Government.[4]

"Managing the price of Government debt" was the function that founded the Bank in 1694. When William of Orange and Queen Mary jointly ascended the throne of Great Britain and Ireland in 1689 they needed cash money to continue the war with France in William's homeland of the Netherlands. The Government Exchequer declined, so a group of people got together to form a joint-stock company, which lent money to the King in return for the loan with interest. The bank, later to become the Bank of England, is thus founded upon a debt, and *the continuation* of this debt, or the continuation of the repayment of this debt, is the motor of our present domestic and international financial economies. Our whole global financial structure is founded upon debt repayments.[5]

Linked to the cost of the loan to the King was the Bank's demand to issue notes – paper money – in return for a royal charter. Previously all value found its form as, or in relationship to, gold. Coin, for instance, would *embody* the actual value in material of that depicted on its face.[6] The new paper notes had little intrinsic value but were contractual agreements against which objects or services could be bought or sold for the value *represented*. Of course these paper promises were backed by gold in the vaults. The "I promise to pay the bearer on demand the sum of ten pounds" printed – still – on British paper notes implied that you could present the note at the Bank and retrieve your ten pounds' worth of gold. This link between gold-as-value and its paper representation was slowly augmented by the Bank through the use of different forms of government securities against which notes could be issued. Tax receipts, revenues on land or commercial contracts, stocks of merchandise, or even potential stocks of merchandise, were to become acceptable forms of security. The Bank began issuing to its scandalized customers *imaginary money* – notes that were backed by other paper promises to pay, sell, or loan services, debts, trades, and obligations at some future time or place. These new obligations against which *imaginary money* could be advanced speeded up and expanded the economy at an extraordinary rate. To all intents and purposes it *multiplied the effect of our coined money.*

By initiating a "fiduciary issue," the Bank denominated paper money in circulation which is no longer backed by bullion in the vaults.[7] Essentially money is backed by a collective act of faith and obligation. The Bank was, and is, a more symbolic institution than we ever realized. We also became conscious that the dematerialization of value from gold to paper promises was continuing out into new instruments and technologies. The current scale of the five principal markets, which trade currency, bonds, stock, derivatives, and commodities, is staggering. For example, the turnover on the currency markets alone is estimated at one trillion dollars a day, which means that in two months the volume of trade dwarfs the annual turnover from manufacturing and retail of the entire planet. Immaterial exchanges of value dwarf the physical trade of goods and capital, even as our own financial dealings dissolve into the swipe of plastic or the click of a mouse.

And yet, ironically, the dematerialization of financial value has accelerated the penetration of the "economic" into all aspects of contemporary life – into healthcare, education, transportation, and broadcasting, which, in Britain at least, were previously state-funded through collective "welfare" strategies and so protected from the vagaries of the "market." Values expressed as money haunt everything: a punch line in a popular TV advert suggests that "we are all bank managers now" and another that "we are all fluent in finance."[8] So, as the signs for financial value become increasingly vast but immaterial, does the central bank's role as guarantor grow inversely to compensate?

The Tate

On the other side of the same coin, or note, we wondered whether it would be possible to situate the Tate – through its ambition and constant expansion – as the principal institution in a parallel "symbolic" economy.[9]

Like the Bank, the Tate connects with a vast network of other exhibitionary institutions and agencies, from museums, galleries, curators, collectors, and dealers, to various funding and sponsoring bodies both nationally and internationally that make up the global economy of art. Does the Tate guarantee the integrity and value of the artworks, objects, images, and knowledges it collects, exhibits, stores, and distributes within this economy? And, in a close parallel with a central bank, is its basic currency becoming increasingly insubstantial and difficult to represent? Artworks and images are dissolving into digital media, fieldwork, and activism; and perhaps this process is further accelerated as "aesthetic experience" dissolves, beyond the regulated symbolic economy, out into the culture of promotion, sponsorship, branding, "City of Culture" status, economic regeneration, advertising, and marketing. (Instances include: the Unilever Turbine Hall commission at Tate Modern; the sponsorship by the online bank, Egg, of "live art" at Tate Modern; BT sponsorship of the Tate website and online commissions; and the distribution of the Tate's own range of paints through DIY superstores.)

Clearly, values expressed through image and information haunt everything. As the signs of aesthetic value become increasingly immaterial, a question arises as to whether, in a close parallel with the Bank, the museum's role as regulator and guarantor grows inversely to compensate.

If the Tate and the Bank appear to have more similarities than differences, there *is* a major structural difference. Based on a gift from Sir Henry Tate, the Tate was founded (as the National Gallery of British Art) in 1897. Coming from a family of grocers, Sir Henry bought the rights to refine sugar and manufacture sugar cubes and, like many nineteenth-century industrialists, he made so much money he did not know what to do with it; he founded hospitals, colleges, and libraries, and he collected works of art.[10] His collection of modern British art was presented to the nation via Parliament as he neared the end of his life, but Parliament initially refused.

Where would the collection be housed? Finally Sir Henry also donated the funds to build a new gallery at Millbank on the Thames, and although it was officially called the Gallery of British Art it inevitably took its founder's name – we know it now as Tate Britain.

You will remember that the Bank was founded on a debt incurred by the King in 1694.

The gift

The contested idea of the gift has been a central theme in anthropology since Marcel Mauss's seminal publication *Essai sur le don* in 1923–24, and more recently its influence has been profound in other social sciences. Mauss's work on the gift proposes an economy outside of or alongside the calculations encouraged by the purely financial – the gift economy pre-dates money and yet has not been erased by its presence. Receiving a gift triggers the obligation to reciprocate; the counter-gift necessitates a return, and so on, endlessly. We could imagine an economy without apparent origin, and therefore we are all already within networks of gift and debt. Giving, and the gift's obligation of an indebted return, assure and realize all manner of social relationships. Through anonymous contributions to and withdrawals from a collective "good" – sometimes characterized as a "cooking-pot" model – individuals become invested in, and therefore beholden to, communal projects. Perhaps here lies the traditional root of nation states through the social welfare projects we mentioned earlier, like healthcare[11] and education, or culture supported through public broadcasting, or "free" access to museums and galleries. Gifting strengthens the interconnectedness of friendships, families, communities, societies, and even nations, and whereas money exchange cancels obligations between people, the gift binds.[12]

The sociologist Pierre Bourdieu (1977) has reworked the anthropological notion of the gift by emphasizing the gift as a gesture of "bad faith," or suffused with "misrecognition." Bourdieu suggests that one of the astonishing characteristics of the gift is our ability to pretend that it is a disinterested gesture, replete with charity, while actually it is a gesture of power and domination, and full of indebtedness. If the gift is surrounded by social obligations of guilt – for not reciprocating appropriately – of indebtedness and obligation, then these are contractual agreements which cannot be recognized as such. An economy which is founded on gifting is based on the misrecognition of the financial value, or the social and cultural force, that the gift entails. Bourdieu and others have characterized such economies as *symbolic*.

Clearly the Tate and virtually all other public institutions of exhibition are completely indebted to private, public, and corporate gifting. Most public collections are the result of private gifts of art, and many public institutions rely on financial gifts to meet exhibition and running costs. These patterns of gifting bind cultural institutions into economic networks of obligation and indebtedness obscured from public scrutiny. These are further complicated by the enormous growth in sponsorship: exchanges where some of the repayments on the apparent gift are specified – my logo on your publicity – but others, as with the true gift, are left unspecified.[13]

The exhibition

All of the above is by way of preparation – evidence of the research that simultaneously enables us to build a context *for* and gives form *to* the exhibition encounter itself. For *Capital* we negotiated three "outcomes" with both the Bank and the Tate, as a way of activating differing levels of engagement between the institution and its audience. They comprised a gift, a publication, and a seminar series.

The exhibition was inaugurated and spectacularly detonated through the issue of a gift, a beautiful, limited-edition, double-sided print. The print consists of an image of a silver spoon borrowed from the Bank's ceremonial service and bearing the Bank's logo, Britannia. The spoon was taken to the Tate and photographed, and thereby copyrighted, by the Tate's in-house photographers; therefore, neither the asset nor its representation belonged to us. The print was double-sided, the handle with crest on one side (denoting the action of giving) and the bowl of the spoon on the other (suggesting receiving).

We negotiated to install *Capital*, which consisted of framed versions of the print, a wall text, a short film, and some contextual reading matter, in the Reading Point at Tate Modern, a room with picture windows that overlooks the City of London, and in the Bank of England Museum. At unspecified times during the day a visitor might be approached by a gallery or museum official. The official would introduce themselves to the visitor and then, with the phrase "*This is for you*," give away the beautifully wrapped, special limited-edition print (figure 6.1). Astonished visitors wondered "Why me?" or "What's this?" Other visitors, looking on and not so lucky, wondered "Why not me?" And the gift-givers themselves felt beholden to explain what they were doing, or what they thought they were doing, and what was happening. Through such a simple gesture, disengaged exhibition behavior – the slow pan along gallery walls, or around vitrines – was transformed into an emotional exchange. Curators, administrators, maintenance people, sales staff, and others – the social infrastructure of any exhibition, gallery, or museum – who nominated themselves as gift-givers entered into a discussion with their visitors as to the nature of their exchange, and what was being exhibited. Were past debts being repaid through the gift, or new debts being incurred?

And it is here, in the exhibitionary encounter between a representative of the museum and the visitor, that the work of the work of art is negotiated. Through the introduction of the gift, we attempted to insert a moment of critical reflection into the habitual flow of things. Through a heightened attention to the chains of debt, generosity, and obligation, what was simultaneously being enacted and exhibited was the social

Figure 6.1 Giving the Gift. Tate Modern, June 2001. Courtesy Neil Cummings and Marysia Lewandowska © Attribution ShareAlike.

contract that generates both culture and finance. Through our gesture of authorizing the giving of the gift, we were using the public money which funded our project and the Tate itself, and giving it back – with interest? – to the previously anonymous visitor, the public taxpayer, who invisibly supports culture and its institutions, to those whose contributions are unaccounted for, because their contributions are not the "magnificence of gifting" of donations, gifts, bequests, or sponsorship of the wealthy and famous, but the invisible support of anonymous investment. It was our, and the Tate's and the Bank's, return to our audience for their generosity.

Of course we are aware that artists' "commissions" have become part of the promotional and funding imperative of any public institution of exhibition, particularly driven by instrumental notions of "outreach," access, and community. Artists have to be aware of the contradictions and obligations that they are entering into, in all circumstances where there is a chance to "exhibit"; our intention is to reveal what has been repressed for so long, and to try and make those obligations apparent.

The second exhibitionary encounter, and the second intervention into distributive networks of *Capital*, was a publication that created a material and theoretical context from which the issue of the gift could be located and the gesture of giving and the reciprocal debt understood. The book contains "backstage" photographs of the Bank and the Tate taken by us throughout our research, complemented by previously unpublished archival material and a sketch history of both institutions. Inside this frame we commissioned three essays, by geographer Nigel Thrift, anthropologist Marilyn Strathern, and political philosopher Jeremy Valentine. The twin themes of the gift and debt were located as the heart of the respective institutions, and the gesture of the gift revealed as the core of *Capital* itself.

The publication gathered much of the research, yet also offered another space of engagement with a different audience through exhibition. Whereas the gift could not be triggered by the receiver, the book required an active purchase, as did the third exhibitionary encounter, a series of seminars on core themes that seemed essential for any economy (either symbolic or financial): those of Gift, Economy, and Trust. Unfolding over three Sunday afternoons, curated in collaboration with Jeremy Valentine, the seminars were chaired by the academic Paul Hirst and lasted for three hours each. Our intention was that there should be short presentations, a glass of wine, and then plenty of time for discussion and exchange. The seminar was turned, like the practice of exhibition itself, into a space of creative production, and not the habitual display of knowledge.[14]

Our intention with *Capital* – through the issue of the gift and, by extension, to all those individuals that enter into its orbit through rumor, publicity, the seminar series, or the book, or even, indeed, this text – was to initiate an engagement with the social imagination. *Capital,* as an artwork, exists in all the interstices of exhibition. Furthermore it set in motion a series of future encounters, debts, punctuations and exchanges, and although the artwork is authorized and guaranteed by the Tate and the Bank, it can no longer be contained or regulated by these institutions. The artwork has entered into a rich and varied exhibitionary life.

Enthusiasm

Exhausted after a series of projects, including *Capital* (2001), *Use Value* (2001), and *Free Trade* (2003), that required endless negotiation with institutions of collection and exhibition, in 2002 we had a chance encounter with Polish film director Krzysztof Kieslowski's first popular feature film, *Amator* (Film Buff), made in 1979. The main character in the film is a leading member of a factory-based amateur film club. Intrigued as to whether such clubs and film-makers still existed,[15] we made a few speculative research trips in the summer of 2002, enquiring into the existence and remnants of amateur film clubs in socialist Poland.

There has been a spectacular transfiguration of Polish political and cultural life since the introduction of the market economy in 1989. It is as if Poland had played out, in a time-lapsed film style, the economic and cultural changes of "western" Europe. Fifty years of social evolution – from a manufacturing to a service economy – has been compressed into just over ten years. Poland is a crystallization of the forces at play in the rest of Europe; it projects a service-driven, consumer-led future, while content to forget its industrial past and hide its manufacturing present. And yet, all the former state-owned industries – for example those generating power, refining steel, or producing chemicals – play a central role in contemporary economic and cultural life. Clearly industry manufactures the goods and energy necessary to generate our material lives, and yet it has simultaneously structured our experiences into "productive" labor and unproductive "leisure" time: traditionally the space of culture. Although, before the economic changes in Poland, even "leisure" was organized through factory-sponsored clubs, various associations, sports facilities, and even state holiday schemes.

Out of this regulated network, perhaps the most popular clubs were those that encouraged the production of amateur film. With 16mm film stock, cameras, and editing tables supplied by the factory/state, a large number of clubs were created throughout Poland from the 1950s onwards. By the late 1960s there were almost 300 clubs. Out of this growing network, and in a mirror reflection of the professional media, film competitions evolved, prizes were awarded, and festivals were organized on a local, regional, and eventually national and international level.

The passions of the amateur, enthusiast, or hobbyist often reveal a range of interests and experiences generally invisible amid the breathless flow of the state-sponsored, or professionally mediated. The enthusiast is often working outside "official" culture and its encouragements, frequently adopting a counter-cultural tone of tactical resistance and criticism.

During our trips to Poland we became aware that most of the factories that housed film clubs had closed, or the clubs themselves disbanded. With help, however, we found a few former club members who were still active, and they, in turn, gave us addresses and telephone numbers of other members and clubs. We began to criss-cross the country, visiting people's houses, extant clubs, and community centers, and with the aid of a portable editing device we watched hundreds of films.

It became apparent to us that the film club enthusiasts were inverting the familiar logic of work and leisure, through becoming truly productive when pursuing their film-making passion and using work to fulfill their own, rather than the factory's or state's, intentions. Perhaps the enthusiast has the same relationship to official cultural production as the gift to financial economies? These grey areas between work and leisure are clearly blurring in our contemporary economies, driven by exchanges of signs, information, experiences, and capital.[16] Cultural production, either luxurious and strictly financial (as in the example of fine art) or outside the reach of profit (as in the practices of the enthusiast or amateur, which were once marginal to the refreshment of capital), has now become central to the "creative industries" and the "new" economies. In these "new" economies the artist or enthusiast is an ideal employee; astonishingly self-motivated, endlessly creative, flexible, enthusiastic, resourceful and, financially, poorly rewarded. So these are some of the themes we began to develop, using the culture of amateur film-making to think through and explore a shift from enthusiasm being a site of resistance, to its becoming a central driver of "official culture" and the very source of the refreshment of contemporary capital.[17]

As we tracked down the films and their makers we were astonished by their ambition. These were not standard "amateur" films of family landmarks such as births, weddings, and holidays, but were an aspiration to cinema. We saw extraordinary films that ranged from two-minute animations and wicked political satires to short "experimental" and "abstract" films, from documentaries on family, village, city, or factory life to historical dramas and ambitious features with great emotional gravity. There is an astonishing range of material, beautifully crafted and largely forgotten – or, more accurately, "doubly repressed." Doubly repressed because the films are tinged with an ideological past incompatible with the ideological present, and because of their "amateur" status they exist below the consciousness of "official" cultural institutions of exhibition – museums and archives.

As a result of our research into these films, their makers and clubs, we found a huge selection of forgotten footage, usually in people's houses, and sometimes literally under their beds. In 2003, joined by curator Lukasz Ronduda of the Center for Contemporary Art, Ujazdowski Castle, Warsaw, we embarked on cleaning, restoring, and digitizing as much of the material as we could find money to support.

The exhibition

As we worked on restoration and digitization, we began to develop ideas for a new project, a means of exploring enthusiasm through exhibition. We were aware of, and wanted to avoid the legacy of, artists' use of found film footage, where the film material is habitually stripped of its context and appropriated as the artists' property. Through discussion, we realized our need to construct a social, material, and conceptual context in which the films could be situated, while all the time being wary of falling into nostalgia.

Almost two years after the research began, the project was first made public in an exhibition entitled *Enthusiasts* curated by Lukasz Ronduda at the Center for Contemporary Art in June 2004 (Cummings & Lewandowska 2004).[18] The exhibition comprised a compilation of official newsreels, a reconstructed interior of a film clubhouse (figure 6.2), a selection of films curated into three hour-long film programs, each presented in a "cinema" exhibition environment, a collection of festival posters, and an "Archive Lounge" of films found but not screened.

The first exhibitionary encounter for the visitor was a room screening Polska Kronika Filmowa. These are short, official state-sponsored films

Figure 6.2 Club House, part of *Enthusiasm*. Tapies Foundation, January 2006. Courtesy Neil Cummings and Marysia Lewandowska © Attribution ShareAlike.

which were shown in cinemas before the main feature, and later on television. The films glorify the productivity of the former communist state: its factories, their workers, material output, state festivals, shopping, cultural events, etc. These films create an introductory ground against which the enthusiasts' films themselves could be appreciated.

The second exhibitionary encounter was through a reconstruction of a fictional film club. Many of the film clubs we visited during our research trips were marvelously evocative; they caught and held the traces of the social and creative history of the members and the films they made. The clubs were usually stuffed with framed photographs, printed film stills, caricatures, posters, certificates, medals, prizes and trophies from film festivals, cupboards stacked with unwanted film reels and videocassettes, redundant projectors, old cameras and recording equipment, film editing desks and chemicals, homemade developing tanks and film dryers, tea- and coffee-making equipment, a fridge, a coat-stand, odd chairs, salvaged furniture, junk, and even rubbish. Our installation of a "clubhouse" – created from materials borrowed from club members, scavenged, or bought at flea markets in Warsaw – was inspired by ethnographic museum room tableaux. A monitor and VHS deck in the clubhouse replayed films by club members documenting club "trips" and holidays, special events, the process of film-making, meetings, and festivals. By inserting loops of self-representation within the fictional "club," we tried to ensure that the collaborative and social nature of the film-making process remained to the fore, while at the same time enabling the "club" to be an actual social space for the exhibition visitor; the clubhouse became the hub of the exhibition, mirroring its status in the culture of amateur film-making.

On our research trips we watched hundreds of films, in many extraordinary circumstances, often with former club members present. We became wary of imposing our own preferences and taste on the richness of the films themselves, and thus tried to become sensitive to their makers' enthusiasms and hopes. What eventually evolved from screenings and discussions were three porous themes: themes of Love, Longing, and Labor. This enabled us to select the films for exhibition and compile them into three hour-long programs, although in contrast to the conventions of artists' use of "found footage" the compiled films were left complete, with their original music and fully credited. Our emergent themes seemed better able to curate the films into comprehension than the arbitrary violence performed by sorting the films into the genres usually deployed (feature, documentary, animation, and so forth).

We had found a means of giving an exhibitionary context to the films and their production, but how should a cinema of enthusiasm be represented in a gallery?

Too often we have seen films and the culture of cinema lazily installed for exhibition. Films are routinely digitized, and projected onto a wall in a black box installed inside the gallery with nowhere to sit, no program, no running time, nothing. We were determined to complement the filmmakers' own cinematic aspirations, and thus we worked with architects Peter Thomas and Catherine du Toit of 51% Studios to find a form of exhibition that could simultaneously express the gap between the humble club and the cinematic desires of the members. What evolved were three beautiful, lush, sensuously curved, vibrantly colored, five-meter-tall, velvet-curtained cinema spaces. Each cinema had appropriate chairs where visitors would feel comfortable, a screen, soft low-level lighting, and a printed program with film notes and running times. Through the program we wanted to hand control of the routes through the elements and spaces of the exhibition back to the visitors themselves. They could sit back and luxuriate in a particular cinema watching the whole program, or wander from screen to screen mixing their own film selection. As with *Capital,* the space of the *Enthusiasts* exhibition became a space of creative production for visitors, mirroring the collaborative practices employed by the amateur film-makers themselves.

In the cinema entitled "Longing" we screened films of personal, political, and sexual love, loss, and longing; we explored themes of alienation, ecological anxieties, a fear of war and violence, and a terrible longing to be elsewhere. In "Love," the films reflected on the joy, banality and celebration of an "everyday" love of life; they dealt with themes of humor and camaraderie, of families, parties, passion, and sex as a radical transgression of the expected. In "Labour," the films traced the beauty, routine, discipline, and horror of work in all its forms; themes of celebration, futility, boredom, and exhaustion are acutely depicted through films made by people caught within the processes of production.

The last major exhibitionary encounter within *Enthusiasts* was with the "Archive Lounge" (figure 6.3). We were conscious that there were many films that could not be accommodated within our emergent taxonomies. An Archive Lounge would enable visitors to watch, via searchable DVDs, all the films found, collected, and digitized but not screened as part of our

Figure 6.3   Archive Lounge, part of *Enthusiasm*. Tapies Foundation, January 2006. Courtesy Neil Cummings and Marysia Lewandowska ⓒ Attribution ShareAlike.

cinema installations. Our intention was to make available as many films as possible, to enable visitors to curate their own programs and recognize that our selection – Love, Longing, and Labor – was part of an interpretive process and not final or in any way authorial.

Enthusiasts: archive

From the seed of the idea of the Archive Lounge developed for the *Enthusiasts* exhibition, we are currently growing a huge and permanent archival extension of the project. Through watching visitors using the Archive Lounge, we realized the possibility for a new kind of exhibitionary space: a space partly opened by new technology, partly through our practice, and partly by a new suite of licenses.

There is an astonishing growth in museums, and in archives and databanks of images, sounds, and information. Indeed, the French philosopher Jacques Derrida (1996) has diagnosed a virulent "archive fever" at work. These new, emergent forms of archival capital have an increasingly powerful grip upon culture and its reproduction. The problem with most existing public archives is that all creative work is born into copyright; every image, text, film, or sound is automatically designated the property of its apparent author – until death plus seventy years in the EU. Copyright is founded on the right of exclusion – what is contractually mine cannot be yours. Through the fixed term of the exclusion, copyright removes creative works from the public domain and denies the legal possibility of the creative reuse of the work by others (except with prior written permission). Now, while there is logic at work between relationships of owners or authors and physical artworks or artifacts – a logic of scarcity and a bounded relationship between people and things – this logic dissolves when applied to media made for reproduction, like film, or immaterial goods, like ideas, or information, or previously distinct media translated into a digital code, which is endlessly replicable at negligible cost with no appreciable loss of quality. Most public film and media archives are built from donated material from public broadcasters or film agencies, or comprise gifts from amateur film-makers. These gifts are usually accepted with an agreement that the copyright, or its management, is assigned to the archive. Some media archives then attempt to turn limited reproduction rights into a revenue stream; they sell rights to broadcast media conglomerates for extraordinary fees. These fees are often well beyond the reach of the publics who fund the archive and donate its holdings. Effectively, our moving-image cultural history, our film and broadcast culture, is being expropriated from the very people who paid for its production – it is like charging thousands of pounds to visit a museum exhibition.

Archives, like collections in museums and galleries, are built with the property of multiple authors and previous owners. But, unlike the collection, there is no imperative within the conventional logic of the archive to exhibit, display, or interpret its holdings. An archive designates a territory and not a particular narrative, but perhaps the archive, too, may be constituted as a creative space for engagement. The material connections contained are not already authored as someone's – for example, a curator's or artist's – interpretation, exhibition or property; rather, it is a discursive terrain where interpretations are invited.

Our experience of working with and struggling to release material from Polish state film archives, or from many public film and television archives in Britain, encouraged us to think about creating a "critical" creative archive of amateur film, which would – to use a term from software development – be "free" or "open-source." With the permission of the film-makers we are currently compressing the films and uploading them onto www.archive.org, an internet public domain resource, where they can be accessed via the *Enthusiasts: archive* website (see below). Uploaded films can be either streamed or downloaded, and therefore exhibited anywhere, at any time. Some films also enable you to re-edit their material or integrate them into new creative works. All of this is possible because the *Enthusiasts: archive* and all it contains is licensed under Creative Commons Licenses.[19] These licenses work as an extension to copyright and grant the licensee the right to use, copy, sometimes modify and redistribute any film, text, or image that carries the CC license. The most important operational clause within each license is that these rights – to copy, modify, and redistribute – must be extended through the licensee's work to others. Through on-licensing, the "viral" heart of the Creative Commons ensures that the source film material and all derivative works will become a legally protected creative resource in perpetuity. Artists and others will be able to watch, screen, download, use, and reuse the material for future creative exchange, enriching rather than depleting the public domain. Enabled through technology and licensing, the conventional archive of inert documentation can be vividly reimagined as a creative space of exhibition. The evolving archive can be found at www.enthusiastsarchive.net.

Through our founding of the *Enthusiasts: archive* as an artwork, we intend to challenge creative practices – to replace exchanges hampered by frustration and restriction with ones facilitated by collaboration and generosity. We want to reanimate the public function of archives, collections, and exhibitions in an age characterized by relentless privatization, and, as with the gift in *Capital*, to initiate new practices of exhibition – practices where, as artists, our "creativity" is not founded on the dominance of the visitor, or where the "studio" is no longer privileged as a space of creative production to the detriment of the exhibition, which is too often imagined as a space of passive spectacle and consumption.[20] Instead, we attempt to collapse those spaces and participants down, so that exhibition is reconfigured as a conscious site of creative exchange for the collaborative negotiation over the "making" and remaking of the work of the work of art. Pursuing this project, we recognize the need to locate our work within exhibitionary institutions, to utilize their authority and resources, and to work with the audiences for contemporary art that they convene. And yet our aspiration for *Capital, Enthusiasts*, and *Enthusiasts: archive* is to test and exceed the institutional grip upon culture and its reproduction. Our artworks are made from and conceived as a nexus of all the forces made possible through the practices of exhibition – simultaneously aesthetic, material, political, financial, institutional, and discursive.[21]

Notes

1   There are clearly enough artworks in the world. Major museums in Britain routinely store about 80 percent of their collections at any given time.
2   We are conscious of building on the legacy of artists who emerged during the late 1980s, who turned their attention to the structures through which art is produced, promoted, distributed, and "consumed" (for example, Julie Ault and Group Material, Andrea Fraser, Sylvia Kolbowski, and a slightly older generation represented by Michael Asher and Hans Haacke) – artists whose artwork became tagged as "institutional critique."
3   This is what the sociologist Tony Bennett (1995) has traced – since the nineteenth century – as the evolution of an "exhibitionary complex" of museums, exhibitions, and trade fairs, with a parallel development of technologies of surveillance, discipline, and control.
4   Britain's National Debt was £12 million in 1700 and is currently estimated at £470 billion.

5   See the US debt clock at www.brillig.com/debt_clock/ (accessed August 2006). The US needs foreign investment of around $505.6 billion dollars a year to service this debt. Without this investment, the US and eventually the world economy would slowly grind to a halt. Briefing paper J.P. Morgan (2002) *World Financial Markets,* New York, 10 December.

6   The philosopher Michel Foucault suggests that money is a "privileged instrument within the domain of representation" (1974, p. 195).

7   Britain removed itself from the Gold Standard in 1931. The gold standard is a monetary system between trading nations in which the *unit of account* is a fixed weight of gold. Typically, under the gold standard paper money circulates as a medium of exchange but the issuer makes it convertible into gold on demand.

8   Personal debt in Britain has broken through the £1 trillion (£1,000,000, 000,000) barrier and is increasing by £1 million every four minutes; the interest we pay on this debt is running at £6 billion every month. www.creditaction.org.uk/debtstats.htm (accessed August 2006).

9   We have little interest in the financial value of art objects; it is obvious that everything can evolve a price and grow a market, even cans of shit (as Piero Manzoni demonstrated in his "Merda d'artista," 1961).

10 See our previous project Free Trade at the Manchester Art Gallery archived at www.chanceprojects.com/ (accessed August 2006).

11 The classic work on gifting and social welfare is Titmuss (1970), in which the author examines the role of altruism in society through voluntary blood donation and distribution. Titmuss highlights gifting and generosity as distinct from other forms of exchange in a market-oriented society.

12 There has been a popular eruption of the symbolic power of the gift characterized by the struggle surrounding Free Libre or Open Source software [FLOSS] and the astonishing growth of peer-to-peer file-sharing networks of exchange. Commons-based peer production, where everyone contributes to a collective good, has reanimated a gift-based economy to produce global systems and services. Note, for example, the open-content collaborative encyclopedia Wikipedia (http://en.wikipedia.org/wiki/Main_Page, accessed August 2006), or the Apache web server software, which is currently running 67 percent of the World Wide Web (see www.serverwatch.com/, accessed August 2006).

13 See Wu, 2002, p. 122.

14 The seminars are archived on the Tate website at www.tate.org.uk/onlinee vents/archive/, accessed August 2006.

15 A related project, *Not Hansard: the common wealth,* took place at the John Hansard Gallery from May 2 to June 10, 2000. The project was an exhibition consisting of a reading room comprising over 2,000 publications, not commercially available, produced by local and national clubs, societies, hobbyists,

collectors, enthusiasts and associations – a sliver of that which is spoken outside of the professionally mediated. The collection was donated to the British Library.

16   Michael Hardt and Antonio Negri make this process explicit in their academic blockbuster, *Empire* (2000). If natural resources are already owned and managed as revenue streams, it is logical that the core processes of bio-power itself will – through the force of law – be turned into resources to profit from. Capitalism begins to mine value from "everyday" structures, habits, and practices – like enthusiasm, conviviality, and generosity.

17   See "The Pro-Am Revolution: How enthusiasts are changing our economy and society" by Charles Leadbeater and Paul Miller, available at www.demos.co.uk/catalogue/proameconomy/ (accessed August 2006).

18   Subsequent versions, reconfigured as *Enthusiasm*, toured to the Whitechapel Art Gallery, London (April 1–May 22, 2005), Kunst Werke, Berlin (June 5–September 4, 2005), and Fundacio Antoni Tapies, Barcelona (October 27–January 15, 2006). See Cummings and Lewandowska 2005.

19   The success of the Creative Commons licenses (www.creativecommons.org, accessed August 2006) rests upon the pioneering work of Richard Stallman and Eben Moglen of the Free Software Foundation. In 1984, they developed the General Public License (GPL) which protects Free, Libre and Open Source Software (FLOSS). The GPL is the foundation of the Creative Commons and most Open Content licenses (www.fsf.org/, accessed August 2006).

20   Here we see connections to many other contemporary artists including Thomas Hirschhorn, Superflex, Becky Shaw, the Copenhagen Free University, Hans Ulrich Obrist, Public Works, and Jeremy Deller, to name but a few.

21   For more information visit www.chanceprojects.com, accessed August 2006.

References

Bennett, T. (1995) *The Birth of the Museum*. London and New York: Routledge.

Bourdieu, P. (1977) *Outline of a Theory of Practice*. Cambridge: Cambridge University Press.

Derrida, J. (1996) *Archive Fever*. Chicago: University of Chicago Press.

Cummings, N. and Lewandowska, M. (2001a) *The Value of Things*. London: August, and Basel: Birkhauser.

Cummings, N. and Lewandowska, M. (2001b) *Capital*. London: Tate Publishing.

Cummings, N. and Lewandowska, M. (2004) *Enthusiasts*, vol. 1. Warsaw: Centre for Contemporary Art.

Cummings, N. and Lewandowska, M. (2005) *Enthusiasm*, vol. 2. London: Whitechapel Art Gallery, Berlin: KW Institute for Contemporary Art, and Barcelona: Tapies Foundation.

Foucault, M. (1974) *The Order of Things*. London: Tavistock.

Mauss, M. (1923–24) 'Essai sur le don. Forme et raison de l'échange dans les sociétés archaïques'. *Année Sociologique,* Paris, 2e série, 1, pp. 30–186.

Hardt, M. and Negri, A. (2000) *Empire*. Cambridge, Mass.: Harvard University Press.

Titmuss, R. M. (1970) *The Gift Relationship: From Human Blood to Social Policy*. London: Allen & Unwin.

Wu, C.-T. (2002) *Privatising Culture: Corporate Art Intervention since the 1980s*. London: Verso.

7

The Politics of Display: Ann-Sofi Sidén's *Warte Mal!*, Art History and Social Documentary

A seminar with Laura Bear,
Clare Carolin, Griselda Pollock,
and Ann-Sofi Sidén.
Edited by Clare Carolin and
Cathy Haynes

The small, rundown town of Dubi in the Czech Republic on the road from Dresden to Prague was once an affluent spa resort and industrial town. It now attracts large numbers of sex tourists, providing what is said to be Europe's longest stretch of roadside prostitution. The women lining the road call out to passing cars, "Warte mal!" ("Hey, wait!"), in German, though their own languages may be Czech, Bulgarian, Russian, or Romany. These women form a significant portion of what some sources estimate are around 10,000 female sex workers active in the Czech Republic. The area around Dubi has long experienced social, ethnic, and economic instability. Its history of transition coupled with the fall of Czech Communism in the so-called Velvet Revolution of 1989 and Dubi's proximity to the recently reunified Germany are significant factors in explaining why the town has increasingly become a centre for prostitution and human trafficking.

In 1999 the Swedish-born artist Ann-Sofi Sidén spent time investigating prostitution in Prague, Cheb, and Dubi in the Czech Republic. She recorded, with a local translator, a series of video interviews with key figures in the sex industry from prostitutes and pimps to the police. She stayed for long periods at the Motel Hubert in Dubi where rooms are rented to prostitutes by the hour. She documented her stay with video, photographs, and a written diary.

The artwork she created from this material exposes the intricate hierarchy of power within Dubi's sex industry defined by gender, ethnicity, nationality, and affluence. *Warte Mal!* employs the visual language of investigative journalism or even home video. At its core is a series of interviews, which appear, against documentary tradition, to be unedited – unmediated, even. However, collaborating with an architect, the artist spun the interview portraits into complex sculptural relationships that surround the visitor and to some extent choreograph their movement and agency. This labyrinthine manifestation of the artwork at times suggested the town plan of Dubi. At other times it recalled sex tourist arcades in other cities around the world. To watch the video portraits, gallery visitors sat inside cubicles that suggested peep-show booths, with the exception that here viewers were exposed to each other through transparent walls. The disconcerting combination of intimacy and distance this fostered was perhaps a main factor behind the artwork's controversy.

Warte Mal! Prostitution after the Velvet Revolution was presented at the Hayward Gallery in London between 17 January and 1 April 2002, and was paired with a solo show of work by Paul Klee. Coinciding with the exhibition, the Hayward held a series of public seminars through which to explore the pressing concerns that the artwork provoked. The first considered the social, historical, and economic relationships between prostitution, human trafficking, and transnational spaces, specifically asking why Dubi became a centre for prostitution. The second debated the political history of struggles around prostitution, power and political reform in Britain. The third, "The politics of display: *Warte Mal!*, art history and social documentary" on 19 February 2002, examined the artwork's politics of representation (figures 7.1, 7.2). This latter event sought to identify *Warte Mal!*'s proximity to television documentary or academic ethnography, and to expose its relationship to art history. The speakers and audience debated *Warte Mal!*'s relationship to visual culture broadly and its particular connection with a modernist literary and artistic tradition attempting to overturn its own conventions – to challenge and expand what art can be – specifically through depictions of the prostitute.

Ann-Sofi Sidén was joined by Laura Bear, Lecturer in Social Anthropology at the London School of Economics, Clare Carolin, curator of the Hayward presentation of *Warte Mal!*, and Griselda Pollock, Professor of Social and Critical Histories of Art at the University of Leeds. This chapter presents an edited transcript of the original seminar of February 2002 – representing, in turn, the artist's, the anthropologist's, the curator's, and the art historian's contributions – followed by a postscript written by each of the speakers at the end of 2004. The political issues at stake seem to us no less pressing, but has the context of the debate changed in the interim? Have the critical interventions of art and social documentary increased? Over time, has the challenge of Sidén's work become less or more important?

Figure 7.1   View of *Warte Mal!* exhibition, Hayward Gallery, 2002. Courtesy of Hayward Gallery. Photograph: Elisabeth Scheder-Bieschen. © Ann-Sofi Sidén.

What the Artist Said

I want to start by talking about the two points of departure that led me to end up in Dubi in the Czech Republic on the border with Germany. First, I was approached by a curator in Holland who wanted to do an independent show in the red light district in Amsterdam and who invited me and other artists to come to Amsterdam where they offered to provide contacts with prostitutes, clients, pimps or bosses, and other people in the trade. So I went to Amsterdam. I'd been there before, and I'm familiar with the theatrical aspect of the glass windows with the girls in them and the men walking past. But for some reason when I got there, I felt I just wanted to get away, and an image kept coming back into my mind. It came from a story told to me by some friends who had traveled through the Czech Republic and Poland just a few years after the Berlin Wall came down. It was an image of a woman standing in the middle of nowhere – in a forest or in open landscape – alone. Or a few women. And the closer you came to a border or a town, sometimes hundreds of them. They are in mini-skirts and obviously they want to stop cars and make some money. This image was so strong because I identified with it myself: I understood the danger of standing there. That isn't because I've been a prostitute but because I hitchhiked a lot when I was young. I'm of the generation that comes on the tail of the hippie movement and a sort of free, expansive, open experience of sex and men. I could do whatever I wanted, I could pick and choose. Sometimes I did bad things and I learned from that. Sometimes I was humiliated. But I was also discovering my sexuality on my own terms, I was choosing it.

For most of the previous six or seven years I'd been living in the United States. I wasn't following what was happening in Europe with the opening up of the Wall and I felt a loss in that.

The image of this girl. I could see her standing there and I know what it is to wait for a car to stop, not knowing who is going to be in that car and what that person is going to do. What was different for me was that I was waiting to go somewhere. The car was going to take me someplace else, to Spain, or to France, or somewhere I wanted to go. But obviously I knew there was a risk involved. Similarly these girls want to go somewhere and to make something of themselves. But the difference is that what's going on on the Czech/German border is a very organized machine which is taking advantage of young women's sexuality. These women don't have the possibility – as I did – to explore their sexuality. They are trapped in this machine. Many of them are slaves. But it's also very complicated, and the longer I stayed there the more this became apparent because there are girls who want to be there, who say "This is my choice, I want to make money this way." I met these girls and they did not seem to be taking it too badly. But there was also the other side.

So I told the people in Amsterdam I wanted to go to the Czech/German border and they helped me a little bit financially. I went there and did the first interview, with Kveta, which is the last interview in the installation. After that interview I thought I wouldn't continue because her testimony was so hard and heavy to hear. I thought I'm not capable of taking care of this. But obviously I did continue.[1]

What the Anthropologist Said

We live in a time when we are fascinated by the real-life details of people's lives. These are a source of entertainment for us in so-called "reality" and "confessional" television shows. They're also a source of facts for marketing research companies who now live with and film families over a period of months in order to sell to them better. In this climate, everyone seems to be interesting for the camera. Now anyone seen through a lens seems to be the bedrock of an entertaining and profitable reality. As a social anthropologist whose discipline is founded on the techniques of participation – listening to and recording people's lives in order to stretch the boundaries of conventional ideas about society – it's very strange to watch this process, this proliferation of images all around us. Anthropological techniques of recording life have spread outside the discipline and are used for very different ends.

Against that context, Ann-Sofi Sidén offers us this exhibition of filmed interviews of people involved in the sex industry in Dubi with whom she lived for nine months. Such an exhibition could easily be seen to fall into the spirit of the time, offering us another standard exposé or a voyeuristic tour. But I want to talk about how this exhibition breaks from current forms of investigating and exploring other people's lives. In particular, I want to look at how it uses the platform of an artwork in a gallery space to question some of the core assumptions of the genres that aim to capture the truth at the core of real life. I will end by discussing how I think it creates a kind of "counter politics of display" through the very viewing experience that it offers. So let me start by talking about what distinguishes *Warte Mal!* from other current forms of investigating and representing lives.

The exhibition cuts through some of the central fictions of the genres of reality TV and academic ethnography. The first of these fictions is the invisibility of the investigator and the objectivity of their eye. Academic and documentary work often leave out the *persona* of the person who records, and the assumption is generally that a reality is presented that is unaffected by the presence of the investigator. But *Warte Mal!*, on the other hand, is an exhibition that constantly points to the ambiguity of the presence of the investigator and *her presence in the framing of the lives we see*. Ann-Sofi Sidén appears in the exhibition as a participant in the lives she records. Her field diary is projected onto a screen and reveals her relationships with the lives of the people who might be called her informants, and we learn of her emotions and her responses to the lives of the women she meets and their responses to her and her translator, with whom one of them, Eva, falls in love. Sidén herself steps into the frame. We see her, for example, dancing on the roadside with Eva. Overall Sidén appears in the exhibition as an investigator, as a friend – sometimes almost the same as the women she meets. She cuts through this pretence of a distant camera or an academic eye objectively recording facts by placing herself and her relationships within the camera frame and the exhibition space. By highlighting the relationships she develops with the sex workers she meets, she undermines the objectification that occurs on confessional TV. Usually sex workers are displayed in this context as examples of a distinct group, rather than as people embedded in the world. It is because *Warte Mal!* is an exhibition and an artwork, rather than an academic text or TV documentary, that Sidén is able to convey the centrality of the position of the observer. Artistic work, by its very nature, is defined by the organizing eye of the artist and her creativity. *Warte Mal!* uses this conventional feature of art to question the objectivity of other genres of production.

Another fiction central to reality TV and social anthropology is that the truth they present is somehow a fixed and finished product. By the time we have finished watching and reading their versions of reality, we feel we have a single organized overview of a situation. But I think *Warte Mal!* undermines this fiction because it exposes different layers of representation. It is built around absent experiences that are never placed on film and it highlights who can and cannot be recorded on film. Sitting in the booths, listening to stories, we can overhear voices from the other booths. Often the accounts from the other booths contradict the story we are hearing in our own booth. Unlike in a documentary, these voices are not coordinated in a debate leading to a conclusion. Instead, the final version of truth never appears. In all of the accounts there are some things we never see. For example, the exchanges of money, sexual acts and violence that are obviously part of the lives of the women in the Motel Hubert remain off the page, upstairs, and unfilmed along with their clients. These absences call into question what can and cannot be shown in the film if it is to remain within the bounds of documentary, rather than other genres such as pornography, for instance. It also makes us wonder who can and cannot be placed under the scrutiny of the camera. Why can we film prostitutes but not their clients, for example? All this leads us to question the very nature of realism in film and in any form of investigation, academic or otherwise. It pushes us to speculate about how inequalities and the conventions of the genre limit the kinds of truths that realism can tell.

But I think the most important effect of *Warte Mal!*, the exhibition, is that unlike any form of academic study or television documentary, it makes us ask questions about our role as an audience. The exhibition brings into view the ambiguity of the position of the audience as consumers of images of other people's lives. Because this is an artwork placed in a gallery, when we see it we are conscious of the reactions of the public all around us consuming these images. Sidén seems to draw our attention to the audience of which we ourselves form a part, and challenges us to consider their – *our* – potentially voyeuristic interest in other people's lives. As we walk around the exhibition we see people sitting in small glass booths and when we first sit in these booths we feel uncomfortable about their similarity to the booths of a peep-show. Equally disturbing is the experience of one of the large projected films. As we watch, we feel as if we are traveling in a car looking out of the window at the lay-bys and the streets with women offering their services to us. We, too, are perhaps in some sense disturbingly like clients in our relationships to these women. Our desire to learn about their lives becomes uncomfortably like a kind of voyeurism. Because Sidén offers us a kind of documentary of ethnographic realism in the context of a gallery, she can disturb our usually solitary, guilty pleasure of being part of an audience on other people's lives. She uses the public space of the gallery to make us question the nature of our relationship to the people that we watch.

Warte Mal! thus offers more than a critique of the sex trade in the Czech Republic, and I suggest that its effect is achieved precisely because it is an exhibited artwork and not a documentary film or an anthropological text.

What the Curator Said

What distinguishes *Warte Mal!* from many of the projects that I have previously worked on is that its engagement with its subject – prostitution after the Velvet Revolution – is, I think, more immediately apparent to the uninitiated viewer than its place within a discourse of and about art. When I first began describing *Warte Mal!* to colleagues involved in the mechanics of presenting and publicizing the show to the public, I found that I needed to think very hard about how the piece should be situated in the wider contexts of art and political and social reality. The question was how to convey the enormous complexity of the experience of seeing this work and its subject matter, and how to situate this in a context that would made sense for the gallery-going public.

On first seeing *Warte Mal!* at the Musée de la Ville de Paris in Spring 2001 I was enormously struck by how vividly the personalities of the interviewees came across. I remember entering the installation with a rough idea of its subject, walking into the booth which contains the interview with Miluse and listening (and watching) the entire thing. Totally engrossed, I then moved on to the adjacent booth – Klaus, Miluse's boyfriend and previously her client – and listened to that interview from start to finish. By the time I arrived in the Dubi room, the main part of the installation, I already felt emotionally drained. On that occasion I don't think I fully registered the horror of the other testimonies: Kveta's, Eva's, Petra's. But later, in the process of transcribing and editing the tapes for the publication that the Hayward Gallery produced to accompany the exhibition (Sidén 2002), I became very well acquainted with these personal histories – so much so that I began to feel the interviewees were people I actually knew. In fact on first seeing the work running at the Hayward, I had the very peculiar sensation of walking into a room full of people I'd been in touch with through correspondence and was now meeting for the first time.

So, to return to the question of how I began to communicate about this work to colleagues and others, what I did – and still find myself

Figure 7.2 View of *Warte Mal!* exhibition, Hayward Gallery, 2002. Courtesy of Hayward Gallery. Photograph: Elisabeth Scheder-Bieschen. © Ann-Sofi Sidén.

doing – was to paraphrase the interviewees' stories. I have found this to be a very effective way of attracting interest in both the work and the subject. This latching on to individual narratives also tends to be the way that reviewers have described the work. People latch onto the individual narratives. Also striking is that their experience of the work tends to mirror my own in as far as one feels the obligation to listen to as much of these stories as one can endure, and that after a time this listening becomes unendurable. What is strange, even shocking to me, is the difficulty that people seem to have in understanding this work as *art* – precisely, I think, because it is so eloquent about its subject and also, it is sometimes implied, because its subject is thought somehow to be beyond the realm of what one should see in an art gallery.

To give a sense of what I mean, here is an excerpt from Sarah Kent's review of *Warte Mal!* in *Time Out* magazine:

Ann-Sofi Sidén's installation is utterly compelling. I spent four hours immersed in the world of sleaze that the Swedish artist explores in videos, photographs and diary entries. This video installation may not be great art but it is certainly obsessive viewing. (Kent 2002, p. 47)

Another reviewer, this time writing for *The Times*, found *Warte Mal!* equally engrossing but also seemed to have trouble understanding it as art. Summing up, Joanna Pitman writes:

> For anyone interested in the human results of geopolitical change in Europe *Warte Mal!* is a potent symbol of the multi-layered tensions in the region that started the century with the promise of something new. I left after two hours feeling dirty, depressed and somehow implicated and nursing a splitting headache. (Pitman 2002, p. 17)

Almost without exception, reviewers and visitors to the exhibition with whom I have spoken describe their experience of the work as a sort of endurance test, making mention of how long they have spent in the installation, as though this was somehow an unexpected and unwelcome investment of their time. By implication they wanted and expected to see a work that would reveal its meaning in a way that was less demanding of their time and attention. It is useful to think about the title of the work here: "*Warte Mal!*", "Wait a minute!" Why do people spend so many minutes in *Warte Mal!*? And why the reluctance to accept the work as art? Is it simply because the gallery-going public (in London particularly) now expects the sort of quick-fix contemporary art that has characterized the past decade and which borrows heavily from the form and language of advertising?

I want to begin to answer these questions obliquely by talking about the American photographer Dorothea Lange, whose work I had very much in mind as I was working on *Warte Mal!* and thinking about its precedents. Lange's best-known photographs were taken between 1935 and 1939 when she was employed by the federally sponsored Farm Security Administration to document and publicize the conditions of the rural poor in America. Writing about her work in 1960, Lange stated that the "benefit of seeing can come only if you pause for a while, extricate yourself from the maddening world of quick impressions battering our lives, the viewer must be willing to pause, to look again, to meditate" (quoted in Hayman & Coles 1998, p. 70).

Lange's best-known photograph is *Migrant Mother* (1936). It was taken during the Depression and its subject is a migrant worker who had fled with her family from the dust bowl of Oklahoma to look for work in California. In journals and interviews Lange speaks again and again about the making of this image. Her approach and attitude to her subject reminds me very much of Ann-Sofi Sidén's. Lange explains:

> I saw and approached the hungry and desperate mother as if drawn by a magnet. I don't know how I explained my presence or my camera to her but I do remember that she asked me no questions. I made five exposures working closer and closer from the same direction. ... She told me her age, that she was 32. She told me that they had been living on frozen vegetables from the surrounding fields and birds that the children had killed. She had just sold the tyres from her car to buy food. There she sat in that lean-to tent with her children huddled around her and seemed to know that my pictures might help her. And so she helped me. There was a sort of equality about it. (Lange & Taylor 1999, p. 50)

Lange was not an "artist" in the sense that Sidén is. She was a documentary photographer. The contexts in which Lange and Sidén have worked are clearly quite different, but I think that the work of both is characterized by an attitude of equality towards their subject. The "artistry" of Lange's work was recognized only towards the end of her life. A retrospective exhibition of her work opened at the Museum of Modern Art in New York in 1965, a few months after she died. Speaking shortly before her death Lange argued that "the real subject of photography is not the actual subject of the photograph but what it provokes" (Hayman & Coles 1998, pp. 127–9). This is a very useful idea to apply to *Warte Mal!*. What will it provoke? What can and will be done with the experience of having seen this work? What will happen next?

What the Art Historian Said

I should like to return to questions already posed in this seminar: namely, What is it that makes *Warte Mal!* an artwork? and Where should this exhibition be placed in the history of representation? I think that these questions are interesting and provocative, and yet they betray a persistent anxiety which pervades our culture about how to ensure that we know what we are looking at. This concern determines the kind of respect or the kind of response that we have to what we see. But is it a bad thing to break down the boundaries between documentary, art, ethnography, and social knowledge? In refusing to be boxed into such categories, perhaps this is precisely what artists such as Ann-Sofi Sidén are exploring. An historical perspective might illuminate this. Instead of thinking about the difference between art and documentary, or art versus anthropology and ethnography, perhaps we could think about a question which is much more fundamental and which concerns regimes of truth: that is, how we are enabled or made to understand the truth through a circulating network of images? Some of these images come from the spaces of popular journalism, common sense repetitions of our culture, from advertising images, films, and anthropologists on television. Others are produced by – or, perhaps, interrupted by – a particular kind of "restating": the knowing and calculated interruption of these normalcies we look to critical art to perform. In this sense, art can contribute to the transformation of social knowledges. Historically, this tradition has taken two directions. The one direction produces what I think Laura Bear has been discussing, which is a certain model of a subject/object knowledge-based paradigm. The subject (whether sociologist, anthropologist, TV documentarist) knows "you," the object of investigation. The other direction – and it is not just an "art" direction because it plays through a number of different practices – is a more effective and situated kind of knowledge, a knowledge which requires an ethics and a politics of who is saying what about whom, or to whom, or with whom, and what are the effects of the way it is being said.

Now, we could situate Ann-Sofi Sidén's work in relation to the development of a tradition of investigative journalism, which we might associate with someone like Henry Mayhew in the mid-nineteenth century. Mayhew, as you may know, went off for the *Morning Chronicle* newspaper to investigate the lives of people living on the edges and in the desperate gaps of new industrial capitalism in the metropolis of London. What is interesting about his investigations is that he reported back the speech of those he spoke to, including trying to transcribe the particularities of their dialects or their inflections of the English language. Soon afterwards anthropology and sociology stopped doing this. They did not want to hear – even in printed form – the actual voice: the anguish, the anger, the irritation, the satire, the irony of those subjects. But I think this tradition asks us, what is it to know about anybody else? How does the encounter with someone different from myself situate me? Am I situated as witness to their social experience, or am I made an observer, dispassionately objectifying them, or even a kind of voyeur? And the question of course is: How does knowledge change me, or change anyone else? Now, if we think of artistic practices as a provocation of discourse by the event that is the artwork, the artwork does not have to contain everything to make something else happen. As many artists suggest, the idea of an artwork is destined to generate interpretations. It wants you to talk about it, not to say "I must find out what it already means." But it also wants to open a space in collective discourse that hitherto was closed down, or censored, or taboo or just became a subject of indifference. So one of the things that I find very interesting about Sidén's work is that it creates a set of situational encounters that belong to this venerable tradition of the provocation to culture to think about something it rather would not.

Prostitution was one of the key themes of nineteenth-century culture. Those great thinkers who were concerned with what made the modern world "modern" fixated repeatedly on the figure of the prostitute who seemed a figure of marginality and, therefore, attracted a sort of mythical identification from those who also found themselves marginal. But equally, and I think particularly in the work of Walter Benjamin, the prostitute was this completely unbearable paradox of both the seller and the commodity in one – something which I think captured the horror of capitalism as it was literally going to penetrate everybody and corrupt every last vestige of humanity. In a sense prostitution is the uncovered world of social destitution and human degradation that is both a product of capitalism and an embodiment of it. So what is going to be our relationship to this?

The great modernists built their artistic careers and their gambits on the prostitutional body: one thinks of Manet's *Olympia* (1863), for instance, or Picasso's *Demoiselles d'Avignon* (1907), or even De Kooning's *Woman* series (1951–3) (because there is a prostitutional association in that of a more biographical kind). Now what I think is different about Sidén's work, which gives it a certain piquancy at this moment, is that the person in the frame with these working-class women is a woman herself. We are in a completely different gendered universe when a woman talks to other women across this space because the nineteenth-century images of modernity were based on cross-class, cross-sexual exchanges: bourgeois men and working-class women. The artists Berthe Morisot and Mary Cassatt could not engage in that particular dialogue: their conception of modernity had to remain somewhere else. But something very interesting is happening when we can actually see Sidén in the space – in the "frame," as Laura Bear has suggested. Different from Brassai, or from E. J. Bellocq, the photographer who took pictures in brothels in New Orleans in the early 1900s.

I want to link this, finally, to a moment that I think was historically very important. It was associated with a feminist moment, a feminist intervention in the possibilities of the art that disrupted and transformed modernism: namely Conceptual Art. I am thinking of a series of very remarkable exhibitions of the 1970s: Mary Kelly's *Post Partum Document* show at London's Institute of Contemporary Art in 1975; Martha Rosler's work on the inhabitants of the Bowery (1974–5); Hans Haacke's work on the Shapolosky real estate scam (1971). I am brought to mind particularly of the film *The Night Cleaners* (1975) that was made by members of the Women's Liberation Movement working with May Hobbs and a group of women who worked as contract cleaners in office buildings struggling for unionization. These kinds of films and artworks precisely had to disengage from what had become the conventional aesthetic frame – that would present their work as "art" – in order to reinvigorate the shock of the encounter between a kind of social and historical "real" and the viewer.

I think what was interesting about nineteenth-century modernism – Manet's *Olympia* or Picasso's *Demoiselles d'Avignon* – was that you, "*the viewer*" (however gendered or sexed you are), are positioned by the presumed structure of the painting as if participating in a particularly prostitutional space. What is interesting about the installation structure of *Warte Mal!* is that it weaves a web around you. It captures you in the threads of discourse, and image, and space in a variety of different ways that equally has that quality – not of documentary that removes the viewer from the picture and gives you a privileged view – but much rather like the paintings of the nineteenth-century moment of modernity. Except that it is putting you in the position of a female investigator, a woman artist, who is exploring – in the sense Sidén herself suggests – what it means for her sense of sexuality and subjectivity to have to listen to the words of young women whose sexuality and subjectivity has been crushed and captured, or "enslaved" within what is called the world of "freedom," the world of "free trade." It brings back a kind of viscous dimension to the question of what the world of capitalist modernity in its untrammeled way has meant. I think the question is provoked by the discourse at the very beginning of this installation of the woman (Miluse) speaking about the benefits as well as the limitations of the Communist era when at least as a single mother she was protected from having to feed her children by selling her body. If there is any sad story about this in terms of history, it is the story that we have been sold about what a great thing it was to have killed off socialism in Europe, to have let capitalism and McDonalds and everything flow into Prague and Warsaw and Bucharest. I think that the work achieves this complex effect precisely because it is made by a woman and precisely because it is art.

Postscript 2004

Ann-Sofi Sidén: *Warte Mal!* has now been shown at the following institutions: Secession, Vienna (1999); Moderna Museet, Stockholm (2000); Musée d'Art Moderne de la Ville de Paris (2001); the Hayward Gallery, London (2002); Kölnischer Kunstverein, Cologne (2003); Baltic Art Center, Gotland (2003–4); and Basis voor Actuele Kunst, Utrecht (2004). At each new showing, I take the opportunity to sit and spend time with the piece. It is like seeing old friends. I know them by heart: each and every character. Even though time fictionalizes – a process that began as soon as I started editing the piece – the immediacy and display of the video recordings have the same impact on me today as they did then. It is as if it all just happened yesterday.

I had begun exchanging letters with one of the girls, but since 2002 we have had no contact. I visited her several times after my work was completed. Last time I saw her she was still working for the same guy in Dubi. Through letters, I found out that she had escaped once, crossing the border using a friend's passport. She went with a German boyfriend/client who was suffering from cancer and lived with him for some months until he was finally admitted to hospital. His friends put her on a train back to the Czech Republic and she went back to working for her old pimp. During one of my visits I insisted on giving her money to pay for a dental work she had had done and complained about having to pay off, but she refused to take it. Instead I had to give the money to the pimp's girlfriend who then paid the dentist. I had never given her money before, directly or indirectly, and after this our relationship changed. She tried several things afterwards to make me give her money. I think this was also discussed with her pimp.

Once she said she had gotten pregnant with the German dying of cancer and that the baby had been placed in a foster home. But when I wanted to open an account for the baby on one of my visits to Dubi there was no baby to see. The individual stories still keep me spellbound, angry and helpless in the same way as when I first assembled *Warte Mal!*.

I am of the belief that any testimony conceals as much as it reveals. With the prism closely focused on one subject, you become aware of many other subjects around it. As the basic understanding becomes clear while watching, the detail of the present keeps changing and consequently also "the whole" of which it is a part. This could be applied to both the viewing of *Warte Mal!* as a piece of art, but also to reality itself.

Griselda Pollock: The encounter with Ann-Sofi Sidén's work *Warte Mal!* was profound. Shortly after seeing it and participating in the Hayward Gallery seminar, I went to the United States where I lectured on the installation and its companion show at the time: an exhibition of the work of Paul Klee. More different two shows could not be – the one exemplifying a personal trajectory through modernist artistic form; the other engaged with video, installation, and some aspect of the documentary tradition in relation to vivid social issues of prostitution in post-Soviet Eastern Europe. I argued that what they had in common was the search for an aesthetic structure by means of which we, the viewers, could be put in a new relation – of knowledge and responsibility – to the world. Present at the lecture in the United States was the artist Carol Jacobsen, whose work also questions deeply the structures of power and the unequal distribution of rights in relation to the oppressive treatment of women, often from minority cultures in US prisons. Her dramatic installations based on photomontage and text have been taken up by Amnesty International in its struggle to reveal the abuses of human rights within American prisons – a continuing fact of American life that was not brought out when the shock discoveries of the abuse of Iraqi detainees in Abu Graib hit the headlines in May 2004. What do we allow ourselves to know and what do we allow sensational reporting of events elsewhere to disguise from us about the constant and daily abuse of human rights that constitute the normalcy of Western societies?

Since *Warte Mal!* was shown at the Hayward Gallery in 2002 information about the extensive trafficking in women worldwide has increased. Notably, there have been many television programs about the horrific trade in women from the former Soviet Bloc, women who are entrapped into the resuscitated "white slave trade" by offers of jobs in catering and club work only to find themselves forcibly drugged and sexually abused, traded on between gangs and groups across Europe. One recent docudrama on British television highlighted the extent of this traffic in women across Europe to Britain and North America. But I hear no outcry resulting from these revelations such as that which attended the publishing of the evidence of regular and routine abuse of male prisoners in Iraqi jails. What is it that renders people impervious to the horror of present-day trafficking in women whom economic necessity drives to seek employment in the service industries of the West only to be brutally degraded and reduced to the most powerless body parts servicing consumers of sexual services who are exclusively male? I am left with the question posed by Sidén's subtly structured interpersonal encounters with gender and the social and economic conditions of post-cold war Europe: what am I, as a woman, if this is what she experiences "as a woman"?

I am fully aware that there is a strong argument for not being hysterical about prostitution, treating it as a form of work, whose conditions and practices need to be regulated for the safety and support of its workers. But the case of trafficked women is not the same. They are not workers by choice and have not any power to decide for or against prostitution as a sex industry. They are enslaved, forced into practices by inflicted brutality, loss of freedom, and threat of death if they try to escape. They are often introduced by force to drug addictions that both tame their resistance and render them more pliable to their exploiters. Trafficking women seems to me a profound crime against human rights and one that speaks clearly of the utter inequality of the sexes in the modern world. If women "choose" within the limits of economic conditions to practice in the sex industry and have the means of organizing into unions and other groupings to attempt to define a space and place for themselves as workers in an industry for which their services are in demand, this is completely different from the current trade in women who are unknowingly trapped into forced and abusive prostitution without hope of escape and entirely at the mercy of gangs of male controllers. In the docu-drama to which I referred above, the determinant of trade was spelt out: demand.

The treacherous field that Sidén's work made visible – provoking cultural debate precisely through herself engaging with a tiny fragment of this world of the sex-trade that so starkly raises the question of gender, power, sexuality and rights – is as "hot" and contested now as it was when she made the work. But far from being a blip in the accommodation of Eastern Europe to the West, it seems that the traffic in women from east to west is now major business. Her work made me engage with this issue: prostitution that has figured as an image for modernity since its inception.

I wonder if she is ready to take this work further. For unless the matter is framed for us by artists who develop economies of representation through which to oblige the viewer to rethink the world thus re-presented, the endemic indifference of phallocentric cultures to the vile abuse of women will continue to permit a traffic in women far more disturbing than that witnessed by Sidén in *Warte Mal!*.

Laura Bear: In the current environment *Warte Mal!* has become even more significant. The circulation of people's "real lives" consumed for pleasure has continued on TV. The economy of London is now linked to the sex trade that emerged with the end of Communism. Down the street from my house young women with Romanian accents lean out of windows smoking. They are taking a break from web-chats with their clients. Sidén's exhibition offered us – and continues to offer us – a counter-politics of display to these trends by the ways it cut through the indifference of audiences and of neighbors. It achieved this by slowing down the experience of viewing. In the exhibition we traveled to Dubi, but we did not do this with the speed of a passing client from across the German border or at the even pace of someone watching a TV program. We had to listen to people's stories, piecing them together and lingering over them until we worked out their relationships. We had to "dwell in" rather than just "travel through" this place. The rhythm of the exhibition pushed us to give some of the span of our own lives to these life stories. We could no longer be a consumer of lives or an indifferent distant neighbour. Instead, like Ann-Sofi Sidén and all good social anthropologists, we dwelt with, learned from and were changed by other human beings. *Warte Mal!* turned the old tool of social anthropology, participant observation, to direct political ends. This is why it continues to have the potential to transform a viewing audience into an engaged public.

Clare Carolin: When *Warte Mal!* was shown at the Hayward Gallery in early 2002 it was relatively rare, at least in London, for contemporary art using the forms and methods of documentary and anthropology to appear in the context of a large- or medium-scale institution. In the preceding years there was no shortage of art of this type being made and shown, but it tended to be seen at international biennials or in more modest – often artist-run – spaces. As the panel discussion and ensuing debate about *Warte Mal!* make clear, the "social documentary" cast of Sidén's work, over and above its subject matter which, as Griselda Pollock explains, has a long history as a subject for modern artists, was perhaps the single most important factor in making the exhibition a controversial entity. Simultaneously, while this combination of factors may have confounded many of its reviewers and visitors, the institutional framing of the exhibition was designed, on the face of it, to contain any controversy generated by the work within the bounds of the scheduled debate.

In the short space of time that has elapsed since *Warte Mal!*'s appearance at the Hayward, and I believe as a direct consequence of the events and legacy of 11 September 2001, "politically engaged" contemporary art which uses documentary, sociological, and anthropological forms and methods to hold a mirror up to increasingly disturbing realities has become completely absorbed into the institutional canon. So much so that Matt Collins (the most familiar face of British TV journalism for the visual arts) was broadcast recently whispering to the camera that "the political is now fashionable." Collins was talking about the work of the artists on the shortlist for the 2004 Turner Prize, all of who used film and video at some stage in their display at Tate Britain, and three of who used it to record real (i.e. non-fictional) subjects. *Memory Bucket*, the documentary film by the winner of the prize, Jeremy Deller, looked at the religious and nationalistic confusions of contemporary America. The film was screened in a straightforward viewing situation – just a screen, no installation around it – and seemed to generate more interest from the press and the public, who on the day I visited the show were crowded three and four deep around it, than any other single item in the display.

It is refreshing to see the reintroduction of overt political content into the institutional frame – particularly given the tendencies in visual arts that preceded it. However, I would contest that there are two critical differences in the approach taken by the exhibitors in the 2004 Turner Prize display and that taken by Ann-Sofi Sidén in *Warte Mal!*. The first has to do with the manner in which the forms and methods of other disciplines are deployed and the second has to do with motivation.

As both Laura Bear and Griselda Pollock make clear in their contributions to the seminar, what distinguished *Warte Mal!* and made it so uniquely absorbing was the skill and subtlety with which Sidén combined the methods of anthropology and social documentary (used in the compilation and recording of the "raw material" of the interviews, photographs, and field diary) with an understanding of how audiences might respond to the material when it was presented in a way that exploited and played upon the natural theater of the art gallery viewing situation. In *Warte Mal!* the complex mechanics of exploitation on which prostitution is dependent, and of which it is part, took the form of an elaborate, but instantly intelligible spatial metaphor. In stark contrast to Deller's relatively straight look at a distorted reality, Sidén's work was the equivalent of a hall of mirrors, in which visitors were reflected and implicated in the issue of prostitution.

Contrast the Turner Prize offerings again with *Warte Mal!* in terms of motivation and you find that at least three of the major video works, Yinka Shonibare's *Un Ballo in Maschera* (2004), Deller's *Memory Bucket* (2004), and Ben Langlands and Nikki Bell's *The House of Osama bin Laden* (2003), were commissioned. This is not to imply that the artists involved were not working with material and themes with which they felt intimately involved, but the commissioning structure is unresponsive to circumstance; it does not allow for major changes of plan, or direction, or heart. As Sidén explains at the opening of the seminar, her motivation for making the work was explicitly personal. She had rejected the commissioning formula offered in Amsterdam in favor of taking her work in a different direction – one she identified with having herself been a lone female hitchhiker in the past. As a result of the time spent in Dubi making *Warte Mal!* she formed close and lasting friendships with many of her subjects and this comes through in the gut-wrenching interviews that are at the core of her work. In turn, the individual stories of these women, when woven together in the installation, gave us a meta-story about geopolitical change, power structures and art itself – which for me remains an unequaled example of a work of art addressing political issues so effectively that the work transcends its status as cultural artifact and becomes more than the sum of its parts.

I would like to think that *Warte Mal!* at the Hayward Gallery and its related program of public seminars was more than a mere consciousness-raising exercise for a minority. For me the power of the work remains undimmed by time, despite the fact that I have not actually seen the tapes for a number of years now. More than any other exhibition I have worked on, it still exerts a slow-release effect provoking regular enquiries and interest. It is reassuring to know that it continues to be shown regularly and to provoke interest in a variety of cultural contexts. I hope that this will continue for many years and that the work will gain new audiences and readings as time goes by, because the problems it addresses show no sign of abating.

Note

1 Transcriptions of the interviews have been published in the exhibition catalogue (Sidén 2002).

References

Hayman, T. and Coles, R. (1998) *Dorothea Lange: Photographs of a Lifetime.* New York: Aperture.
Kent, S. (2002) *Time Out.* Issue 1641, January 30.
Lange, D. and Taylor, P. S. (1999 [1939]) *An American Exodus: A Record of Human Erosion in the Thirties.* Paris: Editions Jean Michel Place.
Pitman, J. (2002) 'Shame of the game.' *The Times 2*, January 16, p. 17.
Sidén, A-S. (2002) *Warte Mal! Prostitution after the Velvet Revolution.* London: Hayward Gallery.

8

From Exhibiting to Installing Ethnography: Experiments at the Museum of Anthropology of the University of Coimbra, Portugal, 1999–2005

Nuno Porto

The purpose of this chapter is to discuss the notion that ethnographic exhibitions may and, I argue here, should, be conceived as experiments in contemporary anthropological practice. There are two movements involved in this proposal. On the one hand, this view suggests that the disciplinary practices which sustain anthropology texts – the canonical materialization of anthropological knowledge – are to a large degree the same as those that sustain the making of ethnographic exhibitions. On the other hand, it pushes the argument further into making explicit the fact that skills which are specific to the making of anthropological knowledge are also crucial to the process of exhibition making, be these ethnographic or otherwise. In order to specify the kind of exhibitionary experimentation involved in these movements, I propose that the notion of "ethnographic installation" may be useful.

Ethnographic installation, I suggest, conveys the experimental mood that has sustained both ethnographic production and exhibition-making processes in much contemporary anthropology. In contrast to the notion of "ethnographic exhibition," ethnographic installation takes as its point of departure the recognition that there is no such thing as a "neutral" point of view or exhibitionary space. Instead, installation requires that concept development, script and scenography are based specifically on what is to be displayed, and the materialization of the concept in a particular venue. My proposal is partly grounded in personal experience of playing a part in creating four exhibitions held at the Museum of Anthropology of the University of Coimbra, Portugal, between 1999 and 2005. Before discussing these exhibitions, I will try to outline the theoretical and practical context involved.

Anthropological Context 1: Switzerland and UK

Such contextualization is necessarily partial. I suggest, however, that although the individuals and institutions involved in examples that I discuss have been operating in relative isolation, their works nevertheless share a wider concern to incorporate reflection on modes of representation into exhibition-making processes. This concern has been termed the "interpretive turn" (e.g. Rabinow & Sullivan 1977) in anthropology and, later, in relation to its more reflexive dimensions, as "an experimental moment" in the human sciences (Marcus & Fischer 1986). These developments raised pertinent epistemological and methodological issues related to anthropological practice, especially those relating to cultural representation and scientific authority. The debate concentrated on forms of textual representation, and identified rhetorical tropes such as the co-presence of ethnographer and subject ("being there," as Geertz termed it (1973)), the reference to subjects as a collective persona ("the Kwakiutl" or "the Balinese"), or the suppression of historical relations with other groups. This work was begun primarily in the US anthropological context, though the identification of a set of "modern tropes" in anthropological work – with serious proposals for overcoming their drawbacks – was also undertaken elsewhere (by Bourdieu, for example, during the 1970s in France (Bourdieu 1972)). In each of these developments – all of which recognized the role of the anthropologist as author – there was an acknowledgment of the anthropologist's work as part of ongoing subjective relationships.

A similar critique was also taking place within the exhibitionary field. A team from the Neuchâtel Ethnography Museum (NEM), Switzerland – notably Jacques Hainard and Roland Kaher – had been fine-tuning a reflexive approach to museum culture through a series of ethnographic exhibitions at least since their *Collections/Passion* exhibit in 1982. They conceived the museum as a site of cultural mediation. Their perspective has over time become "total" in the sense that NEM has come to institutionalize products of their reflexive work which not only center on exhibition processes but also involve wider reflection about the kind of institution museums are, could be, or should be. What was distinctive about such work was the deliberate choice of exhibition concepts that addressed "public culture" issues, the use of experimental aesthetics incorporating a critique of authoritative modes of display and the collection of essays edited for each exhibition project. For example, *Ethno Poche* (*Texpo*[1] from 1994 on) was conceived as an erudite/popular alternative to the expensive, "coffee-table" catalogue common to museum exhibitions. These (non-)catalogues, pocket-book size, have no pictures and are not printed on expensive glossy paper but are instead inexpensive edited volumes in which several authors address the exhibition theme, showing that there is no single point of view and underlining the fact that exhibitions are, as James Clifford emphasized of ethnographic texts (1988), partial at best. Cultural representation and interpretation are intertwined in these volumes and presented as non-authoritative. NEM has also sought to engage further with its (mainly local) audiences, by incorporating their reactions into subsequent exhibitions. This is one of the rare places where a distinctive curatorial practice has overlapped institutional identity.

Other examples of experimentalism in ethnographic museums include the work of Anthony Shelton in the UK, who has deliberately tried to establish a dialogue with the British arts scene by subjecting it to anthropological scrutiny. This was so in his *Fetishism: Visualising Power and Desire* exhibition at Brighton Museum and Art Gallery in 1995, and even more so in his major reformulation of the Horniman Museum's African collections in the *African Worlds* exhibition, the first permanent exhibition of African art and culture in London. The *African Worlds* exhibition features the installation of Egyptian artifacts at the entrance of the exhibition hall, describing them as "African art," thus proposing an alternative descent for African artifacts (in museums and elsewhere), as well as combining this genealogy with "diasporic" artifacts expressly made for the exhibition by contemporary African artists. Both these movements work against the notion of "primitiveness" publicly imprinted in the notion of "African art" (cf. Errington 1994), thus enabling historical collections – such as those at the Horniman – to be used as a means of addressing current concerns of African communities, in Africa or elsewhere.

Anthropological Context 2: Portugal

As well as these broader trends in museum practice, the context for the contemporary work of the Museum of Anthropology of the University of Coimbra (MAUC) necessarily also incorporates matters more specific to Portugal itself. In Portugal, a related reflexive movement has been led by anthropologists working as independent curators. A landmark here was Mary Bouquet and Jorge Freitas Branco's *Melanesian Artifacts* produced for the National Museum of Ethnology (Lisbon) in 1989. *Melanesian Artifacts* was a complex reflection on the nature of collecting in Portugal, setting the practice against the backdrop of the Portuguese colonial empire, world political economy and history. Thus a collection of Melanesian artifacts, obtained by the seizure of a German vessel as it traveled to Hamburg during World War I, became a material anchor for reflecting on the nature of collecting, on the knowledge artifacts may provide and, broadly speaking, on the cultures of collecting.

The project inspired J. A. Fernandes Dias's production (again as independent curator) of *Memory of Amazonia* at Porto. Initially based on an earlier exhibition of the same name at MAUC in 1991 – exclusively based on the eighteenth-century collection of Amazonian artifacts collected by the naturalist Alexandre Rodrigues Ferreira – the reworked exhibition added the notions of territoriality and ethnicity, commented on the historical artifacts with contemporary artifacts and artworks, and linked the historical collections to the debate over indigenous land in contemporary Brazil. As a result, this exhibition led to another – co-curated in cooperation with representatives of Brazilian indigenous communities – held at Manaus, in Brazil, in 1998 (*Memory of Amazonia . . . in Amazonia*).

That Fernandes Dias was responsible for this experimentation was not coincidental: as a specialist in contemporary art, being the sole anthropologist who is Professor at the Lisbon Fine Arts School, he acts as a mediator between anthropology and the arts scene (see Dias 2001). Such mediation, traffic and intertwining is a further facet of the broader movement underway, as has increasingly become acknowledged by both the anthropological and art worlds.[2]

Both in Portugal and beyond, it is possible to recognize, during the 1980s and 1990s, the emergence of the anthropologist-cum-curator as contemporary to the acknowledgment of the anthropologist-as-author. The coincident emergence of these attests to the awareness that cultural mediation is partly a political matter in a broader sense. Furthermore, this awareness occurs in a historical period in which there has been increasing call from source communities – those usually the object of ethnographic representation – for museums to reframe their exhibitions (Arnoldi 1999) or to permit community members to become co-curators of exhibitions (Karp and Levine 1991; Clifford 1997).

This kind of meta-museological exercise is part, therefore, of a broader context of the crisis of anthropology, of wider epistemological and methodological discussions, and of a more general shift toward addressing the public cultural arena and the context of exhibition. It is this last, the context of exhibition, that is likely to be most variable. Attending to specific audiences, competing in particular settings, and dealing with different organizational and funding arrangements, all mean that experimental ethnographic exhibitions which are comparable in conceptual and formal terms may be the product of quite different networks, agencies and interests.

The Arts Scene from an Anthropological Perspective: Material Culture

For British audiences, the *Material Culture* exhibition, subtitled *The Object in British Art of the 1980s and 90s*, may exemplify a move led by artists, art critics, and art historians to go beyond the conventional disciplinary borders of their fields and incorporate theoretical reflection from other disciplines, in this case from anthropology. Held in 1997 at the Hayward Gallery (a major venue for art exhibitions in London), the curators stated that the title was borrowed from "anthropologists and archaeologists to describe the physical products . . . of peoples under their scrutiny" and that it was being used here as "a way of focusing attention in a new way on British art of the past twenty years or so," thereby blurring genres of "painting" or "sculpture" (Archer & Hilty 1997).

In anthropology, a renewed emphasis on material culture was consolidated in the 1990s in a groundbreaking journal – the *Journal of Material Culture* – and a new anthropological interest in art, under the totemic spell of Alfred Gell's *Art and Agency* (1998), in which contemporary arts were subject to anthropological analysis and interpretation. A comparable move had also been taken in the US, inspired by James Clifford's and Fred Myers's insights on the relations between art and culture (Clifford 1988; Myers 1995). These all contributed to an interest shared by both anthropologists and artists in art as – to put it bluntly – a social practice. Susan Hiller's work – both the artworks and the theoretical mediation between art and anthropology – is the pioneering example of such a move from the arts scene (Hiller 1991; Einzig 1996). The context is, therefore, of a growing traffic of concepts, purposes, and practices. Notions of "fieldwork" and "participant observation" became incorporated in artistic practice which, in turn, reclaimed its social purpose as one of mediation and social critique (see, for instance, Küchler 2000, Kwon 2000, or Rorimer 2000).

For the sake of inventory, one would probably also need to include the French experiment on the destitution of the category of "African art," materialized in the much traveled and reviewed *Magiciens de la Terre* exhibition of 1989. Somehow the awareness of the existence of contemporary artists who claimed their African identity paved the way for recognizing anthropological attention to the politics attached to notions such as "African art" and the renewal of analysis incorporating the contemporary arts. The traffic between the arts scene and anthropology may be seen as part of a process of decolonizing disciplinary fields and institutional arenas that are no longer characterized by a single, Western, authoritarian voice.

Institutional Background

To state that exhibitions are related to the museological context of their production is by now a truism. The defining specificity of the MAUC is the fact that it is a university museum – the last operating in Portugal with such status – directly linked to the Department of Anthropology of the same university. In terms of "museum culture" (following Sherman and Rogoff's 1994 expression) the fact of being a university museum haunts the institution with Sturtevant's (1969) question (formulated with the late 1960s US context in mind): "Does anthropology need museums?" While this can mobilize the museum in a positive way, it also accounts for the fact that exhibitions are a marginal part of what the museum is about: the conservation of the collections and the teaching and research cooperation with the University anthropology department are regarded as more important. The Anthropology Museum receives its funding from the University and is technically a section of the Natural History Museum (NHM) of the University's Faculty of Sciences and Technology, to which its technical staff are affiliated. It is directed, on a two-year circulating basis, by one professor of the anthropology department, who is responsible for giving scientific direction, and a permanent member of the staff of the Anthropology Section of the NHM. Funding depends on the Science and Higher Education Ministry policies, which are currently set according to a per capita value of students. Although the NHM staff budget is assured, since it has no students (it is not a teaching unit), the museum has had to rely for the rest of its budget on receiving a percentage of the Faculty general budget. This is very close to nothing (€ 5,000 in 2005). Each exhibition project, therefore, has to raise its own funding from a variety of sources – the university itself, state agencies, and private institutions. The positive side of this otherwise harsh situation is that if material means are gathered for making an exhibition, there are few other constraints. Exhibitions at the MAUC – very much like the teaching content of departmental courses – do not have to respond to issues of popularity, public taste, and so forth. Exhibitions are, therefore, primarily academically driven. This is true of the examples which follow, all of which draw on notions of ethnographic installation and experiment.

Installing Ethnography

If a growing stream of ethnographic exhibitionary practice seems to be identifiable, the question remains as to why anthropologists should deal with the notion of installation. I suggest two reasons: one historical and the other more pragmatic.

Looking back to early ethnographic displays from around the 1920s, the period in which anthropology came of age, it can be seen that the idea that ethnographic objects were somehow art-like has long been present. The art-likeness of *ethnographica* could derive from the primitiveness of their creators, or merely from an exoticist point of view of other cultures. Nevertheless, the double territories between which *ethnographica* moved when displayed in "the West" fueled public interest in these objects, especially after early twentieth-century painters and sculptors detected in them formal solutions for their own artistic practices. In fact, even the debate on the legitimacy of modern colonialism engaged partly in debates on rationality which, in turn, related eventually to the "primitive people's" plastic capacities (e.g. in dealing with realistic representations of humans) and, hence, rationality (see Mack 1994 for the exhibition, in London, of "Kuba art" collected by Emil Torday). In other words, even if not conceived as such by their producers, the display of *ethnographica* has, historically speaking, implied installation techniques, in the sense that the organization of the ordering of objects, the exhibition text, choice of display materials, lighting, colors, sound, and so forth create an "environment" for the objects. This has been, at best, a creative, ill-ruled, customized process with no definitive recipes, which engaged venue, objects, ideas, and public and social networks in a common goal, just as installation art projects do. Therefore, since neutrality – even if intended – is not an achievable goal, an awareness of exhibition design processes becomes crucial for conscious, deliberate and programmatic curatorial intervention in this practice. Installation procedures – both conceptual and practical – may thus be thought of as integral to the mediation process that exhibitions consist of. As Latour points out (1993), unlike a mere intermediary, a mediator partly constructs whatever it mediates. Cultural mediation thus becomes central to exhibitionary practice; and those designing exhibitions need to make decisions about content and forms of display on the basis of exhibitionary purpose rather than, say, the public's preferences or curatorial notions of "aesthetic" presentation.

Therefore, a second, more pragmatic, reason for the adoption of installation techniques in ethnographic displays may be thought of as deriving from the fact that either as "cultural mediation" or as "cultural critique," exhibition projects occur within the dynamics of social contexts, being, necessarily, tainted by the circumstance of local social life. It is not only relevant to make clear what and how to exhibit, but to whom, where, and when. Even if exhibition projects are seldom perceived as such, they tend to be site- (and time-)specific, thus calling for "reframing" when remounted elsewhere not only on account of physical constraints (such as size and shape of venues) but also because of the nature of the venue (e.g. an art gallery, a public museum, or a university museum). Exhibition projects disclose different levels of translation and mediation which are implicit to the process of transforming concepts into something which is worth visiting. Such has been the case of the MAUC exhibitions which I will now go on to discuss.

Installing Ethnography at the MAUC 1999–2005

Angola in Black & White: photography and science at the Dundo Museum 1940–1970 (1999)[3]

This exhibition was based on the photographic archive of the Diamonds Company of Angola (DCA), a chartered company operating in the North Lunda District of what was then Portuguese Angola. DCA had established a museum – the Dundo Museum – in 1936 as a repository for local material culture (mainly Lunda and Tschokwe) which was vanishing because of colonial occupation. The photographic archive mainly concerned the company's museum activities.

Photography was used at the Diamonds Company as a long-distance managerial device. Photographs circulated from the Dundo to Lisbon and back, and were used in monthly and annual reports by different sections of the Company (e.g. health, education, mining). These reports were read and commented on in Lisbon from where instructions, partly based on them, followed to the Dundo, and where exhibitions, also based on the reports and including some of the photographs, were produced.

Central to the argument of the MAUC exhibition was that photographs could be seen as objects that circulated along the managerial networks of the Company; and that, as such, they were means of control. That is, they were presented not mainly as objective "representations" but as tools of record, surveillance and decision making, the "meaning" of which relied on a network of "print colonialism." In the context of the Diamonds Company, they were also a state-of-the-art technology, articulating with its institutional hi-tech culture. To exhibit these photographs was, therefore, also to set out this hi-tech culture, as well as the particular colonial project in which it was implicated.

The exhibition was a relatively high-budget project. In terms of content, it definitely qualified as a "tight-script" exhibition, in the sense that the circuit was sequential, cumulative, and prescriptive. Very little room was left for wandering around as visitors were forced (by layout, furniture, and space design) to flow along the structure of discourse set out.

The production team involved architects who designed all the furniture, a graphic designer responsible for unifying all texts, labels, captions, posters, leaflets, tickets, and catalogue, and photographers who produced enlargements of chosen pictures following local aesthetics and techniques. The research for the exhibition was part of a PhD project, which also drew on scientific guidance from two senior anthropologists and consultancy from another. Graduate students of the department participated in the process of mounting the exhibition, which was divided into three main sections occupying the 450 square meters of the gallery: (1) photography as a means of producing reality; (2) photography as an archival object; (3) photography as a tool for surveillance, displacement, and knowledge production.

A secondary notion involved in the presentation of these concepts relates to the idea of displacement. Visitors, it was decided, should feel that they have moved in time and space and should have the sense, while visiting the exhibition, of being under surveillance – a common sensation expressed in published accounts of travelers to the Dundo during the colonial period. The idea that this was a colonial corporation was translated by the architects into the physical display media. The gallery – consisting of a large hall and the college cloister – was colonized by a 25-meter-long iron and glass wall, exhibiting photographs and their several transformations as archive products, internal reports, and printed publications. At the entrance to the exhibition, visitors faced the back of this wall as they were guided into the cloister, where the first section of the exhibition was divided into two cubes – one white and one black.

Inside the white cube, institutional films on the DCA were shown. The idea was that these films could act as an introduction to the Company, Angola, and colonialism, through a "cleaned" image that the whiteness of the cube underlined. Moving from the white cube to the black cube, the visitor saw a Tschokwe mask – made by Dundo Museum sculptors – displayed under the caption "This is not a mask." On its side, four differently framed photographs of the mask being exhibited – illustrating the specifics of photographic image production (field depth and frame) – were accompanied by the caption "This is not a mask either."

From this play with photographic representation the visitor entered the black cube which was, in fact, a photographic dark room. Inside was a table with a photographic enlarger, and the tanks and chemicals, and several different proofs of the photographs the visitor had faced outside. These indicated different levels of manipulation that the black and white negative may be subjected to (framing, gradient, contrast, and so forth). The point was that photographs are less the "pencil of nature" than a "man-made" artifact.

Exiting the dark room the visitor entered the second section, which presented photographs as archive objects, much as – and this was partly the point – museum objects. To stress the physical nature of these photographs-as-archival-objects it was crucial that they could be seen on both sides since their reverse is stamped with the Dundo Museum's archival number and section. After strenuous discussions, the architects came up with a design solution for this requirement for the visitor to see both sides of the photographs: iron-framed 'cabinet-file' tables with photographs displayed in pivoting glass mounts (see figure 8.1). Each table housed six photographs standing one after the other, rather like an archival card index system. These devices were crucial to the argument of this section, because they displaced vision to the manual gesture of flipping each image over to see the next and, in so doing, revealing its stamped reverse side, and also relating the act of handling to the act of viewing. The use of the devices encouraged the visitor to engage with the photograph as object, and articulated this with an archival use: hierarchy, order, sequence, grouping.

Each room of the Dundo Museum was represented by an enlarged photograph of that room and a cabinet-file table containing photographs of different resolutions of the enlarged photograph. From here, the visitor could enter the hall, where she would first see her reflection in a mirror on which Lamprey's 2-inch quadricule was printed.[4] This provided a motif for the following stands, which displayed "biographies" of anthropometric-like photographs showing the materials that marked their transformation into scientific evidence published in the articles of the Company's scientific journals. The visitor was confronted with the same photograph at different stages, which showed how captions of a single event became abstracted to form scientific evidence. The visitor then moved to the actual 27 boxes of the archive and, finally, to four mirrored stands containing photographs of "distinguished guests" to the museum – among which she would see her own reflection, observing herself as one of them.

Figure 8.1   Photographic display tables at the *Angola in Black & White: Photography and Science at the Dundo Museum 1940–1970* exhibition, Museum of Anthropology of the University of Coimbra, 1999.

Since four-fifths of the wall of the exhibition was made of glass, the visitor was also visible to an external audience, as though part of the exhibition. Except while inside the cubes, the visitor was both exposed to other visitors and enabled to survey others. The panoptical feeling expressed by nearly all published accounts of Dundo visitors of the colonial period was, thus, transposed to this space and linked to the experience of perceiving the photographs. In order to stress the physicality of the exhibition's wall – in marked opposition to the text-saturated cloister section – the display in the large hall relied on selected texts from the pages of books and journals, leaving all other information to the leaflet given to the visitor at the entrance.

Latour's distinction between a "mediator" and an "intermediary" (mentioned above) was crucial in the argument. The installation literally framed the perception of these photographs as part of surveillance technologies and practices carried out by the Diamonds Company of Angola. As photographs were also used in scientific work at the Dundo, the discourse which organized their display came to reformulate them as a material link between power and knowledge. Inasmuch as the sense of being surveyed was drawn back into the visitors' experiences, content and form melted with one another, thus framing the visiting experience.

Babà-Babu: Stories of a Cradle *(2004)*[5]

Between 2000 and 2003 the MAUC Ethnography Gallery underwent major refurbishment work. No exhibitions were mounted during these years and, because of budgetary cuts, the exhibitions planned to go ahead in the restored gallery had to be shelved. *Babà-Babu* – the first exhibition after this period – was devised as an extremely low-budget exhibition. Only half of the gallery was used (the cloister rooms were closed) and a single object was put on display: a Hindu cradle built in the former Portuguese colony of Goa in 1904 (figure 8.2).

After two years of suspension, it was crucial that this exhibition should attract school audiences back to the museum. How to do this while also avoiding a child-driven exhibition project was the challenge. The approach taken was to engage different levels of perception by bringing aesthetic presentations of ethnographic materials into dialogue. *Babà-Babu* was an aesthetically oriented installation that, at the same time, could act as a means for commenting on Hindu culture and on historical links between Portugal and India.

The cradle was chosen mainly for its aesthetic appeal: it is a wooden artifact, enamel-painted, with a decorative frame of 3×3 cm hand-painted Hindu divinities (as if the user – the sleeping baby – was being placed under the protection of the gods). The cradle was commissioned in Goa

Figure 8.2 Views of the *Babà-Babu – Stories of a Cradle* exhibition, Museum of Anthropology of the University of Coimbra, 2004.

by a military official for his baby daughter. However, as it was later deemed to take up "too much room in the house" it was offered to the MAUC in the early twentieth century.

The installation project evolved into an open-script project clearly addressing the debate between art and artifact: the cradle was presented as an art object in a first section, then dissected as an anthropological source for the understanding of Hindu culture. For this purpose the gallery was divided into two main oppositional spaces: first the visitor would enter the gallery and approach its empty darkened room. In a black stand, the cradle was carefully illuminated – as a piece of jewelry – with directional spotlights, orienting the viewer to details of its painted figures or manufacturing particulars. Passing the object, in a luminous room, the visitor would be metaphorically set inside the cradle: the 3×3 cm paintings were photographed and enlarged into 60×60 cm figures, replicating, in the gallery room, the frame of the cradle. The center of this second room was filled with pillows where the visitor could sit, admire the paintings, and read about them on the leaflet given at the entrance – a device that allows for a "clean" (i.e. caption-free) display without compromising information. At a third, complementary section, documentary films on Hindu culture were continuously shown on a loop. Visitors could wander from one room to the other layering (so to speak) the partial information that each of the sections provided.

The sound in the gallery was provided by a selection of Hindu lullabies produced by a Goese amateur music ensemble resident in Lisbon who authorized the use of their music free of charge. On weekday mornings, the Educational Services team presented the exhibition to the schoolchildren. Hindu narratives – mainly focusing on the characters painted in the cradle's frame – were told and then performed by the children. In the afternoon and at weekends the exhibition was open to the general public.

The experiment with *Babà-Babu* had two aims: to make a dignified exhibition with a near-zero budget, and to make such an exhibition work as an experience for the visitor. Again, the "ambiance" was carefully planned, playing with vision and sound, exploring the contrasts between intimate contemplation and accession of accurate cultural information. Notwithstanding the emotional environment created, part of this information centered on the biography of the cradle's owner, showing the historical context of the cradle coming into possession as part of a colonial process. The main exercise – that art and artifact may not be incompatible – was clearly accomplished. Visitors, whose curiosity was sparked by the art-like installation, were then eager to learn more about the cradle, the paintings, and Hindu culture, and they could do so in the next section of the exhibition.

Without net – Ruy Duarte de Carvalho, Paths and Detours *(2005)*[6]

Without net focused on the work of the contemporary Angolan anthropologist, poet, writer, and film director Ruy Duarte de Carvalho (1941–). The exhibition was planned within the program of the University Cultural Week of 2005 which centered on the lusophone world and featured a tribute to de Carvalho. During the week there was an international seminar on his work, and two theater plays based on his texts were performed. The common denominator in de Carvalho's complex work, which over more than thirty years spans film, poetry, fiction, and anthropological analysis, is its focus on the Kuvale people of southern Angola.

Without net is a line from one of his poems. The full poem was displayed at the entrance, serving as a guideline to the exhibition.[7] It describes the sense of being without a known safe ground that is experienced by the anthropologist in the field. It can also be read as a comment on de Carvalho's work, all of which concentrates on and is inspired by the Kuvale way of life, whether in explaining the specifics of this nomadic pastoral people, or in commenting on contemporary Angola or on the world and life in general.

The materials available for the exhibition were (1) de Carvalho's books (including literature, poetry, and anthropology monographs), (2) his field photographs (organized in two dossiers each containing about two hundred plastic sheets, which in turn contained four photographs each), and (3) his films and related plate photographs.

The key concept of the exhibition project became to present these materials in a "Kuvale aesthetics," focusing on de Carvalho's work by making it visible to the public and in turn drawing on it to update the meaning of the MAUC's southern Angolan artifacts. Like *Babà-Babu*, this was a low-budget, fairly "open-scripted" exhibition, divided into three main sections.

The exhibition opened with the poem, and then presented two stands, one of which contained de Carvalho's poetic publications and the other his analytical ones. The stands were framed by an excerpt from a recent "ethnofiction" text on the Kuvale, printed on the gallery wall and also presented by the author on audio. From there, the visitor moved to a gallery room that was completely empty except for hanging plastic sheets containing de Carvalho's field photographs, organized in terms of different aspects of Kuvale life ("landscape," "religious practices," "cattle," etc.). This was intended to evoke the empty space of the southern Angolan deserts in which the Kuvale move around, and was inspired by the fact that the Kuvale usually hang their belongings. The idea was to provoke a mix of estrangement caused by familiar artifacts (9×12 color photographs organized by theme) and strange content. The visitor would have to face cultural estrangement engendered by the presentation of familiar objects in an unfamiliar and difficult-to-comprehend world. The visitor, that is, was to be left without a net.

From this part of the exhibition, with its emphasis on a close, dedicated, and detailed view provided by the photographs, the visitor was drawn into the cloister room where some of the same images were now projected onto the walls, together with excerpts from de Carvalho's poems, fiction, and analytical texts; and, at the end of the room, his films were shown. In addition, a selection of photographs of the film-making period (late 1970s and early 1980s) was placed opposite a selection of southern Angolan objects from the MAUC's collections, similar to those in the films and photographs. Like the field photographs in the previous section, these objects were also hung, in line with "Kuvale aesthetics." By moving to the end of the cloister room, the visitor also moved from de Carvalho's present work to the past (film being his gateway from agronomy to anthropology in the mid-1970s) and simultaneously was presented with Kuvale transformations over the thirty years. This shift in time-frame was also emphasized by the shift from current color photographs to black and white photographs and films.

The purpose of the installation of materials and the description of each section was explained in the visitors' leaflet. Again, the visual nature of materials and their display was emphasized. Overall, this installation presented the ensemble of de Carvalho's work through an interpretation of that work, while leaving plenty of room for the development of personal visiting scripts. A visitor could concentrate on the field photographs, then take a seat and watch the films, or focus for a while on the slide show, move from there to the artifacts, from these to the plateau photographs on the facing wall, or create another personal script. The setting did not impose a rigid perceptual sequence as the totality of de Carvalho's work was on display, each section creating partial relations with others.

Nomads *(2005)*[8]

The research on de Carvalho's materials from the southern Angolan Kuvale motivated another exhibition, which also opened at the University Cultural Week on the Lusophone World – a world whose material culture is, so to speak, materialized in the MAUC's collections. *Nomads* was a meta-museological exercise in the sense that it was based exclusively on some of the most valued museum objects that have been traveling around the world for the last twenty years.

Nomads occupied a single room of the gallery (figure 8.3). The objects were displayed on the custom-made (extremely expensive) plywood boxes in which they had formerly been transported. First impressions were of a warehouse – some kind of liminal space where the boxes had been opened and objects inspected – while, at the same time, the objects were carefully illuminated to provoke a dramatic effect. On the room's wall, places and travel dates were listed anarchically, suggesting a used travel case. Catalogues of the exhibitions at which the objects had been shown were displayed in just the same way as the objects themselves, so showing them to be valued as much as the "treasures" selected. The purpose of the installation was simply to present these objects as valuable not so much on account of their "antiquity" or "rarity" but as objects of knowledge which have a long biography inside the MAUC. Such objects, *Nomads* showed, operate as ambassadors of the University on their travels elsewhere in the world. For this reason, sufficient resources should be provided to care for them and to update research upon them.

Nomads had no other interpretive device, nor any script. The visitors stood in front of the installation and, if searching for more information, could handle the catalogues of other exhibitions and browse information about the objects on the spot. If not, they could just look at the exhibition and be confronted with the disorienting sense that it provoked.

From Exhibiting to Installing Ethnography

In a perfect world, an account of exhibition-making processes would be restricted to dealing only with form and content, interpretive devices, artifact selection, script layout, and spatial organization. Resources are usually not referred to, as if their availability was not integral to the social process within which exhibition making occurs. Yet the social networks

Figure 8.3   *Nomads* exhibition, Museum of Anthropology of the University of Coimbra, 2005.

that sustain exhibition making necessarily include the institutional frame of the venue. As a university museum, one of the roles of the MAUC is to provide its exhibition audiences with state-of-the-art reflection on contemporary issues, addressing, with this concern in mind, its historical collections. Since its preferred public is the university population it should provide a voluntary and complementary form of education, which also means that exhibitions compete with many other forms of "leisure" and that, therefore, exploring the specifics of an argument developed in a closed space, using "the real thing," may be turned into a significant experience unmatched by any other form of media presentation. From this perspective, some of the major assets and resources of the MAUC are the collections which may be interpretively updated for commenting on the present situations of people identified as being represented in these collections. Lest we forget, ethnographic objects were – somewhere in their past existence – part of actual social practice and to privilege this view enables their inclusion in an object-oriented perspective on contemporary situations.

If ethnographic exhibitions may be minimally defined as a process of displaying objects as fundamental to the mediation of social relations (which is in itself a thoroughly social and cultural practice), then, to have a department of Aathropology in close-knit relation with a museum is an important resource for the latter too, since the teaching and research environment provides clues for the choice of display themes and the aesthetic approaches that installations may employ. Even if exhibitions of the MAUC – from 1999 to 2005 – have received decreasing amounts of funding, this does not make exhibition impossible but means that it must be planned according to the lesser financial means available. During this period, exhibitions have involved fewer "fireworks" and less stunning technology but have entailed more concept development. So far, "less" has been turned into "more" via effective but inexpensive ethnographic devices.

Installing, rather than exhibiting, has been refined as a specific knowledge-practice at the MAUC. It conceptualizes itself in opposition, for instance, to what supermarkets do, which is to put objects on *display* (also within a script organized in a closed space). Translated to this museological setting, installation is experimental in the sense that it implies qualifying the social relations between persons and objects by framing them as a site of specific sensorial and cognitive experience that cannot be replicated anywhere else. This requires experiments with the materials used, with their display and layout, and an ongoing reflection and play with sound, vision, and body movement, so constructing displays that may be situated somewhere along an imaginary axis between total closure of the visiting script and its total openness within the limits of the discipline's knowledge. Each project has been conceived in its entirety – as a unique exercise that draws on its formal and conceptual links with other non-museological materials such as the printed ("catalogues," leaflets, posters, and even tickets) or those of the media (such as radio and television advertising which is free of charge for this kind of event and institution). Such a conception is intended to make clear the core concept on which each installation is grounded. What results is that mediation reverberates beyond content and articulates – and hopefully translates – it into durable materials.

Each exercise is thus conceived as an experimental situation, as a partial interpretation of a theme, as a sort of conditional mood that values, among many other possible perspectives, the fact that, as objects of knowledge, ethnographic objects may mediate contemporary issues and that these can be approached, in the museum, through an anthropological practice.

Notes

1   *Texpo* (a blend of "text" and "expo") is the name given by the Neuchâtel team to the edited volumes on the exhibitions. Until 1994 they used the designation *Ethno Poche* (Pocket ethnography); they then decided to stress the fact that exhibitions are about concept discussion, which can be done through either an exhibition or a book.
2   Both anthropologists have gone on to produce more exhibitions as independent curators. These include Bouquet's *Man-Ape, Ape-Man* at the Natural History Museum, Leiden, the Netherlands, 1993, and her *Sans Og Samling*, Oslo, 1998. Fernandes Dias's work with contemporary African artists recently materialized in the exhibition *Looking Both Ways* (New York, Lisbon 2004–5), and in the launching of the website from the project *ArtAfrica* (www.artafrica.gulben kian.pt/, accessed August 2006).
3   Technical data: research: Nuno Porto; scientific supervisors Nélia Dias and Manuel Laranjeira; scientific consultant: Mary Bouquet; installation conception: Nuno Porto with José António Bandeirinha (architecture); graphic design: João Bicker; photographs: Agostiniano de Oliveira and José Pedro (Diamang photographers); new prints: Paulo Mora.
4   J. H. Lamprey, in a short article entitled "On a Method of Measuring the Human Form" (1869), proposed the use of a 2-inch grid frame against which subjects should be photographed to record anthropometric data to a common standard. Lamprey's system was intended to facilitate accurate comparisons between "specimens of various races," and this method – either explicitly or not – influenced much nineteenth-century anthropological photography.
5   Technical data: research and texts: Maria do Rosário Martins and Maria Arminda Miranda; installation conception and assembly: Nuno Porto and João Bicker with Carlos Antunes (Atelier do Corvo – Architecture);

documentation: Maria Augusta Rocha; preventive conservation: Ludovina Todo-Bom; object classification: Maria do Rosário Martins and Carmina Silva; graphic design: João Bicker; photography: José Menezes; sound: music by the Ekvât band and the Surya band.

6 Technical data: conservation (objects from the MAUC collections) Maria do Rosário Martins; preventive conservation: Ludovina Todo-Bom; classification (objects from the MAUC collections): Maria do Rosário Martins and Carmina Silva; education project: Maria Arminda Miranda; Documentation: Maria Augusta Rocha; installation concept and assembly: Nuno Porto and João Bicker with Luis Quintais; selection of materials: Ana Rita Amaral, João Bicker, Luís Quintais, Nuno Porto, and Rute Magalhães; graphic design: João Bicker; photography: Ruy Duarte de Carvalho (field photography 1990s) and Rute Magalhães (field and plateau photography 1970s and 1980s); sound: Ruy Duarte de Carvalho (voice).

7 "Without family / without trust / nor ethnic group / without weight even / to lose / foot / this entire circus is made / without net. / Falling, therefore, no. / Without net / alone." "O Outro," from *Ordem de Esquecimento,* in *Lavra Incerta,* Luanda, Editorial Nzila, 2001, p. 98 (translated by the present author).

8 Technical data: conservation: Maria do Rosário Martins; preventive conservation: Ludovina Todo-Bom; classification: Maria do Rosário Martins and Carmina Silva; education project: Maria Arminda Miranda; documentation: Maria Augusta Rocha; installation concept and assembly: Nuno Porto and João Bicker; graphic design: João Bicker.

References

Archer, M. and Hilty, G. (1997) Material culture: a user's guide. In *The Object in British Art of the 1980s and 90s.* London: Hayward Gallery, no page numbers.

Arnoldi, M. J. (1999) From the diorama to the dialogic: a century of exhibiting Africa at the Smithsonian Museum of Natural History. *Cahiers d'etudes africaines,* XXXIX (3–4), 155–6: 701–25.

Bouquet, M. (1993) *Man-Ape, Ape-Man.* Leiden: Nationaal Natuurhistorisch Museum.

Bouquet, M. (1998) *Sans Og Samling/Bringing it all Back Home to the Oslo University Ethnographic Museum.* Oslo: Scandinavian University Press.

Bouquet, M. and Branco, J. (1989) *Artefactos Melanésicos, Reflexões Pós-modernistas.* Lisbon: IICT.

Bourdieu, P. (1972) *Esquisse d'une théorie de la pratique, et trois esquisses d'ethnologie kabyle.* Paris and Geneva: Droz.

Clifford, J. (1988) *The Predicament of Culture: Twentieth-Century Ethnography, Literature, and Art.* Cambridge, Mass.: Harvard University Press.

Clifford, J. (1997) *Routes: Travel and Translation in the Late Twentieth Century.* Cambridge, Mass.: Harvard University Press.

de Carvalho, R. D. (2001) *Lavra Incerta.* Luanda: Editorial Nzila.

Dias, J. A. F. (2001) Arte e antropologia no séc. XX: modos de relação. *Etnográfica,* V (1): 103–30.

Einzig, B. (ed.) (1996) *Thinking about Art: Conversations with Susan Hiller.* Manchester: Manchester University Press.

Errington, S. (1994) What became authentic primitive art? *Cultural Anthropology,* 9 (2): 201–26.

Geertz, C. (1973) Thick description: toward an interpretive theory of culture, in *The Interpretation of Cultures: Selected Essays.* New York: Basic Books, pp. 3–30.

Gell, A. (1998) *Art and Agency: an Anthropological Theory.* Oxford: Clarendon Press.

Hainard, J. and Kaehr, R. (eds.) (1982) *Collections Passion.* Neuchâtel: Musée d'Ethnographie de Neuchâtel.

Hiller, S. (ed.) (1991) *The Myth of Primitivism and Other Modernist Myths.* London: Routledge.

Karp, I. and Lavine, S. (eds.) (1991) *Exhibiting Cultures: the Poetics and Politics of Museum Display.* Washington, D.C.: Smithsonian Institution Press.

Küchler, S. (2000) The art of ethnography: the case of Sophie Calle. In A. Coles (ed.), *Site-Specificity: the Ethnographic Turn.* de-, dis-, ex-, no. 4. London: Black Dog.

Kwon, M. (2000) Experience vs. interpretation: traces of ethnography in the works of Lan Tuazon and Nikki S. Lee. In A. Coles (ed.), *Site-Specificity: the Ethnographic Turn.* de-, dis-, ex-, no. 4. London: Black Dog.

Lamprey, J. H. (1869) On a method of measuring the human form, for the use of students in ethnology. *Journal of the Ethnological Society of London,* 1: 84–5.

Latour, B. (1993) *We have Never been Modern.* Hemel Hempstead: Harvester Wheatsheaf.

Mack, J. (1994) *Emil Torday and the Arts of the Congo.* London: British Museum.

Marcus, G. and Fischer, M. (1986) *Anthropology as Cultural Critique: an Experimental Moment in the Human Sciences.* Chicago: University of Chicago Press.

Myers, F. (1995) *The Traffic in Culture: Refiguring Anthropology and Art.* Berkeley: University of California Press.

Rabinow, P. and Sullivan, W. (eds.) (1977) *Interpretive Social Science: A Reader.* Berkeley: University of California Press.

Rorimer, A. (2000) Lothar Baumgarten: the seen and the unseen. In A. Coles (ed.), *Site-Specificity: the Ethnographic Turn.* de-, dis-, ex-, no. 4. London: Black Dog.

Shelton, A. A. (1995) *Fetishism: Visualising Power and Desire.* Aldershot: Ashgate.

Sherman, D. and Rogoff, I. (1994) Introduction. In D. Sherman and I. Rogoff (eds.), *Museum Culture: Histories, Discourses, Spectacles.* Minneapolis: University of Minnesota Press, pp. ix–xx.

Sturtevant, W. C. (1969) Does anthropology need museums? *Proceedings of the Biological Society of Washington,* 82: 619–49.

9

Raising Specters: Welcoming Hybrid Phantoms at Chicago's Museum of Science and Industry

Anne Lorimer

Introduction: Putting the Ghost Back into the Machine

If an experiment is a practical experience through which human knowledge is confirmed or disrupted, in what sense could a museum exhibition be described as experimental? "Experimental" has, in the context of the arts and other media, come to mean something like "novel" or "cutting-edge": an exercise anticipated to be risky, but performed for the sake of expanding (or defining, through failure) the boundaries of a medium or genre. The term also emphasizes those aspects of practice in which maximal unexpectedness is courted: unlike a routinized and rigorously pre-defined scientific experiment, experimentation in the artistic sense may not only yield unpredictable results, but also shift the conceptual grounds on which to evaluate the results. By thus drawing our attention to media and to processual instabilities, experimentation can teach us something about mediation – the dynamic, mutually structuring relationship between symbolic forms and larger social and material processes. Thus, for example, if we take seriously the media through which scientific knowledge gets represented and received at a site of popular culture, such as Chicago's Museum of Science and Industry, we can learn new things about how scientific entities become imposed on and appropriated by people's everyday projects. Throughout the 1990s, the Museum of Science and Industry (MSI) was for me a series of naturally occurring experiments, in which, as an anthropology graduate student, I observed, interacted with, and interviewed visitors, floor staff, and exhibit creators. In this chapter I will focus on a single exhibit, *Learning and Learning Disabilities: Explorations of the Human Brain* (figure 9.1), and on a single respect in which this experimental exhibit disrupted what its creators thought they were trying to do. Seeking to account for this rupture reveals how the social projects of science museum staff and visitors rely on an older notion of mind, spirit, or ghost that still haunts the *Brain* exhibit.

Figure 9.1   Entrance to *Learning and Learning Disabilities*. Photograph courtesy of Archives, Museum of Science and Industry.

MSI's *Brain* exhibit was widely (indeed, award-winningly) judged to be innovative, and varied strikingly from a "traditional" museum exhibit in the nature of its media. The exhibit as a built space contains relatively few "authentic" artifacts, of which perhaps the closest examples are an attractive silvery-pink plastinated brain specimen, a thin brain cross-section, and several video recordings in which individuals with learning disabilities discuss their experiences and capabilities. Instead, its creators planned its many multimedia interactive exhibit units to challenge visitors to fulfill various set tasks that cannot be completed without triggering, within visitors' own brains, authentic exemplars of the cognitive processes that each exhibit unit describes. The authentically present "real things, real processes" – to use a slogan current among MSI professionals at the time – are thus the exhibits' visitors and their brain activity. Medical exhibits always have the potential to create mappings between exhibited anatomies and visitors' own; for example, MSI visitors to the nearby *Body Slices* exhibit create what are often emotionally fraught mappings between themselves and the cross-sectioned cadavers preserved in aqueous solution between panes of glass. But whereas those interactions tend to construct persons as vulnerable and repulsive flesh, the *Brain* exhibit offers visitors the opportunity to objectify instead their cognitive powers: I have seen girls, for example, take pride in (and subsequently often recount) surpassing the score of older family members, or insist on not only discerning the correct answer but also registering it on the exhibit unit's interactive screen. Senior exhibit developer Sara Graeber[1] intended the *Brain* exhibit to vary not only from traditional museum media, but also from other current representations of the brain in public culture: "To me there are too many medical exhibits that tell you the bad news of someone who's lost all these abilities, and [visitors] come away with a very, very morbid sense from it." Graeber's goal, which succeeded dramatically, was to take a topic often perceived as threatening, and instead present it in a welcoming environment, organized thematically around the images and bright colors of a children's birthday party. Yet the exhibit also produces an uncanny effect that was unintended, indeed undesired, by its creators, an effect that emanates from its white plaster statues and its long photographic mural of people dressed and painted all in white, their images emerging from a stark black background. As Graeber confirmed: "Some people say that there's a ghostly look to it, which is not one of our intended outcomes.... Some visitors have said that [the white figures] look ghostly." Why might an exhibit that was intended to be welcoming wind up a site for ghosts?

I argue that in investigating this question, we can learn not only about the processes whereby exhibits are produced and received, but also about why scientific imagery in public culture may be fraught with cultural loadings that would be disavowed from the point of view of those responsible for scientific content – as when contemporary representations of the brain appear still haunted by an older linking of mind to spirit or ghost. If this specter has not been laid to rest, it is not simply because of the sheer weight of prior symbolic systems, but rather because the ghostly mind is being strategically invoked as part of people's ongoing praxes and projects. In this case, scientists and educators, searching for a way to make their exhibit less threatening, experienced a collective, "magic" response to their chance glimpse of fabricators' artwork because, I will argue, such artwork had qualities which represent a kind of transcendence of this threat, qualities which become explicit to art-world professionals, though not to museum educators. The artists themselves connect their artwork's visual lineage to images in which identifying persons with brains is a means of transcending race. Persons working in or visiting MSI's public space likewise strategically transcend racialization by identifying their selves with their brains. In identifying with the brain, visitors are also identifying with a kind of ghostly afterworld, like that of the public sphere – specifically here, the milieu of a science museum, in which an educational ideology foregrounds visitors' cognitive selves, while traces of other persons (those who dictated content, devised scripts, or were cast as statues) likewise circulate and speak with little apparent physical co-presence, as if equivalent to thoughts or memories. Equating one's brain with one's mode of being-in-the-world is liberating in certain respects, yet also associated with disempowerment, as when it compensates for lack of material resources. The brain exhibit crystallizes and thereby reveals a symbolic melding of brain and ghost into a virtual, technologically invulnerable persona. Such melding is made possible by an aspect of symbols which, as Lévi-Strauss noted (1966, pp. 18–21), is excluded from our ideology of rigorously predefined scientific concepts: they bring with them traces of their prior usage, and each incarnation in a new material form can invoke meanings which, although unintended, become incorporated as part of the symbol's richly effective meaning, sometimes thereby thematically reconciling problems which are irresolvable, such as that of life and death (cf. Lévi-Strauss 1963, p. 220). It is this aspect of symbols that allows "experimental" exhibitions to go beyond what could have been thought out beforehand, and to offer instead new forms of knowledge and practice.

Bodily Threats and a Welcoming Spirit

To obtain an overview of *Learning and Learning Disabilities,* visualize its floor plan laid out in the shape of an enormous cross-sectioned human head, so that moving into the central space of the exhibit enacts moving from the outer skull more deeply into the brain itself. Dotted around the carpet of this inner space are six giant plaster heads, modeled from the eyes down. These lower heads each form a base for an array of educational and interactive materials, which thus visually stand in for the head's upper portion. Each head wears as a crest a different color photograph, appearing in profile as if it were its head's dome, and each showing how children at a birthday party engage in activities that involve a particular cognitive function. Below this crest, the plaster head base supports pieces of interactive exhibitry, each intended to stimulate that very same cognitive function among visitors. Above each giant head a plaster brain hangs suspended, as if it had floated up from the lower head underneath. These various floating brains are each painted in a complex array of bright, pastel, and metallic hues, showing how the exhibited cognitive functions can be mapped onto neuroanatomical sectors. In contrast to this colorful interior area, the exhibit's periphery is dominated by monochrome statues and photographs: this periphery corresponds to the brain's enclosing skull. Two openings in this periphery wall are intended to represent eye sockets. At each, a white plaster statue is topped from the neck upwards with a video monitor showing the figure's head, played by an actor. This persona, Joel, greets visitors, welcoming them to the exhibit and contextualizing the birthday party inside as his own childhood memory. This strategy was designed to make "a bright and positive common environment" for a topic exhibit developers feared might alienate visitors. As Graeber explained in an interview on June 25, 1990,

> Many television programs about the brain have a point of view of talking about the brain-injured... You'll see someone on television who can remember everything, or can remember nothing, or can see something on one side of his head but not understand it on the opposite side... Those are pretty frightening things.... I felt that what we wanted to accomplish in part [was] having people feel that they could approach this subject... you know, "okay I'll try this once, I'll try and look into this subject." We had to do something different from showing a lot about brain injury, because it's all pretty scary, what you see there and being such an unknown in your own

head that you can very easily wonder, "well, what's lurking in my own head?" I'm not really sure I would want to know.

In contrast to these threats of loss, stigma, and lurking inner unknowns, the exhibit creators wanted to provide "a supportive atmosphere."

My first interview with Sara Graeber left me trying to grasp how an exhibit environment might simultaneously be conceptualized as reassuring and yet suggest a place inhabited by ghosts. A step toward solving this puzzle occurred later that afternoon, when I happened to collect a text written by exhibit developers at another Chicago museum, also dealing with anatomy, mortality, and the person:

Fieldnote: June 25th 1990, The Field Museum of Natural History

Off the entrance hall to the left is an Egyptian tomb: a reconstruction of the Tomb of Unis-Ankh. The tomb is a part of "Inside Ancient Egypt." A plaque says: "Anything that the spirit of the dead person might find useful or necessary in his new life could have been kept here. These jars and pots from our collection are typical, but there might also have been furniture, games, hunting equipment, cosmetic items and sealed jars containing oils, wine and beer. . . . *The Mummy's Life in the Afterlife.* Many of us think the Egyptians were obsessed by death. That's because most of what we know about ancient Egyptians, and most of the objects in museums, come from burials. We may feel that funeral objects are morbid, but for the Egyptians, the whole point was to create a life after death that was very much like life on earth. Our burial scenes will show you the many steps Egyptians took to assure a comfortable and joyful eternal life for their loved ones."

In the decision process as Graeber was narrating it, much like the Egyptian funeral process as narrated by Field Museum exhibit developers, comfort and joy were to come first and foremost from familiarity, providing cognitive reassurance and hence emotional reassurance:

[The] subject of the brain is so difficult, and so unknown to everybody, that it's like a terra incognita. Now if you're going to venture into someplace that you don't know, you like to take some things with you that are going to help you along the way. . . . The birthday party we present gives people something from their own world that everyone knows and can relate to and enjoy as a way to find out about their own brains.

Narrating the series of decisions that the team made, Graeber framed the team's mission in terms that I, in transcribing the interview that evening after my first visit to the Field Museum, could not help hearing as evocative of preparing someone for a trip to the land of the dead. Here is a way in which ghostliness functions as comforting: unlike the other anatomical exhibits, in identifying with the forms of humanity exhibited in *Explorations of the Human Brain* one remains a person – wearing clothes and jewelry, engaging in familiar activities and dialogue with others – and indeed that personhood is being celebrated.

In the decision process as Graeber was narrating it, the birthday party was appealing because its form was said to be familiar to all members of the museum's public:

> We had been considering other subjects. Things like cooking, or driving your own car. There's lots of eye–hand coordination things, or mental things, that would work but all those didn't reach the audience the way we wanted it to. They might reach adults...you know, a certain level of education. They might reach a certain ethnic group, but none of them worked well enough for us to select it. So we came up with the birthday party.

If birthday parties have meaning for so many persons, this is in part a function of their widespread statistical distribution: meaning is simply a matter of associative familiarity. But this distribution is in part a consequence of another kind of link between birthday parties and persons: birthdays are a cultural form in which to appropriately celebrate any person (or personification). In this respect, the birthday party is a perfect rebuttal to the threat posed by other exhibits and television programs: whereas brain injuries represent a threat to the person's coherent subjectivity, birthday parties celebrate a personhood that is both continuous and culminating. "A birthday party", suggested Graeber, "is really a celebration of how your brain has changed over a year's time. You can be a whole new person based on the learning that you do."

The effect of this additional, unplanned level of meaning was experienced by the exhibit creators as "magical," a term that I think refers here to the effect of a concrete symbolic form to operate on multiple levels, resolving multiple conflicts perhaps even before these have been explicitly formulated.

The notion of personhood appeared as an exhilarating solution at another crucial moment, in which the team envisioned the exhibit's most ghostly element: its mural.

> Executing the mural was really a delight, I mean it was really a creative dream.... Before it didn't really...it didn't have people on it initially. Through a day's worth of thinking of what we were going to do there, and one of my colleagues said "it just has to be people". (Graeber, interview)

Can the exhibit's ghostliness be accounted for by simply considering the symbolic use of "personhood" to circumvent the brain's associated threatening images? Identifying the brain with personhood does not necessarily cancel the threat associated with the brain as a biomedical entity. Rather, it can increase the threat by pointing to the high stakes: your very personhood is at stake, all the more fragile for being located in a chunk of soft tissue. What is logically needed, then, is an image of personhood that transcends the flesh: in other words, in order to persuade visitors to approach the brain scientifically, it may help to simultaneously offer them images of ghosts.

Indeed, the brain exhibit can be coherently read as offering just such an image, countering the corporeal threats that appear in other nearby exhibits – perhaps the ones which exhibit creators came through on their way "up here" – particularly *Body Slices* and the now defunct, sinisterly titled *Good Teeth and Good Health Go Together*. Such a reading of these exhibits can be constructed by attending to a contrast between qualisigns (Munn 1986): on the one hand images of corporeal vulnerability, decay, and stigma are identified with fleshy-toned cross-sections of human anatomy (in the case of *Body Slices*, these are cross-sections of actual, imperfectly preserved human cadavers); on the other hand, endurance and invulnerability are marked by hard white bones and teeth. Visitors are frequently and loudly disturbed by the cross-sectioned cadavers, but not by their neighbor, the disarticulated skeleton. This contrast recalls Hertz's monograph on secondary burial (1907): the dead are threatening and unhappy while still fleshy, but once reduced to bones, become benevolent, transcendent spirits. The hard white statues likewise support this idea of a departed person whose personality has transcended the flesh and become invulnerable. Statues can thus function as a solution to the threat posed by the sliced corpses: one young boy who hated visiting the latter exhibit, and whose father had drawn a line on his chest explaining "This is where they cut you, here," kept pleading to be told that "they only do it to statues." Such a solution is what the brain exhibit offers: "from a distance, the first thing you encounter are people: the white mannequins outside" (Graeber, interview). While this link between the white figures and white bones may seem farfetched, it should be remembered that the exhibit's mono-chromatic perimeter was designed to symbolize the brain's surrounding housing – a human skull.

But this notion of a personhood that transcends the flesh is not part of the decision-making process as narrated by Sara Graeber – even though it does logically resolve the predicament her account sets forth. How, then, did this spectral persona make its entrance? Who offered MSI a ghost to put back in the biomedical machine?

The Ethereal Afterlife of Studio EIS

It is the mural, remember (figure 9.2), which Sara Graeber identified as both the exhibit's ghostliest component and a favorite moment of the exhibit development process, a "creative dream." The mural originated in the MSI design team's visit to Studio EIS, a Brooklyn firm co-owned and directed by brothers Elliot and Ivan Schwartz, who specialize in crafting

Figure 9.2 Photographic mural and statues fabricated by Studio EIS. Photograph courtesy of Archives, Museum of Science and Industry.

life-size figures, cast from human models, for corporate and museum clients, including the National Civil Rights Museum. During this visit, one of the brothers recounted, MSI's design team happened to notice an image unintended for their eyes, which triggered a new imaginative possibility and practical solution:

> When they came to the studio there was a photograph above the door back in there which suggested to them a possible way in which to resolve one of their spaces. It's a photo showing about thirty or so figures, very tightly grouped together. And there, there's one running wall that was about seventy-five feet, and they said "we *need* to have something back there, it'd be great to have figures representing people"; and we said "well, it's a great idea, but seventy-five feet of figures, three deep would cost you half a million dollars or something." So we said, "Well, look, you know it can be accomplished photographically and so why don't we do that?" So that's what actually happened. We then figured out how we were going to do this and we kind of sold each other on the idea that this was the way in which to go.

It is clear that both the clients and the fabricators were creatively open to the magic of contingent events, allowing themselves to be inspired not simply by the concept of "people," but rather by a concrete sign (cf. Lévi-Strauss 1966, pp. 1–33): a particular photograph of white statues against a black background.

This photograph had been taken, not as part of the studio's work, but for the brothers' own aesthetic interest: about to send off a large batch of client-commissioned statues, they were struck by the massed statues' powerful presence – an impact which would inevitably be lost once the statues were dispersed into various museum contexts – and wanted to keep an image of this moment in which their creation amounted to something more than these separate purposes for which it had been created. While the brothers run Studio EIS as a business to support Ivan's painting and Elliot's photography, their fine and commercial arts are linked beyond mere funding. Indeed, when the director of exhibitions at the International Center for Photography wanted to condense themes of Elliot's art, he drew on a photograph that takes as its object a model being cast for one of the studio's sculptures:

> When Schwartz photographs living subjects, he treats people as sculpture, presenting them as objects that seem at once alive and dead. In *The Modern*

> *Prometheus*, a man draped with protective cloth sits with plaster covering his eyes and much of his face ... Schwartz ... plays off Mary Shelley's subtitle for her novel *Frankenstein*, in which man defies nature in an attempt to reconstruct life using his own creative powers. (Hartshorn 1987, p. 2)

Elliot Schwartz himself drew my attention to this exhibition catalogue.

The photograph's resonance in this fine arts context reveals an aspect of the studio's commercial work: like Frankenstein and his monster, it amounts to a use of technology to create a persona which is not human, but is made by and from humans, and which transcends the mortality of individual flesh. This same symbolic operation, in the context of MSI's Human Body Zone, alters the nature of what it means to identify the self with anatomy. It does so by relying on a dual potential of human anatomical embodiment: on the one hand, anatomical embodiment defines us as mortal bodies, but on the other hand, it permits the self to achieve objectification in more durable forms, such as photographs and sculptures cast from life, that can linger and multiply in a kind of afterlife. Elliot Schwartz identified this value the statues have:

> They're sort of dead, they're not dead; yet they're alive, they're not alive; they're here, they're ... you know, they sort of exist in a number of different planes. And I, I like that aspect of them. They really have a quality of a human being inside the clothing. They have a very, very, convincing, sort of, *after*-effect. You feel as if, a person *has been there*. They excite people.

It is as if the statues take the deadness of corporeality – and of corporeal absence – and transform it into a power to achieve transcendence, converting the negative value of bodily dissolution into the positive value of an after-effect that can circulate socially (cf. Munn 1969).

The particularities of the Schwartz brothers' work were not as available to project manager Sara Graeber, who did not make the trip to New York; in discussing the statues, she referenced a more famous American sculptor, George Segal, whose work raises a complementary set of concerns: the discourse surrounding his work emphasizes how casting technology transcends the evanescence of particular interpersonal moments, turning them into something that can be anatomized. Like Studio EIS, Segal specialized in monochromatic white figures cast from life, which the artist considered especially striking when positioned against a black background, and these figures too are often described as possessing "ghostliness" (Edwards 1999,

p. 5; cf. Fletcher 2000, Prather 2000). Segal has suggested these sculptures provide an analogue for quotidian yet ineffable moments of human experience:

> What I'm trying to do in my work is somehow fumble around for the language to talk about what's the equivalent of five seconds of consciousness. You and I sitting here, our legs are crossed, we feel the pressure of our foot, we have a physical sense of who we are; we also have all these ideas in our head, ideas it takes a lifetime to gather. (Segal in Edwards 1999, p. 4)

As this and other portions of the interview series suggest, Segal understood consciousness to be more than merely cognition or emotion: it is tied in with the body as intrinsically material, dependent on an individual mortal trajectory. Yet his sculptures in turn transcend lived moments of the organic body, attaining an enduring form in which they can circulate as objects of a more public consciousness.

Phantoms in Public

In this section, I want to suggest an affinity between the image of the brain as ghostly persona, and how persons are understood to participate in the public sphere. This affinity arises through particular historical and cultural circumstances, including antiracist imagery, urban crowds, the gallery form, and the particular forms of agency available to service workers.

Let me begin by clarifying that although the mural Studio EIS created for MSI originated in a photograph of sculptures, the brothers did not feel the actual mural's white figures to be merely statues manqué:

> I don't have any question, when I look at these pictures, I know there's a person in there. They don't represent sculptures to me. You know, the *eyes* cannot be *painted*, obviously, and you really sense...it's sort of like looking through the mask, that there is a person in there. Even though they kind of look like some sculptural thing, the way they're set up, black against white. (Elliot Schwartz, interview)

Rather, the photographs of these figures linked to another lineage of publicly circulated imagery:

The image that came to mind when we started working on that were these images from *Psychology Today* a long time ago. Where you would *essentially obliterate* the *color barrier*, by changing somebody to something. It's not really neutral, but it is a neutral color when you think of it – from black to white. You know, stark white as if painted as opposed to flesh. (Elliot Schwartz, interview)

In twentieth-century American public culture, antiracist imagery and discourse sought to distinguish those outward signs, which functioned as social markers of "race," from the mental states and capacities held to determine a person's true worth. In so doing, such discourse and imagery drew on a longstanding moral prioritization of spirit over flesh (cf. Augustine 1950); however, insofar as any such explanatory ghost had been, in the course of the Enlightenment, expelled from its housing in the human anatomical machine (La Mettrie 1943), secular antiracist authorities necessarily localized the spirit as mind, and the mind as functioning brain, in alignment with established scientific practice (e.g. Boas 1965, pp. 102–4).

But if a ghost lacks anatomical validity, it also possesses something that the brain does not: ghostly images are socially recognizable *as persons*, possessing faces, clothing, speech, etc. Insofar as a brain is an internal organ ("wet and gray and mushy... just sitting there inside your head" (Tomorrow n.d.)), its public exposure functions as a kind of affront to personhood, reminding us of the grimmer ways in which we can be reduced to flesh. Wet, gray, mushy brains are, for example, displayed within a neighboring exhibit of cross-sectioned preserved cadavers, eliciting from visitors loud disgust and horror; these sections are also legible as racially marked. The race-transcendent mind can be more safely shown by creating a composite in which the brain is represented by visual imagery of a social persona, while that persona is altered by abstracting from it the rhetorically salient feature of color. Such imagery makes it possible to imagine the ghostly brain as itself a person. This ghostly brain manages a kind of personhood peculiarly adapted for the public sphere. Warner has argued that the distinguishing peculiarity of persons in the public sphere is their lack of embodiedness: they must have bodies that are unmarked, correlated with their lack of interestedness (Warner 1990, 1993). Similarly, the persons in the brain exhibit have become spatiotemporally unmoored, as part of their strategy for addressing visitors. Consider the case of a woman I saw absorbedly attending to a mannequin whose video monitor was asking her to simultaneously rub her belly and pat her head. She complied; but when the monitor said: "Uh huh, that's good!" as if to praise her performance, she suddenly became self-conscious, glanced around, caught my eye and that of her male companion, and laughed, as did we. What was funny? I suspect the exposed absurdity was that the actor displayed on the video screen could not, in fact, be praising her individual performance: the human co-presence he seems to provide is really a trace of some prior time. It is as if, within the space of the exhibit, time flickered back and forth between that prior time and our own visit: the time of the professional recording and the time of visitor–exhibit interaction occupy the same place, but we can no longer alter that prior time. And if we cannot alter or experience intersubjectivity with our surroundings, then our represented presence becomes problematic, uncertain, and evanescent. In this respect, a phantom public sphere makes phantoms even of the populace it claims inhabits it.

If the public is sometimes described as a phantom (Robbins 1993), this is in part because, analytically, the public, being illimitable (Warner 1990), can never be fully present in any actual gathering. Such gatherings may however be ritually framed as revealing signs of, or acting upon, this larger entity (as when visitors to Chicago's 1893 Columbian Exposition report their own participation as a sign of American racial progress (Reed 2000), or an MSI guide hopes his conduct will counteract racist beliefs among hinterland tourists) – just as MSI exhibits claim to display other normally inaccessible forces underlying everyday life, such as human interior anatomy, or the industrial division of labor. Such framing is part of how, historically at MSI and Chicago's two world's fairs, crowds of visitors have themselves been construed as among the attractions that make such sites worth visiting.

Thus the December 1965 issue of MSI's official magazine, *Progress*, featured photographs of crowds and long lines. By the 1990s, however, such depictions had been replaced by images and slogans of mind and brain, rendering the Museum visit as a pleasurable learning event taking place within, or bursting out of, an individual person. Indeed, promotional graphics during this period focus on and treat analogously the Museum dome and the dome of the visitor's skull, each seen lifting open. In such imagery, the brain functioned symbolically as a concrete abstraction (in Valerio Valeri's sense): a physical object that could both thematize one aspect of a complex situation (the MSI visit becomes "learning") and express all instances thorough a single essence (since each visitor is crucially equipped with a brain). When visitors described MSI's efficacy, they too spoke of taking children there to "expand their minds," or finding as an adult that its exhibits had become "embedded" in one's "brain." One teenager explained that "the Museum enlightens your brain" because you "learn a lot" of "things involving science," and you learn it "in a fun way." But this visitor also reported "watching people": the crowds, which, like the exhibits, can be interpreted as privileged representatives of the "real world" outside. MSI's public, he commented, features "different cultures... black, white, everybody... and they're all interested in what's here." By participating in pleasurable science learning, he experienced himself as participating in a community that transcends race. And indeed many Chicagoans, especially those living in or near low-income African-American neighborhoods, construe MSI as a rare chance to share space with a multiracial, transnational public: to measure oneself against racially privileged peers and know oneself a contender, entitled to safe public space and to spectacle; to go on racially proscribed dates; or to meet strangers, as Tabitha Glass recalled, "from all over the world.... It makes you a well-rounded person who can fit in in any situation. I have a lot of fond memories that I'll take with me to the grave."

Tabitha once told me she "grew up in the Museum." Her imagery above conveys how memory becomes an instrument for converting social situations into an inalienable possession, one that remains part of one's personal identity through even the ultimate bodily hazard, death itself.[2] Such construals of memory are consistent with nineteenth- and twentieth-century American tropes in which the personal mind becomes a microcosmic container of impacts made upon it by jostling urban milieux, tropes which evolved in tandem with, and draw on, cultural technologies such as photography, exhibition galleries, and world's fairs (Orvell 1989). Indeed, her grandmother, Tabitha recounted, had attended and photographed the 1893 Columbian Exposition (whose only remaining structure is the Museum of Science and Industry); and Tabitha considers co-presence with her relatives' memories and their deliberately diverse acquaintance gave her a lived experience of history and society, contributing to her own cosmopolitan identity.

Identification of personhood with mind or brain is thus consistent with a rich awareness of one's social matrix, while simultaneously emphasizing autonomous agency even for those socially disempowered. This paradox was brought home to me by Keith Hughes, whose artistic life, like

Tabitha's, centers on creating self-aware forms of cosmopolitanism from historic African-American identity. For his day job at MSI, Keith led visitors touring a future exhibit's construction site. Between tours one day, he mentioned feeling frustrated by his inability to protect himself from the site's dirt and dangers; in particular, he felt anyone on the site ought to be issued a construction helmet. When I asked whether he had submitted a proposal through MSI's "Bright Ideas" employee suggestion box, Keith told me he had not invested much effort, since his previous suggestions had been stymied by bureaucratic inertia. I expressed surprise, having heard that demonstrators' ideas do result in changes, for example changes in the tour's script. Keith explained that while the script changed every day, outfitting tours with hard hats would require money and resources not directly accessible to himself and his colleagues; they can change the script because "your brain is accessible to you, and the ideas that pertain to the construction site are accessible." Ironically, on the one hand Keith must rely on his brain as his prime asset, while on the other hand, guarding this asset carefully would entail using the means he defines as outside his brain's scope: a construction helmet, to prevent head injury and brain damage. Within MSI's power structure as Keith experienced it, bright ideas are insufficient to maintain the conditions of their own production.

Through these commentaries by Keith, Tabitha, and the anonymous visitor, as well as MSI's promotional graphics, we can start to see an affinity between the image of the brain as ghostly persona and the (limited) forms of transcendence people experience through their participation in public space. Inhabiting MSI is said to stimulate the brain, creating immediate intellectual pleasure and expanding one's mind through scientific knowledge and cosmopolitan *savoir-faire*. The resulting brain is socialized, not simply a biological organ which can be revealed by slicing tissue; to behold the brain's contents and its capacities for cognition, we must watch actors projected on screens or in photographs, enacting an individual's memories. This cultured yet individual mind is valued as an inalienable aspect of one's persona – if one brackets biological vulnerability and persons' problematic agency over the material infrastructure in which they are embedded. But such bracketing is, after all, commonly character-istic of ghosts: they are invulnerable, because already dead, and so disembedded from the material world that they may pass through its walls as inconsequentially as non-vandalizing visitors pass through a museum exhibit.

Conclusion: Raising the Specter

Early work in the anthropology of science (Martin 1987, 1994) demonstrated that scientific representations of the body are loaded with implicit moral metaphors, metaphors that map between physiological entities on the one hand and socioeconomic formations or personae on the other. However, such work did not focus on explaining how those metaphors, which often are ones which would be disavowed by scientists, became *part* of these scientific representations: for example, are they scientists' subconscious? Some larger subconscious? Random noise? If we want to understand why scientific representations have the particular symbolic resonances they do in the public sphere, then we need to look at mediating processes, which involve the labor not simply of scientists, but also of, for example, medical illustrators, big game hunters, and taxidermists (Stafford 1991, Haraway 1984, Taylor 1992).

Crafting representational media, such as the *Brain* exhibit's mural and statues, entails a division of labor, in which such objects are appropriated – both by visitors and by those creators at different points along the path or network – as part of people's ongoing praxes and projects (Pfaffenberger 2001). This point matters for two reasons, both important for not only ethnographic analysis but also the politics of ethnographic writing. Firstly, through this process, aspects of meaning are picked up and transformed. Examining mediating processes thus involves questioning the adequacy of sociocultural models wherein those who craft such representations are considered as merely "executing" concepts intellectually originated by scientists, artists, or planners (Ingold 1997). Secondly, it provides a way for us to talk about the cultural construction of biology without invalidating our ethnographic object as a case of false consciousness created automatically when society projects itself outwards (Durkheim & Mauss 1967). Rather, people are drawing on particular symbolic forms because these forms have practical uses in particular situations. By tracing these images' histories, we can also restore their grounding in political contestation, such as the social context of race and public space sketched above.

Scientific concepts and mediating images circulate, to a large extent, under rather different regimes of meaning. Lévi-Strauss distinguished scientific "concepts" from the bricoleur's concrete "signs" in that, unlike specially manufactured concepts, signs draw on a messier history, each fresh occasion haunted by past usage (1966, pp. 18ff.). Located at a border between these two regimes, technoscientific exhibits are doomed to translate concepts and engineering feats, ideologized as well defined, into aesthetic and symbolic forms corrupt with excess.

Barbara Maria Stafford has anatomized an Enlightenment discourse in which sensorily experienced cultural forms are to be mistrusted insofar as they take on an autonomous agency, exceeding their proper role as transparent conduits for cognition, "obliterating the independence of physiological functions and thinking" (Stafford 1996, p. 5); in such an ideology, "design" is indeed about cognitive intentionality, which disciplined imagery merely executes. When I briefly recounted the story of the exhibit-altering Studio EIS trip to Spencer, who had since become MSI's senior designer, his disapproving response was that this team had let themselves be seduced "by their eyes," rather than being guided by their conceptual goals. His critique illustrates a common fear among people acting as authorities at MSI: that aesthetic forms, instead of acting as a transparent conduit or facilitating vehicle for underlying concepts, will steal the show: that exhibit creators, exhibit forms, or exhibit receivers will fail to act in a semiotically disciplined manner (Lorimer 2003).

Examining concrete instances of visitors' and creators' actual linguistic and aesthetic practices, however, reveals a more complex, multidimensional form of semiosis – a semiotics of the concrete, which creates hybrid readings, grafting together concept with form. What I am arguing in the case of the *Brain* exhibit is that, taken as both concept and technological media, the *Brain* exhibit fuses science-based representations of the brain with older notions of mind, spirit, and ghost, evoking images of an invulnerable technological afterlife. While the plaster statues do not conceptually *represent* persons enjoying a cerebral and invulnerable afterlife, something of the sort is implied by their hybrid collaboration. Such hybridization, which I have discussed elsewhere (Lorimer 1997), occurs *sub rosa*, in the playful commentary of both museum professionals and visitors. Even Spencer mobilizes hybrid forms in order to critique a dangerous gap between form and content: when another exhibit creator had suggested that bulky and noisy mechanical apparatus needed on board the airplane could be concealed within the overhead carry-on luggage compartments, Spencer enacted the hypothetical utterance of a small child visitor: "The suitcases are rumbling and hissing, Mom." This kind of linguistic practice creates a hybrid between exhibit technology on the one hand and the exhibit's real-world referent on the other, so that the exhibit becomes *about* exhibit technology and its aesthetic qualities. The plaster statues topped with video monitors were not, Sara Graeber carefully explained, intended to represent people whose heads had been replaced by televisions; the exhibit creation team's preferred technology for creating an impression of speech and facial movement had been to project images onto the statue's facial area, but this technology proved too expensive. Yet such semiotic hybridization does emerge in the final exhibit, as when one father ambling past commented to his son: "Hal, these people got TVs for heads. How d'ya like that." New media thus trigger more complex and resonant meanings than those intended and, in Frankenstein fashion, transplanted media transform meanings, fusing science-based representations of the brain with older notions of mind, spirit, and ghost, to evoke a cerebral, invulnerable, and technological afterlife. This fusion is underwritten by a hybrid reading of the exhibit's official content as grafted onto the aesthetic remains of particular other persons once alive, present, and patiently allowing themselves to be encased in plaster in a Brooklyn studio.

I argue that both exhibitions and experiments can be described as a process of discovery which comes from translating concepts into material form, in order to see how different aspects of this materiality may interact with each other in complex, not fully anticipated ways, and to thereby gain new insights into both these underlying concepts and the nature of immanent materiality itself. In this sense, any exhibition is an experiment – if appropriated as such. But for whom are MSI's exhibits an experiment in this way? In her critique of museum evaluation, Ghislaine Lawrence (1991) has described how in certain behaviorist moments of visitor studies, museums become like the mazes scientists run rats through, observing their responses. Unlike behaviorism, contemporary sociocultural anthropology insists on attending to and learning from the reflexive models which are emergent in the phenomena it studies, and amidst which it is necessarily situated. Yet, ironically, while I became deeply indebted to exhibit creators, my methodological commitments left me unable to give exhibit creators what they were most interested in obtaining from an outside researcher: a means of evaluating what they had done.

What I want to suggest here, then, is that exhibits be evaluated as experiments, as described above. What this means is evaluating them not simply on how well they pass on the canonical knowledge of science, but rather on what *new* knowledge can be created by observing the rich interplay of materiality, semiosis, and sociality that takes place within the space they have created. Exhibition experiments, I suggest, are exhibitions judged according to a different standard, in which sensory modalities and processes of translation become tools for observing concepts not as abstracted intentions, but in the fullness of their social and material life. For this reason, exhibition experiments can teach us new things not only about museology, but about the larger world of science and popular culture, within which the exhibit functions as a circuit.

The exhibit creation process narrated here was itself sufficiently reflexive and experimental that themes of eeriness, darkness, technology, and human remains which art critics find in Elliot Schwartz's photography (Hartshorn 1987; Haus 1991) could infiltrate and resolve the ambiance of *Learning and Learning Disabilities.* Usually, Elliot commented, Studio EIS "delivers to the client that which he has thought in his or her mind," in a linear temporal progression. "It is not our intention that raised the specter of any of this stuff to begin with. We are in a sense executing other people's ideas." In this case, however, MSI exhibit developers' openness to their aesthetic experience in the fabricators' studio altered the division of labor, creating a looping hybridity between form and content that allowed the exhibit to become deeply culturally resonant. To understand science as popular culture, and especially how its representations become patched into people's projects, we need to take seriously the media through which science gets represented, and received. We learn about the public sphere and its possibilities, as well as about human cognition, through concrete encounters.

Acknowledgments

Various stages of research and analysis were guided by Nancy Munn, Michael Silverstein, and Bill Hanks, and funded by the Wenner-Gren Foundation for Anthropological Research and the American Association of University Women.

Barbara Stafford's seminar on medical illustration persuaded me both intellectually and aesthetically that fabricators do far more than copy concepts. Alaina Lemon helped capture data. Ira Bashkow conversed about Death and Science over non-fatal oysters. Lindsey MacAllister, dedicated archivist, hunted down my hunches, and found far more. I am especially grateful to Sharon Macdonald, who along with Paul Basu and Viv Golding has been extraordinarily generous and supportive from the moment I showed up on her virtual and actual doorsteps. Others who took my cold calls, and to whom I am now deeply indebted, include Andria Frink, Anne Hornickel, and Elliot Schwartz.

Notes

1 All names, except for those of publicly known artists, are pseudonyms.
2 For Tabitha, death can be framed as another transformative experience, as when she formally announced over the telephone: "My grandmother made her transition this Saturday."

References

Augustine, Saint, Bishop of Hippo (1950 [c. 427]) *The City of God.* Trans. Marcus Dods. New York: Modern Library.

Boas, F. (1965 [1911].) *The Mind of Primitive Man.* New York: Free Press.

Donohoe, V. (2005) Pop go the expectations: collection includes other creative facets of sculptor Segal. www.luag.org/pages/viewfull.cfm?ElementID=170 (accessed August 2006).

Durkheim, E. and Mauss, M. (1967 [1903]). *Primitive Classification.* Trans. Rodney Needham. Chicago: Chicago University Press.

Edwards, A. (1999) Interviews with George Segal. Transcript excerpts available at www.pbs.org/georgesegal/ihow/inhisownwrds.html.

Fletcher, V. (2000) Commentary on George Segal's Bus Riders. http://hirshhorn.si.edu/collection/gallery/segal.html (accessed August 2006).

Haraway, D. (1984) Teddy bear patriarchy: taxidermy in the Garden of Eden, New York City, 1908–1936. *Social Text,* 11: 20–64.

Hartshorn, W. E. (1987) *Elliot Schwartz: Nocturne for Drums.* Exhibition catalogue. New York: International Center of Photography.

Haus, Mary 1991. Elliot Schwartz: stranger than fiction. *ARTnews,* 90 (2): 69–70.

Hertz, R. (1907) The collective representation of death. In his *Death and the Right Hand.* New York: Free Press, pp. 29–88.

Ingold, T. (1997) Eight themes in the anthropology of technology. *Social Analysis,* 4 (1): 106–38.

La Mettrie, J. Offray de (1943 [1748]) *Man a Machine.* La Salle, Ill.: Open Court.

Lawrence, G. (1991) Rats, street gangs and culture: evaluation in museums. In G. Kavanagh (ed.), *Museum Languages: Objects and Texts.* Leicester: Leicester University Press, pp. 9–32.

Lévi-Strauss, Claude (1963 [1955]) The structural study of myth. In his *Structural Anthropology.* New York: Basic Books, pp. 206–31.

Lévi-Strauss, Claude (1966 [1962]). *The Savage Mind.* Chicago: Chicago University Press.

Lorimer, A. (1997) Brats, authorities, and telephones: using "voicing" to analyze linguistic fragments overheard in privileged public sites. Paper presented at 1997 AAA panel "Fieldwork Methodologies for Privileged Public Sites."

Lorimer, A. (2003) "Reality world": constructing reality through Chicago's Museum of Science and Industry. PhD dissertation, University of Chicago.

Martin, E. (1987) *The Woman in the Body: a Cultural Analysis of Reproduction.* Boston: Beacon Press.

Martin, E. (1994) *Flexible Bodies: Tracking Immunity in American Culture from the Days of Polio to the Age of AIDS.* Boston: Beacon Press.

Munn, N. D. (1969) The effectiveness of symbols in Murngin rite and myth. In R. Spencer (ed.), *Forms of Symbolic Action.* Seattle: University of Washington Press, pp. 178–214.

Munn, N. D. (1986) *The Fame of Gawa: A Symbolic Study of Value Transformation in a Massim Society.* Cambridge: Cambridge University Press.

Orvell, M. 1989. *The Real Thing: Imitation and Authenticity in American Culture, 1880–1940.* Chapel Hill: University of North Carolina Press.

Pfaffenberger, B. (2001) Symbols do not create meaning – activities do, or, Why symbolic anthropology needs the anthropology of technology. In M. Schiffer (ed.), *Anthropological Perspectives on Technology.* Tucson: University of Arizona Press, pp. 77–86.

Prather, M. (2000) Curator of post-war art at the Whitney Museum of American Art in New York interviewed for "Remembering George Segal" on *Newshour with Jim Lehrer,* June 14, 2000. Transcript available at www.pbs.org/newshour/bb/remember/jan-june00/segal_6-14.html (accessed August 2006).

Reed, C. R. (2000) *"All the World is Here!" The Black Presence in the White City.* Bloomington: Indiana University Press.

Robbins, B. (ed.) (1993) *The Phantom Public Sphere.* Minneapolis: University of Minnesota Press.

Stafford, B. M. (1991) *Body Criticism: Imaging the Unseen in Enlightenment Art and Medicine.* Cambridge, Mass.: MIT Press.

Stafford, B. M. (1996) *Good Looking: Essays on the Virtue of Images.* Cambridge, Mass.: MIT Press.

Taylor, J. (1992) The public fetus and the family car: from abortion politics to a Volvo advertisement. *Public Culture,* 4 (2): 167–83.

Tomorrow, T. (n.d.) This Modern World: The trouble with brains. www.cafepress.com/tomsworld.4829742.

Warner, M. (1990) The "res publica" of letters. *boundary 2,* 17 (1): 38–68.

Warner, M. (1993) The mass public and the mass subject. In B. Robbins (ed.), *The Phantom Public Sphere.* Minneapolis: University of Minnesota Press, pp. 234–56.

10

Exposing Expo: Exhibition Entrepreneurship and Experimental Reflexivity in Late Modernity

Alexa Färber

Since the 1980s, "reflexive exhibits" have become an increasingly prevalent experimental form. They are characterized by the asking of questions rather than the presentation of facts, and typically achieve this characterization by means of setting up multiple positions on a subject, or deconstructing historical and social processes, and seeking to produce debate (see Macdonald 1998, p. 234). Moreover, such reflexive exhibits usually reflect on the nature and processes of exhibiting itself.

World's fairs came into being in the nineteenth century as part of the same exhibitionary impetus that produced the public museum (Roth 1990; Wörner 1998; Plato 2001). While there is a sense in which they were always experimental – in that they were temporary representations of nations, typically using novel technologies and architecture – the same "reflexive turn" that we see in relation to other forms of exhibition is also evident in world's fairs in the late twentieth century. This is clear, for example, in Penelope Harvey's account of Expo 1992 in Seville (Harvey

1996). It was also the case – though with some intriguing new twists – in the last of the world's fairs of the twentieth century: the millennial Expo 2000, held in Hanover, Germany.

This chapter explores the notion of experimental reflexivity as a crucial mode of incorporating late modern capitalist workings in professional exhibition practice. Through an analysis of the work and self-positioning of entrepreneurial exhibition designers, I will argue that the example of Expo 2000 is a more general expression of strategic experimenting and reflexivity in professional exhibition entrepreneurship. The chapter is based on work that I carried out as an ethnographer during the production, running, and aftermath of Expo 2000, specifically on interviews that I conducted with exhibition designers and visitors and participant observation in the exhibition itself. My discussion of the status and effects of experimental reflexivity in the enterprise of creating innovative exhibitions (what I call "exhibition entrepreneurship") is also informed by my reflections on the parallel practices in anthropology, or more specifically in ethnographic writing. This traffic between ethnography and exhibition is not, however, only the prerogative of the ethnographer of the exhibition. As will be shown below, one feature of exhibtion entrepreneurship at Expo 2000, and surely of many other realms of cultural production, is a drawing on ethnographic ideas and practices which understand the subjective experience of the ethnographer as both a resource and an object of ethnographic experiment. While this – and the idea of experiment for its own sake – is frequently celebrated in both the artworld and anthropology, my analysis of professional practices at Expo 2000 highlights the entanglements of experimental reflexivity in the workings of late modern capitalism, and gives cause for further reflection on the motives for, and implications of, this form of experimental reflexivity in entrepreneurship more widely, including in ethnographic practice.

Below, I first discuss the notion of "ethnographic experiment" before introducing Expo 2000 and my work. I then focus on two of its different instances of experimental reflexivity as a mode of exhibition entrepreneurship: the "Themenpark," a "thematic area" concerned with "knowledge" (which also raises questions about disciplinary knowledge) and a book about the Expo, called *Hyperorganismen*. I argue that, while the "Themenpark" lays out the structural and discursive context for the actual exhibitionary work, the book about the Expo is not merely a by-product of Expo, or a catalogue of it, but a representation of an apotheosis of aspects of the new forms of experimental reflexivity, and thus counts as a medium and proof of professional entrepreneurship. Through these two instances, I seek to examine the various features of such new forms of professional exhibition practices and self-positioning through experimental reflexivity, their production, consumption, motivations, and entanglements.

Ethnographic Experiment

Ethnography generally involves a re-presentation of data that has been generated by the author him- or herself. This subjectively generated data has usually been produced through participant-observation and experiences gained within a socially and culturally foreign context; and this is transformed into ethnographic writing by framing it historically, socially, and culturally. At the heart of ethnographic writing, then, lies subjective experience objectified through (self-)reflexive operations.

Even if fieldwork takes place "at home," ethnographic perspectives are employed to try to create a degree of distance. Such perspectives include defamiliarization by epistemological critique and defamiliarization by cross-cultural juxtaposition (Marcus & Fischer 1986, pp. 137–68), the aim being to disrupt common sense and "make the reader conscious of difference" (ibid., p. 137). The evoking of a sense of difference must simultaneously bear witness to the former involvement with and actual distance from the cultural other in order to count as legitimate ethnographic knowledge.

In their analysis of the forms and historical contexts of ethnographic writing in the twentieth century, Marcus and Fischer point out the experimental character of the representational practices at work. Since the 1960s, ethnographic writing has showed a growing awareness of the contingencies involved in its textual production, and the beginnings of attempts to "experiment" and "achieve...an *effect* of innovation" by playing with and disrupting conventional forms (Marcus & Fischer 1986, p. 40). With an emphasis on dialogues or collage-techniques on the one hand and explicitly fictionalized narratives on the other, a growing number of ethnographic texts try to subvert matters such as the conventional author's position (among others Dwyer 1987; Abu-Lughod 1993; Price & Price 1995). Symmetry (between the researcher and the object of ethnography), transparency (of the research process and textual production), and poetic revelation (as a kind of hyperrealist representation) thus count among those experimental techniques that turn the ethnographic experience, if not to say the ethnographic self, into an object of experiment. Since the 1980s, such techniques, especially those emphasizing subjective experience, have further expanded and become increasingly evident in other realms of cultural production, especially in the arts (see Foster 1996 on the assimilation of cultural difference). As I show below, it is also evident in such a "classic" institution as a world's fair.

Expo as More than Expo

"The Expo is the Expo," sociologist Gerhard Schulze claimed before Expo 2000 had even opened its doors. Such events, he writes, "splash around people like bathwater at body temperature, hardly perceptible, hardly causing any irritation…They signify nothing beyond the surface" (Schulze 1999, p. 93, trans. Richard Gardner). Although an Expo certainly produces a glossy surface – evident not least in its role in polishing the urban political, economic, and federal republican image, and in marketing to international participants – more than ten years of controversial debate about its meaning and costs indicates that there might be more to it. Moreover, Schulze's critical characterization does not explain all of the exhibition areas and even less the representational work involved.

Ethnographic work on exhibitions has shown that the representational work involved in creating an exhibition develops a dynamics that leads to a complexity and diversity that resists narrow interpretation (Macdonald 2002a, p. 260). There is an excess of meaning produced in the act of making an exhibition that inflects upon the representation itself. Matters such as media attention, the seeking of personal gain, or recognition by exhibition professionals, and the creation of networks for future engagements, all constitute part of an exhibition's performativity. For exhibition professionals this tension between requirements on behalf of public authorities and private sponsors for clear-cut and often "glossy" messages and their multiple professional ambitions is both part of their motivation and commitment, and also their dilemma. This is perhaps especially so in the case of a world's fair, given its obvious status in public image policy. The historical legacy of the world's fair as a catalyst for the spread of racist, nationalistic, and positivist representations (see for example Rydell 1984; Benedict 1983) adds to this ambivalence and prompts cultural critique within the institution itself.

It was against the background of such earlier world's fairs, and criticisms of them, that Expo 2000 was planned as a "new kind of expo" (Expo

2000 1999, p. 36). This sparked my own anthropological curiosity. In what ways would Expo 2000 seek to be innovative? What kinds of representational practices would it deploy? And, how would such an institution – aware of its problematic predicament – express cultural critique?

According to the official account of what was innovative at Expo 2000, one of the most significant changes was supplementing the traditional exhibition areas, such as the national pavilions and the cultural program, to include two additional elements, the Worldwide Projects (a permanent network of civil activities/projects undertaken in different countries around the world) and the Themenpark. Through these, Expo 2000 tried to incorporate critical perspectives on the political and social dimensions of world's fairs and (global) society. I discuss this further specifically in relation to the Themenpark below. Before doing so, however, I comment on some of the particular challenges for an ethnographer of conducting an anthropological analysis of an institution such as Expo.

World's fairs are an ambivalent field of research for social anthropologists (see for museums and festivals Bouquet 1995, 2001; Handler & Gable 1997; Kirshenblatt-Gimblett 1998). They are characterized by a high degree of self-referentiality even while they retain a whiff of their past roles in colonialist objectification and the celebration of modernity. Many of their products, exhibits, and events today are marked by a constructivist understanding of culture. Thus, nowadays, national pavilions – the classic exhibit area of world's fairs – typically seek to counter the ways in which nation, culture, and ethnicity were presented earlier by engaging in ironic self-portrayals. Or they try in various ways to critically illuminate the historical, political, and social significance of the institution of the world's fair itself. In her work on the 1992 Expo in Seville, Penelope Harvey also observed the blurring of boundaries between the representational practices at work at the exhibition and those implicated in anthropological theory; and she points out that it is not surprising that there should be such an overlap, for both anthropology and world's fairs have been formed through the same kinds of social and cultural processes, and share concerns with concepts such as "culture" (Harvey 1996, p. 47).

At Expo 2000 in Hanover I found the overlaps to be literal too. During my fieldwork (May 1999–November 2000), not only was I usually welcome as an anthropologist to conduct interviews with exhibition designers, managers, staff, and national representatives, but I was also asked to give my (anthropological) opinion on the exhibition design and contents. This gave me a sense of how anthropological knowledge was expected to offer an appropriate perspective on the exhibition and on those responsible for it (Färber 2006). And so it was no surprise that while I was examining the making of parts of this world's fair, I encountered former fellow students now applying the anthropological knowledge we had acquired together in class outside the academic field. Reflexive knowledge of the kinds popular in anthropology permeated many aspects of Expo 2000, both in relation to analyzing and criticizing the institution of the world's fair itself and in doing the same with respect to social, socioeconomic, and geopolitical questions. This reflexive perspective was expressed in different forms, including an exhibit portraying the history of world's fairs, the "Worldwide Projects" network and, especially, parts of the Themenpark. While the former could be understood as the expression of the reflexive turn in exhibitions as described above, the latter showed in addition aspects of experimental self-reflexivity. In the context of Themenpark there were instances of "ethnographic experiment" in which subjective experience which had generated data (in this case, the exhibition) was then subjected to a process of objectification (in this case, the publication of a supplementary book). This entails a version of the "defamiliarization" or "othering" used by ethnographers in constructing their texts; and, as in anthropology, it can be used in exhibition entrepreneurship too, to provide a particular kind of professional legitimation for the task undertaken.

Themenpark Knowledge

While "Themenpark" is perhaps most accurately translated into English as "thematic area," the name itself was – in typical playful and reflexive fashion – also a play with the idea of the "theme park," a related institutional form from which the world's fair has borrowed and also tried to differentiate itself. At Expo 2000, the Themenpark was an exhibit arranged by the Expo GmbH (limited company) on a 100,000-square-meter site. It was conceived as a public–private partnership, a relatively novel form of organization, which was intended not only to bring economic benefits but also to incorporate the critical perspectives and contents of non-governmental organizations and of scientific and artistic collaborators. The innovative working practice involved in creating the Themenpark was, according to its director, intended to be a "mirror of a civil society, ... a mutual idea factory of the constitutive groups and groups of society"

(Roth 2000, p. 2, trans. R. G.). This official representation of the Themenpark working structure and its aims echoes a vision of exhibitions as
not only commenting on society but mirroring and taking part in political, scientific, and social debate (Ames 1992). It was also intended to
provide the first German world's fair with a contemporary, democratic,
cosmopolitan, and "green" image.

Under the direction of the historian and folklorist Martin Roth, eleven
themes were developed that were designed to echo the Expo's slogan
"Humankind–Nature–Technology" and the United Nations' Rio Declar-
ation on Environment and Development, Agenda 21 (see Beier 2001). One
of these themes was *Knowledge–Information–Communication* (henceforth
Knowledge), in which categories such as "art" and "science" were chal-
lenged and their boundaries simultaneously blurred and re-enacted. This
construction of a space that was both disciplinary and interdisciplinary
was made possible within the limited time-space framework of the exhibition, where exhibition makers had to work together on a specified project.
This provided the basis for practices of experimental reflexivity, and, like
ethnographic experiments, was also displayed in a publication on the
exhibit – *Hyperorganismen.*

Knowledge consisted of two parts: a hi-tech swarm of robots and a science
tunnel, both addressing the (popular) discourse on knowledge society (see
Rötzer 1999; Willke 2002). The first, produced by an artist group called
Beobachter der Bediener von Maschinen (BBM; "Observers of Operators of
Machines") in collaboration with a "scenographer team" from ZKM, the
Center for Art and Media, in Karlsruhe, was an "artistic" approach with a
playful, sculptural form. The other – contributed by the scientific organization the Max Planck Society (MPG) – was a more conventional display of
scientific achievements. This initial evocation of an art–science difference
was, however, later, purposefully, blurred. Let me describe how and also
outline some of the ideas about knowledge involved.

Located in the so-called "queuing area" in front of the main part of
Knowledge, the science tunnel consisted of a 170-meter-long metal "tunnel." On the right side of the tunnel, three-dimensional natural science
models – including some "authentic" items, such as a meteorite – were
scattered at intervals of about ten meters. Cordoned off and with small
labels, these looked like conventional museum presentations and were
scarcely noticed by any visitors. On the left side, the tunnel also included
short videos, computer animations and films about physics, astronomy,
biology, and other areas of natural science. These attracted a little more

attention than the static exhibits, though most visitors remained focused on the hall, which could be glimpsed through portholes in the tunnel wall, with the star attraction: the swarm of robots.

On the threshold of the main exhibition hall, standing in front of a black curtain, an Expo security guard asks visitors to be silent and careful in the dimly lit room behind him. He names the sponsors and gives a short introduction to the idea of the exhibit. He explains that the concept of the swarm was intended to be a metaphor for the complexity and interconnectedness of knowledge. Representative of this concept, according to the explanation given, was the swarm as known from the animal kingdom, or rather, the swarming behavior of animals. The robots "behave" according to this principle.

The nearly gymnasium-sized room behind the curtain is almost completely dark, only the upper half being bathed in intense blue and violet light. An "other-worldly" atmosphere is intensified by strange musical sounds. Through the darkness 72 robots, which also provide some weak light through their transparent plastic hulls, 1–2 meters in diameter, slowly move. Sequences of pictures are internally projected onto the hull: a film showing a fish swarm, pictures of human eyes, then, in quick succession, images of fast-reacting technological systems, such as an ATM, cartoon characters, computer-animated pictures of the brain, and picture frames revealing the sponsors' names (the telecommunication company, Alcatel, and the publishing and media company, Burda). While these pictures skip from one hull to another, silently, the robots glide at snail's pace, one following the other, but without their direction being clear (figure 10.1).

Although the sculpture was based on the most advanced technological achievements, as explained in the catalogue and by the guard, the idea informing this exhibit was drawn not from scientific knowledge but from a puzzle. As artistic director Olaf Arndt put it in an interview with me, science has not yet been able to explain the swarm and animals' swarming behavior (Arndt, Berlin, November 24, 2000). So the swarm as a metaphor for knowledge spoke to a lack of scientific certainty, and more generally contributed to a Themenpark emphasis on the complexity of knowledge as a (scientific) metaphor – echoing the fact that part of the growing importance of scientific knowledge in contemporary societies lies in its self-created ambivalence of being the cause of problems it then has to solve. Scientific knowledge struggles with its own complexity as do people in their daily lives (see Beck, Giddens, & Lash 1994).

Figure 10.1   Robots in *Themenpark Knowledge* at Expo 2000, Hannover, Germany. Courtesy of Reuters/Michael Urban.

From my repeated observation in the exhibition hall I could detect that the visitor's encounter with these objects followed a certain dramaturgy: first they moved carefully, following the robots until they noticed the machines' reactions to their presence. Then they discovered that they could influence the robots' direction of movement by detecting the robots' contact point, a small opening on the lower edge of the hull. Thus, the machines reacted to the visitors as would alert living creatures. This ability to react was apparently what made the swarm so attractive and encouraged people to interact with the objects. People sought to work out: when does a robot stop? Where will it head if I stand directly in front of it?

Despite these kinds of knowledge-seeking questions, it was evident that visitors approached the moving sculpture as an artistic performance, and conceptualized their experience as though transported into a room inhabited by aliens from another planet. Although the artist group wanted the exhibit to be experienced without further explanation, the security guard's introduction and a leaflet explaining the theme were deemed necessary when it became clear that the exhibit concept was rarely grasped by visitors. Asking them what they learned within the exhibtion hall about the subject of knowledge, only a few people talked about the swarm exhibit in terms of information networks and knowledge. Instead, they described it as an astonishing and entertaining experience. By contrast, most of them talked about the science tunnel as containing scientific themes and subjects.

The *Knowledge* exhibition hall, then, could hardly have made the distinction between art and science any clearer. It was reflected in the evocative versus didactic exhibition strategies of the swarm versus the science tunnel. While the swarm metaphor served as an evocative medium to transfer an idea and an unresolved question, the conventional display of the science tunnel was a didactic attempt by a worthy institution to impart information. For visitors, the robots were experienced in terms of "wonder" (Greenblatt 1991) and the quasi-"magical" – they were to be experienced rather than understood in detail. The science tunnel, on the other hand, sought to produce effects of recognition in establishing links to prior knowledge in an experience that Greenblatt describes as "resonance" (ibid.).

Despite these evident differences, the exhibit makers themselves did not draw such a clear distinction between art and science. Olaf Arndt explained how he had attempted to answer the Expo's and business partner's requirement to make unequivocal messages accessible to a mass audience without losing the main idea of the swarm. Projecting pictures that would illustrate the idea of networking onto the robots' hulls thus became subordinate to the swarm – and in Arndt's view thus artistically secondary – a matter that was one of the hardest battlefields within the whole project (interview with Arndt). Equally, the Max Planck Society saw their scientific aspirations compromised by the medium, especially by any attempt at explaining scientific complexity. The compromise here was also the use of pictures – in this case of attractive and even scientifically "incorrect" images rather than ones that were "correct" but uninteresting (interview with Andreas Trepte, MPG München, July 24, 2001).

This blurring of the border between the science exhibit and the art exhibit, hardly visible at first glance and only understandable through the exhibit makers' commentaries, reflects a "dilemma of popularization" (Korff 2001, p. 14) in which visitors bring their own expectations as to the appropriate communication structures of different forms of display. While there has long been overlap in the display of science and art (even, for example, in the first science center, the Exploratorium (Macdonald

2002b)), what is characteristic in this new case is a double movement in which an interdisciplinary "art–science" space is specifically brought into being, and disciplinary boundaries are highlighted, transgressed, and recreated. It is this movement that on the one hand turns art–science into accessible and consumable cultural products. On the other hand, this seemingly playful awareness of disciplinary boundaries and their possible transgression is today a neccessary professional competence of exhibition professionals.

How much this reflexive movement is incorporated into professional self-positioning may best be illuminated by a closer look at the main players involved in *Knowledge*. The artistic group, Observers of Operators of Machines, located in the Hanover region, was active in anti-Expo events beforehand, and must be counted among the city's leftist subculture scene. At the same time, Olaf Arndt and his colleagues have in different constellations received funding from business, cultural foundations, and private sponsors for their earlier work. After having tried in vain to receive support from the local cultural foundation for an artwork that would contribute to the city's cultural program during Expo 2000, they took the opportunity offered by the Themenpark to work inside the institution. This "step inside" was not made without debate and some misgivings within the group, but Arndt finally considered it much more interesting to experience how far one could go within the organization Expo 2000 rather than to criticize it from outside (interview with Arndt).

Arndt found, however, that Expo 2000 working conditions differed from those he had experienced in other art production projects. In the Expo structure, the artist group – which Arndt prefers to refer to as a "collective" – was designated a scenographer *team*, and as such it had a designated place in the Expo hierarchy and had to deal with the demands of business and scientific partners, not only in conception and content, but also by having to work within official German safety standards (Bruckner 2000). As Arndt puts it, reflecting on the group's motivation to accomplish the work under these conditions, he and his collaborators could only resist as a collective by conceiving the structure they worked in as an "enemy, against whom they defended their gold," their artistic idea (interview with Arndt). One way in which they also sought to maintain their credibility as an artist collective was by reflexively creating a space of art–science.

Much of this disciplinary play, however, took place outside the institutional framework of the world's fair, and as part of a broader field of cultural production and more specifically of *artwriting*. George Marcus and Fred Myers borrow this term from David Carrier (1987) to indicate a discourse that establishes itself as the preeminent social space for critical self-reflection (Marcus & Myers 1995, p. 30). Artwriting by critics, scholars, and journalists has become such an important context that "it has been reflexively absorbed within the work of art producers themselves" (ibid., p. 27). This incorporation of cultural critique into the artwork itself points to the fact that artistic objects or performances "only accumulate culture value to the extent that they are inscribed in 'histories'" (ibid.). In order to return to the artworld from the mass cultural field of Expo 2000, the artist group sought to inscribe such a history through a legitimating narrative of ethnographic experiment. This took the form of a book: *Hyperorganismen*.

Hyperorganismen: Hypertext and Semi-revelation

One of the other concerns of the artistic group was to get new projects financed, and to provide a more lasting legacy with the right kind of artworld credentials to help them do so. Expo was widely described as a flop. This was not only by those who identified its political shortcomings, but more especially in the national media where it was widely regarded as culturally uninteresting and shown to be financially unsuccessful, with fewer than half of the anticipated 40 million visitors attending and a budget deficit of about €1.2 billion. Against such a background, the artists sought to distance themselves from this mass event and their own contribution to it. This was, in my view, a key motivation for the decision by Arndt and his colleagues to produce a book, *Hyperorganismen*, about their work on Expo. Through this book, *Knowledge*, the exhibit they had developed as a *scenographer team*, was turned into an object of critical reflection of the *artist collective*. Here they could demonstrate irony toward Expo and justify their reappearance in subcultural and art scenes. With the help of techniques such as transparency and revelation, the Expo experience could be presented as an ethnographic experiment – as both intimately experienced and culturally other.

Hyperorganismen is an indubitably "alternative" and "arty" book, a specialized rather than a mass product, made available only in specialized art and subcultural libraries. Alongside typical exhibit photos it includes images of sketches on scrap paper, computer generated views of rooms, snapshot photographs, tables of contents turned into statistical and geographical maps, and a comic strip (figure 10.2).

The photographs reproduced in the book only show segments of the exhibition interior, the framework of Expo 2000 visually disappearing almost completely. The main motif of the book is revelation into the normally hidden and this is evident, for example, in shots of the exhibit's control room, where monitors, a soft drink, and a bag of peanuts can be seen.

Rather than concentrating on the finished product, as would a typical exhibition catalogue, *Hyperorganismen* focuses on *processes* and *contexts* – from the complex portrayal of the process of the exhibit's production to indications of a network between authors and publishers, disciplines and texts. This also has the effect of highlighting the artistic group's theoretical network. The book contains chapters by individual authors, chosen to represent diverse areas of knowledge, from literature and quantum physics, nanotechnology and philosophy, to ornithology, nutrition, and orthography. Making exhibitions and tourism are mentioned as topics, too, and can be read as direct points of reference to the world's fair, though they seem rather out of place in the overall framework. There are other somewhat extraneous topics, such as software programming, the

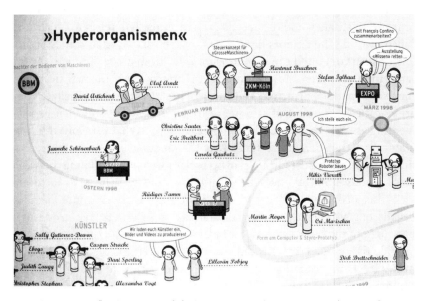

Figure 10.2 Reflecting on exhibition process in *Hyperorganismen.* Courtesy www.judithzaugg.ch.

formation of autonomous political groups, and electronic music, which seem to be there mainly to add to an aura of critical technology culture.

In addition to this visual and structural evocation of the production processes, professional networks, and theoretical references, the artists reflect ironically on the conditions of the exhibition's creation in their introductory articles (Arndt et al. 2000; Bruckner 2000). This includes critical reflection on the content and structural difficulties involved. The meetings with project partners and Expo representatives, as portrayed in the texts, resemble a battlefield rather than a collegial creative process at a café table (as the sketches reproduced in the book suggest). Quotes from personal and official minutes and from working meetings are included, also adding to the sense of glimpsing the hidden and to a reflexive procedure in which the experience-based knowledge – garnered by Arndt and colleagues at the Expo – is transformed into explicit knowledge that is rationalized and commented upon. This has the effect of including the reader in an atmosphere of conspiracy. However, although on the one hand the impression is given of transparency, this apparent "laying bare" simultaneously tends to mystify the team's working practices as an artistic creation process (see Bismarck 2003, p. 92).

This ambivalent gesture of transparency makes the work at Expo retrospectively into a trip to an alien world; or, in other words, Expo becomes retrospectively alien and distanced. The reflection here refers to an already "alien" world. The authors have gone through this world, but they are no longer a part of it, and can therefore criticize "from a safe distance." At the same time, however, the positions of the members of the artistic group themselves and the principles of their own practices are rarely visible. They are not made an object of critique or ironic distancing, and their experimenting as such remains oddly unreflected upon. What is involved in this ambivalent transparency, I suggest, is the creation of a kind of "return ticket" into the artist group's own social context, vacillating between autonomous political movement and sponsorship. The artistic group seeks this, I contend, in order to secure not only necessary future financial benefit but also symbolic and cultural capital. The reflexive procedures presented in the book – the objectification of their own Expo experience – provide the resource for this capitalization on their Expo participation. It makes the Expo experience an ethnographic experiment, and thus turns a commissioned task into art.

For Arndt and colleagues, Expo 2000 had become the cultural "other" to which they had undertaken a research trip and returned with a treasure of experiences they could further utilize. For the director with overall responsibility for *Knowledge*, Stefan Iglhaut, and the overall director of the Themenpark, Martin Roth, experimental self-reflexivity extended yet further. This is evident in their joint contribution to *Hyperorganismen*.

In their contribution, they begin by explaining the principle of the *Knowledge* exhibition itself, the alienation of the visitor through the objects, the provocation of astonishment and amazement, and the intention to generate a diversity of meaning among visitors analogous to the "swarm" metaphor (Iglhaut & Roth 2000). This is followed by a dialogue between the two about what promoted, hindered, or influenced the production of the exhibit. The authors confront one another with the question whether the exhibit worked at all, what decisions they find right or wrong in retrospect, and where they remain undecided. Ideas they discarded are mentioned, as are the reasons for discarding them, and new ideas are developed. Mutual criticism is voiced, as is criticism of the team and poor media reception.

The authors direct the reader's attention back to their own manner of working. In their dialogue they make explicit, analyze, and criticize the implicit practical knowledge of exhibition practice in a very subjective manner. As in a public diary, they document their experiences or thoughts and distance themselves from that for which they were responsible; and they do so by employing tropes of transparency and revelation. At the same time, they use stylistic techniques, not to unsettle the reader's sense of the authenticity of what they are saying, but to support it. This is done by presenting the text in the form of cellphone short (text) messages (SMS), including dates and time of day (or night). Nevertheless, and perhaps unintentionally, this form of presentation appears fictional, for one instinctively perceives that the messages are much too long and concentrated for the spontaneous medium of the short message. Here, again, the transparency and revelation are partial.

Transparency and revelation are, inevitably, only partial, as James Clifford has pointed out in relation to ethnographic texts (Clifford 1986). Nevertheless, a feature of experimental ethnographies has been to draw attention to this very fact, and in so doing to question the "truth" of what is presented. The exhibit makers' text does this too, on the one hand by authenticating a reflection on the exhibit practice (by means of openness and style) and on the other hand by creating by the same means doubts about its authenticity, maybe even declaring it fictive. This self-reflexivity also has the effect of making the participation of Iglhaut and Roth itself into an "ethnographic experiment" – something to which they can have an ironic and distanced relationship. Their participation can be rationalized as an experiment that could be repeated again at any time because, in retrospect and from a safe distance, the experiences made there can be evaluated. A major point of experiments, after all, is to try things out, to see whether they work or not, and to learn from the experience. Their self-commentaries – and in a sense especially their self-criticisms – show evidence of just this kind of experience-based learning. As such, they are, perhaps, particularly effective as "return tickets." Moreover, they help to position their authors as creative, reflective and significant players in the late-modern world of cultural production. In this self-positioning the artwriting works as an efficient medium, while the narrative of the ethnographic experiment seems to respond, as I will show below, to late-modern working conditions and requirements of professionalization.

Ethnographic Experiment as a Resource in Late-Modern Society

By applying ethnographic procedures of experience-based reflection and to some extent revealing themselves publicly, curators meet an apparent public demand to know how an exhibit is made and how the curators "tick." This kind of transparency also meets a public pressure to lay bare everything for which tax and other funding was spent.

With regard to the benefit in symbolic and financial capital that collaboration on Expo 2000 promised all involved, "experimenting" can be understood as a form of practice which meets the demands of cultural production today. The experiment is a structure that does not so much construct or produce content, as allow it to "appear" or "materialize," and then provide the opportunity for commentary and possible generalization. This notion of experiment can be seen as emerging from an overlapping form of artistic practice and cultural critique, in which art, and discourse upon it, are collapsed into one. This collapse is achieved by designing a particular kind of evocative and provocative exhibit and opening up a reservoir of theoretical points of reference. It is worth pointing out, however, that all of this occurs most strikingly in the text about the exhibition rather than in the exhibition itself. Reflexive and analytical knowledge thus appears in the tried and proven medium of a book – mediated by and in artwriting.

At the same time, curators position themselves within a differentiation of the "curator system" that has been observable since the 1990s. This system is distinguished no longer so much by the individuality and performance of the artist as by those of the curator. As Locher puts it: "What earlier distinguished an artist's work, namely style, his handwriting, his name, today applies to the curator's work" (Locher 2002, p. 226, trans. R. G.). The uniqueness of the curator is what now guarantees attention and corresponding funding.

While this may well indicate a growing similarity between curatorial and artistic practices, these are not necessarily fully symmetrical, for a redistribution of symbolic capital is also involved in which the artistic is increasingly subsumed to the curatorial. As Locher puts it: "Artistic strategies in the institutional field are moving ever further up into management. With each step of this 'semantic' ascent, the artist becomes poorer and less important" (ibid., p. 228). The appropriation of this new, creative, reflective, and distanced status for curators, as exemplified in Iglhaut and Roth's contributions in *Hyperorganismen*, is part of this process.

The kinds of self-reflexive ethnographic experimenting described in relation to Expo 2000 act as evidence of such an appropriation of creativity, reflexivity, flexibility and, I would add, risk-taking professionalism. Declaring the world's fair retrospectively a professional challenge, considering one's own contribution to it a risk (as the title – "No risk, no fun" – of Iglhaut and Roth's text suggests) makes clear how in this field of cultural production the late-modern model of the entrepreneurial self is at work.

The entrepreneurial self can be seen as characteristic of late-modern models of labor and manpower, representing the "new spirit of capitalism," as Boltanski and Chiapello (1999) have demonstrated. On the one hand it is characterized by those features highlighted in the logic of the "Cité en projets" (Boltanski & Chiapello 1999, 2003), namely, networking, the analysis of networks, flexibility, polyvalence, activity and autonomy, seeking a higher (social) goal, the creation of trust and enthusiasm (Boltanski & Chiapello 2003, p. 63). The logic of the entrepreneurial self is thus based on techniques of self-resourcing and self-management, which aim to turn professionals into "their own enterprise" (Wuggenig 2003, p. 150). Wuggenig shows for the fields of economics and the arts how technologies of the self blend into project work. He speaks about a new form of "disembedding" which results in the "insecurity of a pursued class" (ibid., p. 152) – a metaphor which resonates quite well with the SMS-dialogue of Iglhaut and Roth.

At the same time, the entrepreneurial self has to demonstrate a competence to make crisis and failure a "productive principle of its practices" (Verwoert 2003, p. 51). In this sense Expo's economic and public failure was part of the risk accepted by the players involved. However, both the artist group and the curators knew how to ensure that the financial and symbolic failure of Expo 2000 would not become their own failure. In their retrospective narrative of Expo this "unsuccessful" event turned out to have been a challenge (rather than a risk) to their professionalism that offered the opportunity to give proof of creativity, reflexivity, flexibility, etc. It is here that the ethnographic experiment, incorporating experimental reflexivity, comes into play – to give proof of and mediate exhibition entrepreneurship.

Self-resourcing is made possible by the "ethnographization" of one's own work. Ethnographization allows workers to objectify their personal involvement, the product produced, and its institutional framework – a framework that in the case of exhibitions itself involves more and more public–private-partnership obligations and a growing demand for flexible forms of work. Working in such collaborations then becomes, especially retrospectively and through ethnography-like analysis and presentation, an experiment. This logic of experimental reflexivity, based on the conception of the ethnographic experiment, culturally legitimizes exhibition entrepreneurship and the "insecurity of the pursued class" (ibid.).

If this is the case, what may have been counted as innovative in the ethnographic experiment and as a locus for cultural critique has to be understood and criticized as being deeply inscribed into the cultural logic of late capitalism. The "family resemblance" (Marcus & Myers 1995, p. 28) between artwriting and anthropology as cultural critique may then be perceived as structural. Also, the experimental blurring of disciplinary boundaries has to be understood as a consequence of this underlying cultural logic of the fields of cultural production. What is at stake here is the locus of cultural critique, which in the form of experimental reflexivity seems to correspond too much to the structure that it would aim to distance itself from. If the museum has been the laboratory of modern society (Korff & Roth 1990) – and exhibitions today are still loyal to that legacy, as exemplified in *Themenpark Knowledge* – these institutions should prevail not only as effects of late-modern techniques of experimenting. They should account for the social effects of experimental reflexivity in making it – within exhibitions themselves – an object of cultural critique.

References

Abu-Lughod, L. (1993) *Writing Women's Worlds: Bedouin Stories.* Berkeley: University of California Press.

Ames, K. L. (1992) Finding common threads. In K. L. Ames, B. Franco, and L. T. Frye (eds.), *Ideas and Images: Developing Interpretive History Exhibits.* Nashville, Tenn.: Sage Publications, pp. 313–24.

Arndt, O., Peter, S., and Wünnenberg, D. (2000) Vorwort. In O. Arndt, S. Peter, and D. Wünnenberg (eds.), *Hyperorganismen. Essays, Fotos, Sounds der Ausstellung "Wissen" des ZKM im Themenpark der Expo 2000.* Hannover: Internationalismus Verlag, pp. 9–17.

Beck, U., Giddens, A., and Lash, S. (1994) *Reflexive Modernization: Politics, Tradition and Aesthetics in the Modern Social Order.* Cambridge: Polity Press.

Beier, R. (2001) Inszenierung von Zukunft. Visionen und mediale Strategien der Expo 2000. *Historische Anthropologie,* 9 (1): 115–25.

Benedict, B. (1983) *The Anthropology of World's Fairs: San Francisco's Panama Pacific International Exposition of 1915.* Berkeley, Calif., and London: Scolar Press.

Bismarck, B. von (2003) Kuratorisches Handeln: Immaterielle Arbeit zwischen Kunst und Managementmodellen. In M. von Osten (ed.), *Norm der Abweichung.* Vienna and New York: Springer-Verlag, pp. 81–98.

Boltanski, L. and Chiapello, E. (1999) *Le nouvel esprit du capitalisme.* Paris: Gallimard.

Boltanski, L. and Chiapello, E. (2003) Die Arbeit der Kritik und der normative Wandel. In M. von Osten (ed.), *Norm der Abweichung.* Vienna and New York: Springer-Verlag, pp. 57–80.

Bouquet, M. (1995). Exhibiting knowledge: the trees of Haeckel, Dubois, Jesse and Rivers at the Pithecanthropus Centennial Exhibition. In M. Strathern (ed.), *Shifting Contexts: Transformations in Anthropological Knowledge.* London: Routledge, pp. 31–55.

Bouquet, M. (2001) The art of exhibition making as a problem of translation. In M. Bouquet (ed.), *Academic Anthropology and the Museum: Back to the Future.* New York and Oxford: Berghahn, pp. 177–97.

Bruckner, H. (2000) Schwarm-, Schreib und Klangmaschinen. Über einige Hörerlebnisse. In O. Arndt et al. (eds.), *Hyperorganismen. Essays, Fotos, Sounds der Ausstellung "Wissen" des ZKM im Themenpark der Expo 2000.* Hannover: Internationalismus Verlag, pp. 25–35.

Carrier, D. (1987) *Artwriting*. Almherst: University of Massachusetts Press.

Clifford, J. (1986) Introduction: partial truths. In J. Clifford and G. E. Marcus (eds.), *Writing Culture: the Poetics and Politics of Ethnography*. Berkeley: University of California Press, pp. 1–26.

Dwyer, K. (1987) *Moroccan Dialogues: Anthropology in Question*. Prospect Heights, Ill.: Waveland Press.

Expo 2000 (November 1999) *The Future: User's Guide*. Hannover: Expo 2000 Hannover GmbH.

Färber, A. (2005) *Die Weltausstellung als Wissensmodus. Ethnographie einer Repräsentationsarbeit*. Münster: Lit Verlag.

Foster, H. (1996) The artist as ethnographer. In H. Foster, *The Return of the Real: the Avant-Garde at the End of the Century*. Cambridge, Mass., and London: MIT Press, pp. 171–203.

Greenblatt, S. (1991) Resonance and wonder. In I. Karp and S. D. Lavine (eds.), *Exhibiting Cultures: the Politics and Poetics of Museum Display*. Washington, D.C.: Smithsonian Institution Press, pp. 42–56.

Handler, R. and Gable, E. (1997) *The New History in an Old Museum: Creating the Past at Colonial Williamsburg*. Durham, N.C., and London: Duke University Press.

Harvey, P. (1996) *Hybrids of Modernity: Anthropology, the Nation State and the Universal Exhibition*. London: Routledge.

Iglhaut, S. and Roth, M. (2000) No risk, no fun. Ein SMS-Gespräch am 17., 18. und 19. August 2000. In O. Arndt et al. (eds.), *Hyperorganismen. Essays, Fotos, Sounds der Ausstellung "Wissen" des ZKM im Themenpark der Expo 2000*. Hannover: Internationalismus Verlag, pp. 295–309.

Kirshenblatt-Gimblett, B. (1998) Confusing pleasures. In *Destination Culture: Tourism, Museums, and Heritage*. Berkeley and Los Angeles: University of California Press, pp. 203–48.

Korff, G. (2001) Das Popularisierungsdilemma. *Museumskunde*, 66 (1): 13–19.

Korff, G. and Roth, M. (eds.) (1990) *Das historische Museum: Labor, Schaubühne, Identitätsfabrik*. Frankfurt am Main and New York: Campus Verlag.

Locher, H. (2002) Die Kunst des Ausstellens – Anmerkungen zu einem unübersichtlichen Diskurs. In H. D. Huber, H. Locher, and K. Schulte (eds.), *Kunst des Ausstellens. Beiträge, Statements, Diskussionen*. Ostfildern-Ruit: Hatje Cantz Verlag, pp. 15–30.

Macdonald, S. (1998) Afterword: from war to debate? In S. Macdonald (ed.), *The Politics of Display: Museums, Science, Culture*. London: Routledge, pp. 229–35.

Macdonald, S. (2002a) *Behind the Scenes at the Science Museum*. Oxford and New York: Berg.

Macdonald, S. (2002b). Exhibitions and the public understanding of science paradox. September 1. http://www2.hu-berlin.de/kulturtechnik/files/MacDonald.pdf.

Marcus, G. E. and Fischer, M. M. J. (1986) *Anthropology as Cultural Critique: an Experimental Moment in the Human Sciences.* Chicago: University of Chicago Press.

Marcus, G. E. and Myers, F. (1995) The traffic in art and culture: an introduction. In G. E. Marcus and F. Myers (eds.), *The Traffic in Art and Culture: Refiguring Art and Anthropology.* Berkeley and Los Angeles: University of California Press, pp. 1–51.

Plato, A. von (2001) *Präsentierte Geschichte: Ausstellungskultur und Massenpublikum im Frankreich des 19. Jahrhunderts.* Frankfurt am Main: Campus Verlag.

Price, R. and Price, S. (1995) *Enigma Variations.* Cambridge, Mass.: Harvard University Press.

Roth, M. (1990) *Heimatmuseum. Zur Geschichte einer deutschen Institution.* Berlin: Mann.

Roth, M. (2000) Kraftwerk der Ideen – Kathedralen der Zukunft. In M. Roth (ed.), *Der Themenpark der Expo 2000. Vol. 1: Die Entdeckung einer neuen Welt.* Vienna: Springer Verlag, pp. 1–7.

Rötzer, F. (1999) *Megamaschine Wissen. Vision: Überleben im Netz.* Frankfurt am Main: Campus Verlag.

Rydell, R. W. (1984) *All the World's a Fair: Visions of Empire at American International Expositions, 1876–1916.* Chicago: University of Chicago Press.

Schulze, G. (1999) *Kulissen des Glücks. Streifzüge durch die Eventkultur.* Frankfurt am Main: Campus Verlag.

Verwoert, J. (2003) Die Ich-Ressource: zur Kultur der Selbst-Verwertung. In J. Verwoert (ed.), *Die Ich-Ressource: zur Kultur der Selbst-Verwertung.* München: VolkVerlag, pp. 7–24.

Willke, H. (2002) *Dystopia. Studien zur Krisis des Wissens in der modernen Gesellschaft.* Frankfurt am Main: Surhkamp Verlag.

Wörner, M. (1998) *Vergnügen und Belehrung. Volkskultur auf den Weltausstellungen 1851–1900.* Münster: Waxmann Verlag.

Wuggenig, U. (2003) Die Kunst auf dem Weg in die blaue Ökonomie. In J. Verwoert (ed.), *Die Ich-Ressource: zur Kultur der Selbst-Verwertung.* München: VolkVerlag, pp. 137–68.

Index

Note: page numbers in italics denote figures or illustrations where they are separated from their textual references